The Essential Guide to *Talking with Gifted Teens*

Ready-to-Use Discussions About Identity, Stress, Relationships, and More

Jean Sunde Peterson, Ph.D.

free spirit
PUBLISHING®

Library of Congress Cataloging-in-Publication Data
Peterson, Jean Sunde, 1941–
     The essential guide to talking with gifted teens : ready-to-use discussions about identity, stress, relationships, and more / Jean Sunde Peterson.
          p. cm.
     Includes index.
     ISBN-13: 978-1-57542-260-2
     ISBN-10: 1-57542-260-3
     1. Gifted children—Education. 2. Gifted children—Counseling of. 3. Educational counseling. I. Title.
          LC3993.2.P48 2008
          371.95—dc22

                                                                                    2007024867

ISBN: 978-1-57542-260-2

Edited by Catherine Broberg and Meg Bratsch
Cover design by Marieka Heinlen
Interior design by Lois Stanfield

10 9 8 7 6 5
Printed in the United States of America

Free Spirit Publishing Inc.
6325 Sandburg Road, Suite 100
Minneapolis, MN 55427-3674
(612) 338-2068
help4kids@freespirit.com
www.freespirit.com

Free Spirit offers competitive pricing.
Contact edsales@freespirit.com for pricing information on multiple quantity purchases.

Dedication

. . . .

to Reuben

Acknowledgments

. . . .

Immediate and extended family, new and longtime friends, colleagues, and many, many students have taught me about development—and about giftedness. I cannot recall a time when I was not around bright people who were growing and changing. That process has fascinated me. I have appreciated and been influenced by these stimulating, challenging, highly idiosyncratic individuals.

I am especially indebted to my husband, Reuben, highly committed to his own work as an educator, for his unwavering support of my teaching, writing, and other interests. We have grown and changed together. I also want to thank my children, Sonia and Nathan, for being patient with me when they were young, sharing me with my teaching career and waiting for summer, when our lives would change dramatically for three months.

Since the first *Talk with Teens* book appeared in the early 1990s, counselors, counselors-in-training, and a variety of classroom and gifted education teachers have given me feedback and ideas for future revisions. Their adaptations, struggles with unclear concepts and guidelines, and excitement over successes have all informed me. I have especially appreciated the feedback and suggestions of Terry Bradley, in Boulder, Colorado, over several years and have included three of her many creative ideas in this book—the paired activity in "Self in Perspective," the stress-ball activity in "Sorting Out Stress," and the children's book activity in "Angry!"

I am relieved that the field of gifted education is embracing the idea that the social and emotional development of gifted kids is important. I am grateful to pioneers in this area for thinking, exploring, studying, writing, presenting, consulting, organizing, counseling, leading, and publishing helpful resources, among them Nick Colangelo, Barbara Kerr, James Webb, George Betts, Michael Piechowski, Dewey Cornell, Linda Silverman, Joanne Whitmore, Tom Hébert, Sal Mendaglio, Tracy Cross, Lawrence Coleman, Jane Piirto, Donna Ford, Sylvia Rimm, Ed Amend, Andrew Mahoney, Susan Jackson, Helen Nevitt, and Judy Galbraith. Through personal contact and/or through their writing, I recognized these as kindred spirits during my initial years in the National Association for Gifted Children. Some have been consistent and important contributors to the Counseling and Guidance Division of NAGC during my years with that organization.

I want to acknowledge Penny Oldfather for supporting the discussion groups I organized when I coordinated a program for gifted students in Sioux Falls, South Dakota, for five years. Group work was a fairly new idea in the field at that time, and her approval, as director of the Unique Learning Experiences program, was crucial to the viability of the group component I developed. Principal Fred Stephens, a former school counselor, supported this strand in the program, and I want to acknowledge him as well. My friend Norma Haan, a former college roommate and a longtime clinician, was a ready consultant.

Last, I want to acknowledge Free Spirit Publishing. Based on my earlier very positive experiences with Judy Galbraith and her staff, I anticipated accurately that the editing process for this book would be multi-layered and rigorous—and highly supportive. I particularly want to acknowledge the conscientious work of Cathy Broberg and Meg Bratsch, content editors, and Darsi Dreyer, copy editor. They were alert and not afraid to challenge me during the long process of birthing the book. Experts in various fields served as consultants and reviewers for Free Spirit along the way as well. I am grateful to all of these individuals for their guidance.

Contents

List of Reproducible Pages

(Downloadable PDFs available at www.freespirit.com/Essential-Guide-forms. Use password justtalk2)

Preface

The Essential Guide to Talking with Gifted Teens is a book that has come full circle in many ways. It was my work with gifted students that inspired an approach to group work that was outlined in two books published more than ten years ago. Those books were called Talk with Teens About Self and Stress and Talk with Teens About Feelings, Family, Relationships, and the Future. The original books were written for the general population, since the preventive, development-oriented discussion group format is potentially beneficial for all teens. Since that time, however, social and emotional development has received increasing attention in the field of gifted education. Though we understand that gifted teens face the same developmental challenges as the rest of the school population, how they experience development may be different. Their own and others' expectations regarding their development are likely to be different from what others experience. Therefore, this book assumes that highly capable teens can benefit from opportunities to talk about developmental hurdles in a group comprised of only gifted teens.

When it was time to revise the books, my publisher and I agreed that two volumes were still needed but with different foci: one for use with the general population—called Talk with Teens About What Matters to Them—and one geared toward gifted teens. This is the volume created for group work with gifted kids.

The Essential Guide to Talking with Gifted Teens incorporates some of the best elements of the earlier editions—in the sessions selected and in the detailed guidelines for group work, including the emphasis on expressive skills as related to social and emotional concerns. I believe these skills are important to future relationships and often are not attended to adequately in schools. Most significant, however, are new topics that reflect issues especially important to gifted teens. Current information about the social and emotional development of gifted kids, based on the latest research and literature, also is included throughout the book. The background information for many sessions has been updated and made more pertinent to the experience of gifted teens. Suggestions and sample questions have been improved and extended, with giftedness in mind.

I encourage you to let me know about your group work with gifted teens, how specific session topics and suggestions have worked for you, and what new activities or ideas you have used to adapt the sessions to your context.

You can email me at: help4kids@freespirit.com or send me a letter in care of:

Free Spirit Publishing
6325 Sandburg Road, Suite 100
Minneapolis, MN 55427-3674

Jean Sunde Peterson

Introduction

About This Book

Description and Benefits

Gifted education teachers often focus mostly on the academic needs of their students, developing an advanced curriculum in a special program or ensuring that curriculum and instruction are differentiated for gifted students in classrooms. Traditionally, much less attention has been given to gifted students' social and emotional development. *The Essential Guide to Talking with Gifted Teens* is intended to meet the need of gifted teens to "just talk"—to share their feelings and concerns with supportive peers and an attentive adult. Whether or not normal developmental tasks, life events, or personal circumstances affect students' attendance, classroom performance, or behavior, the sensitivity and intensity of gifted teens may add an extra layer to their internal response to these challenges. Yet, because they are perceived as highly capable and may appear to be doing well, many adults assume that gifted children and teens are handling social and emotional concerns adequately. Furthermore, gifted teens are often reluctant to ask for help, believing, like the adults, that they should be able to deal effectively with personal problems, difficult circumstances, low morale, or low motivation by themselves. Even when family life is discouraging, deeply engrained achievement habits may allow high-achieving gifted students to continue to demonstrate excellent classroom and talent performance, again contributing to the assumption that support isn't needed. Fundamentally, little is known about the inner life of gifted teens. Adults rarely ask how these students are experiencing various aspects of life, including the day-to-day challenges of social, extracurricular, and academic life at school as well as normal developmental changes.

My experience with approximately 1,300 group sessions with gifted teens has taught me that, collectively, they have a wide range of concerns that often are not apparent to others. For many, adolescence is not an easy time. Even remarkable performers, who delight the adults around them, are growing and developing—with self-doubts and uncertainties about the present and future. Gifted underachievers may not feel as self-assured as some of them seem. Gifted rebels may feel in control only when others stay at a distance, avoiding their speeding, looping tetherball. The ready-to-use semi-structured sessions provided here can serve as a curriculum that nurtures the social and emotional development of these and other gifted teens. The sessions have been used in programs for gifted students in public and private middle schools and high schools, in summer university programs, and in yearlong residential schools. The suggestions, activities, and written exercises in this book, along with the focused but flexible format, have been thoroughly tested.

I have witnessed the benefits of these guided discussion groups for gifted students of many ages. The groups can accomplish the following:

- allow gifted teens to focus on how and where they are, in the present, not on how or where highly invested adults may believe they ought to be

- produce inspiring results in both well-adjusted gifted students and those with significant risk factors

- help gifted students normalize "weird" thoughts, sort out personal conflict, put self- and others' expectations into perspective, and lower stress levels

- provide an opportunity to explore the notion that sensitivities and intensities are associated with giftedness

- give students who are cynical and negative about school an experience that makes it bearable

- help group members learn to anticipate problems and find support for problem-solving

- serve a preventive function by improving self-esteem and social ease (High levels of either of these should not be automatically assumed in gifted kids. Students feel better about themselves as they become comfortable and allow their real selves to show and be affirmed during group meetings.)

- give educators and counselors an opportunity to interact with many gifted students about social and emotional development at one time, maximizing time and impact

Although researchers exploring the concept of giftedness have often focused on assets rather than burdens associated with high ability, a growing trend is to look at the latter as well. Researchers in the field of gifted education are often educational psychologists, and many have explored areas such as motivation, self-regulation, cognition, problem-solving ability, higher-order thinking, the process of learning, differentiated curriculum, and underachievement as related to motivation. Others have studied gifted students' subjective experience of social development qualitatively, discovering and pursuing new research directions as a result. The session topics in this book have been chosen on the basis of research, clinical literature, and collected anecdotal reports.

For the sake of brevity and reading ease, *gifted teens* will be the phrase used to identify the target population here. A more current and more appropriate phrase would be *teens who are gifted*. The term *gifted* will be used throughout the book as a descriptor (not as a noun), rather than the phrase *gifted and talented*, in line with the national organization's name (National Association for Gifted Children) and most pertinent scholarly literature. In this book, *gifted* will refer to any kinds of exceptional talents that represent the top of a bell curve in a particular domain.

Genesis

For twenty-five years, I was a teacher in public schools. For nineteen of those years, I taught mostly English literature and language to junior and senior high school students in the United States and Germany. My years in the classroom tuned me in to the social and emotional world of teens, and I observed and interacted with many who were gifted. When they wrote essays, interacted with me during yearbook meetings, worked with me in foreign-language club activities, or lingered after class, they taught me about adolescent development—and about sensitivities and intensities. Of those who were intellectually gifted (demonstrated largely through their writing insights and skills), some were high achievers and some were underachievers.

In general, students across a range of ability levels readily accepted my invitation to respond in writing to the literature we were reading. In fact, we did not discuss literature much orally; instead, they wrote in their journals about what they were reading, and I responded in the margins. There was no "correct" interpretation. They were encouraged to immerse themselves, think about the characters, apply perspectives related to other subjects and to their own world, gain insights, and learn through the process. We used class time for providing background material to help them understand the contexts of what they were reading. We sometimes discussed what they were reading, but students seemed to appreciate their autonomy in drawing conclusions themselves. In their journals, they asked questions about what they didn't understand. I like to think that all of my students benefited from this approach, but the gifted ones seemed particularly to thrive. The process was open-ended, with no limits on their insights, creativity, or depth.

There were many reasons for this teaching approach, and some of them relate to the discussion groups I later developed. Namely, students need information, and they need to develop skills. I wanted my students to learn to express themselves on paper and to become self-reflective, independent thinkers. I also wanted to hear from everyone equally, not just from the highly verbal and assertive. I employed an interactive, constructivist approach to foster immersion in learning, with hands-on classroom activities, media and community resources, vocabulary-in-context exercises, classroom dialogue, and reading. We learned together, and the students became more and more comfortable with complexity and ambiguity. Some of these strategies are similar to those I recommend for the development-oriented discussion groups described in this book.

I soon saw that the gifted students wanted to *be known*—to be recognized for their individual worth and uniqueness, not just for their intellect or talent. Some stayed after class to talk about difficult personal matters. I believe that gifted teens are hungry for acknowledgment and nonjudgmental listening. I learned that there were many important things they did not discuss with peers, and some of these teens did not have a comfortable enough relationship with a parent to ask tough questions or express concerns.

I was certainly reminded that gifted students were not exempt from troubling life events, difficult family situations, and challenges related to social and emotional development. The parents of some were divorced, unemployed, addicted, ill, absent, neglectful, or abusive. In contrast, some had parents who hovered protectively. Most important, these bright students were experiencing universal developmental challenges, although perhaps qualitatively differently from others their age. They fought with siblings, had "crushes" and breakups, and were anxious about the future. Some struggled with the hypocrisy of the adults around them and the sad state of the world as they saw it, and they responded to these and other issues with sadness, problematic behaviors, frustration, irritability, lack of motivation for schoolwork, and sometimes depression. They had difficulty managing their complex, fragmented lives. Sometimes they felt like exploding from tension. They needed someone to talk with. They needed affirmation for their humanness. They needed to have feelings and experiences validated.

Eventually, in another school, I had an opportunity to create an extensive small-group program for gifted students. Group work had never been done there. I thought back to the gifted teens in my classes. I certainly had seen the need for support and attentive listening. I decided to offer a group experience, focused on concerns related to social and emotional development.

The groups did not catch on immediately, but by the second semester, after more than one carefully crafted invitation, there were three groups, with about ten students each. The next year there were six groups, and then ten, with two hour-long groups per day, coordinated with the noon lunch schedule. Usually once each year I invited administrators, counselors, and student teachers to join us—with no group experiencing a guest more than once, and always with only one guest—in order to learn a little about proactive small-group work (in this case, with gifted teens) and perhaps to view gifted individuals more holistically. Group members were eager to "demonstrate their group." I was careful to choose a topic for those sessions that would not require a great level of trust (for example, "What do you wish teachers understood about teens like you—in general?"). Almost invariably, the guests would comment to me later that they had never thought that gifted students might feel misunderstood and narrowly viewed.

The students faithfully attended group meetings even though attendance was voluntary. Some came to school when they were not feeling well because they did not want to miss group. Most attended the weekly group meetings for three full years, without any lack of topics to talk about. We hardly ever discussed academics, per se, but we did address the stress related to the classroom and competitive activities. Group members became close through steady, undramatic weekly contact, and when a personal or institutional crisis arose, the groups were a ready support system. The students taught me, they taught each other, and they learned about themselves. The topics were not particularly heavy, but they resonated. The students relaxed and "just talked." Some students indicated, in formal, written feedback at the end of each year, that their group had offered crucial guidance in some aspect of life. Others said their group had helped them survive a difficult year. Almost all mentioned that it was important for them to hear that other gifted teens had concerns. The most shy members said they had gained from hearing others talk about growing up. Even normally gregarious group members wrote that they realized they were not alone in dealing with personal challenges. *The Essential Guide to Talking with Gifted Teens* grew out of the manuals I eventually created for the groups.

In other locations, I continued to form middle and high school groups with various populations. Concurrently, I finished doctoral studies in counselor education, began university-level teaching and research, and became a licensed mental health counselor, working in one or more settings, including private practice, school counseling, alternative teen facilities, and substance abuse treatment, for several years. I often worked with highly able children, teens, and families, continuing to learn about the social and emotional development of gifted individuals. I am now teaching in a university setting, helping counselors of tomorrow tune in to the affective needs of gifted students. From the highly capable graduate students in our selective program, I am learning about giftedness as it is experienced after high school and college.

Purpose

The purpose of these guided discussions is to support the social and emotional development of gifted teens. Whether through small- or large-group discussion, they become increasingly self-aware, and that in turn helps them to make better decisions, solve problems, and experience healthier relationships. They learn to affirm their complexity and make sense of their emotions and behavior. They feel more in control of their lives.

This support comes in the form of an environment where group members can express themselves. All teens need practice putting concerns and feelings into words. As bright as gifted teens are, and as much as some of them talk socially, they may not be skilled at communicating feelings and concerns clearly, genuinely, and effectively. Learning to talk about what is important to them and to listen attentively to others will enhance their present and future relationships. Adolescence is a good time to learn these skills. Small groups, in particular, offer two important opportunities that may be lacking elsewhere:

- a noncompetitive environment where no grades are given and where everyone is fairly equal (When focusing on social and emotional development, there is a relative absence of social hierarchy—and arrogance.)

- a safe place to talk about the journey of adolescence with others who share the experience (Everyone is navigating an uneven sea, with complex feelings, frustrations, and anxieties.)

Gifted teens gain social skills through interacting with each other in the presence of a nonjudgmental adult. The teens learn what they and others have in common, learn to listen, gain experience in initiating and responding to conversation, and become aware of how they are seen by others. All of these gains can enhance social ease and self-esteem, both of which can help make school a more pleasant, more comfortable place. In the current era of accountability, small-group work may also be viewed as a strategy for improving attitudes and test performance of gifted underachievers.

The format of *The Essential Guide to Talking with Gifted Teens* is not designed specifically to teach group skills or to acquaint teens with the vocabulary of group work. However, many such skills and some aspects of group dynamics will likely become familiar. The extensive introductory material here actually offers a solid overview of techniques related to group facilitation.

With guided group discussion, process is more important than product, and one goal is to enhance the skill of articulating social and emotional concerns. The focus, objectives, and suggestions for content and closure contained in each session provide a framework for solid, substantive, invigorating group experiences.

It is important to understand that the purpose of these group discussions is not to "fix" group members. Even though the questions are designed to provoke reflection and introspection, the emphasis is always on articulating feelings and thoughts in the presence of others who listen and care. These groups are not meant to be therapy groups. Yes, group work in any form has potential therapeutic value, and some noticeable changes in attitude and behavior often occur in the kind of groups promoted here. However, even when it appears that these changes have occurred because of the response and support of a group, other factors, such as changes at home, the healing effect of time, or developmental leaps, may also have contributed. Nevertheless, being involved in a group might help, and even be crucial, in times of personal crises, whether or not others in the group are aware of the distress. It is important to note here that mental health professionals can use many of these sessions in group therapy and in family counseling to foster communication and personal growth. Indeed, though few in number, providers who specialize in working with gifted clients do exist, and some do group work with gifted youth.

As is the case whenever adults stand firmly and supportively beside teens, establish trust, and participate in their complex lives, you will serve your group best by listening actively, with the focus fully on them, and offering your nonjudgmental presence as they find their own direction.

Meeting ASCA Standards

The national standards for school counseling programs, developed by the American School Counselor Association, focus on academic, career, and personal/social development of students. The focused discussions outlined in this book address standards in each of these areas, with giftedness in mind.

In relation to academic development, various sessions can help gifted students develop positive attitudes toward school, toward teachers and administrators, and toward learning. Group members become more aware of their learning preferences. Topics related to post-secondary options and transitions help students anticipate the future.

Related to career development, almost all discussion topics are intended to enhance self-awareness, including personal strengths and interests. Such self-awareness is a key ingredient in finding career direction, particularly when gifted teens struggle with *multipotentiality* (multiple interests and talents and career choices). A basic premise

of this book is that bringing gifted teens together in small groups helps them make comfortable interpersonal connections—through listening and responding, supporting and being supported, and appropriately expressing feelings and opinions. They break down cultural and socioeconomic stereotypes and learn about the perspectives of others. Interpersonal skills and sensitivity to others will enhance working relationships in the future. Group members reflect on the work attitudes of significant adult models in their lives and are encouraged to imagine themselves in future work contexts. They also learn about post-secondary educational settings and are able to ask questions and receive important information. Group facilitators are provided suggestions for organizing career-oriented experiences outside of school as well.

Most important, this book focuses on personal/social development—on simply growing up. Session topics encourage self-reflection about identity, feelings, and peer, family, and community relationships, not only in terms of universal developmental tasks, but also acknowledging that giftedness has potential impact in these areas. Members develop skills in a group, a social microcosm, potentially enhancing their lives in the present and after the school years. In addition, group members learn about emotional and physical vulnerabilities related to technology, high-risk social situations, relationships, and stress, and they consider ways to be social without putting themselves at risk.

Assumptions

The format and content of *The Essential Guide to Talking with Gifted Teens* reflect the following assumptions, which you may want to keep in mind as you lead your group.

1. Gifted teens have a desire to be heard, listened to, taken seriously, and respected. They want to be seen complexly—more than simply performers or nonperformers.

2. Because of their place on a bell curve of ability, they have a sense of differentness.

3. Some who are quiet, shy, intimidated, or untrusting often do not spontaneously offer comments, but they, too, want to be recognized and understood as unique, complex individuals.

4. All gifted teens need and appreciate support, no matter how strong and successful they seem to others. All have doubts about themselves at times. All feel socially inept and uncomfortable at times.

5. All feel stressed at times. Some feel stressed most or even all of the time. Many feel stressed because of overcommitment, overscheduling, or overinvolvement. All are concerned about the future.

6. Whether or not it is demonstrated outwardly, all have a high level of sensitivity to themselves and to their environment.

7. All are sensitive to family tension. Some are trying hard to keep families afloat or intact, and they may be given heavy responsibilities because of their abilities.

8. All probably have some sort of image to protect.

9. All feel angry at times.

10. All gifted teens, no matter how smooth and self-confident they appear, need practice talking honestly about feelings.

The Nuts and Bolts of Group Work

Group Settings

The session structure is appropriate for both small-group and large-group discussion, although some topics work better with small groups. Sessions are arranged in a purposeful progression for a long-term series, but may certainly be rearranged to create a short-term program or focus. Materials should be selected to fit context, purpose, and need. Here are some settings in which the sessions might be used:

- school-counseling and advisory groups for students of high ability
- summer enrichment programs for gifted teens
- residential schools for gifted teens
- leadership retreats, programs (those attending are likely to have demonstrated, or have the potential for, highly able leadership)
- music, athletics, or other organizational retreats for group-building
- at-home family discussions

Length of Meetings

Ideal meeting length varies, depending on the age of participants. Thirty- or forty-minute meetings probably suffices for students in grades six and seven—a bit longer, if hands-on activities are included. Eighth-graders and high school students usually appreciate a full hour (or class-period length)—after they settle in and gain trust. I recommend that groups that meet over lunch be allowed to leave a few minutes early from the class they're in before the group session, so that they can get their food before classes are dismissed and maximize the time available for discussion.

These sessions are also useful for weekend retreats or extended sessions for gifted teens. (I once used them for twice-weekly ninety-minute sessions at a state Governors School with groups of fifteen to sixteen.) Sequencing sessions so that activities alternate with focused discussion, with unstructured social time mixed in as well, is important, of course, as is maintaining stable group membership.

Large Groups

The Essential Guide to Talking with Gifted Teens can be useful in a self-contained classroom for gifted students or classrooms at residential or other schools for gifted students. Weekly discussions, or a daily series of units limited to a week or two, can be part of the curriculum. Homeroom, administration periods, or community time can use one or two activities or discussion catalysts effectively if the time allowed is adequate (at least twenty minutes). Sometimes gifted students are placed in the same homeroom for the purpose of group discussion geared toward social and emotional development.

Small Groups

Group Size
For small-group work, ideal group size varies according to age level. For younger gifted students, a group size of six to seven seems to work best. Regardless of age, however, I do not recommend more than eight students. These are general guidelines. My counseling students and I have experienced successful small-group discussion with as few as three students, who bonded well and developed trust after other members moved away.

Meeting Location
For small-group work, I recommend a small room (instead of a classroom). Such a space is more likely to be private and uninterrupted, to have fewer visual distractions than a classroom, and to promote a sense of intimacy. I also prefer to sit around a table—not only for comfort, but also because many sessions involve writing. Sitting at student desks also usually works well. Lying or sitting on the floor for an entire session actually becomes less comfortable than sitting in a chair for some. Group dynamics differ, of course, depending on whether a particular class or group has thirty members or ten, but the focus and most of the strategies here work with both sizes of groups. Since a discussion of an activity sheet can easily take an hour with a group of eight verbal students, adjustments must be made when activity sheets are used with larger groups. For example, full-size classes can be divided into small groups (three to five members) for sharing, with appropriate directions for discussion.

Group Composition

Most of the guided discussion sessions in *The Essential Guide to Talking with Gifted Teens* are appropriate for gifted kids at any point in adolescence. Ideally, groups are "closed," with membership not changing after the group begins. Each time someone is added, a group usually must focus again on developing trust, since it is a "new" group. Losing a member also changes group dynamics. Therefore, group organizers need to consider students' school-attendance patterns when determining group size. Some gifted teens have poor attendance.

I have found that the best groups are often those whose members do not know each other well outside of the group. They seem to feel free to share, and they do not have to preface all comments with "Well, someone in here has heard me say this before, but . . ." It shouldn't be assumed that gifted students are well acquainted with each other. Gifted teens who are involved in some activities may not be acquainted with gifted teens in other activities, even when both activities are under the athletic or music umbrella, for instance. And gifted teens with heavy home responsibilities or after-school jobs may not be involved in activities at all. On the other hand, I have had well-functioning groups where most of the members knew each other well. The groups helped them know each other better. Even best friends may not typically discuss topics like those in this volume.

However, depending on the size of the student population you draw from, you may not have a choice. If some members of your group know each other, it is important to move the group beyond the natural division of friends and nonfriends. Having a focus, with specific activities and written exercises, helps to ensure that the students who are friends do not dominate or irritate the others with "inside humor." Encouraging them to change seating each time can also be helpful, although it is important to make that a group norm at the outset, since groups—especially middle school groups—may be resistant to doing that later.

I like to promote the idea of using the groups to break down social barriers. In general, I prefer a membership balance between achievers and underachievers, at-risk and not at-risk, highly involved in school and not so involved, and representatives of various ethnic and socioeconomic groups. The mix helps members to break down stereotypes and discover common ground.

If several groups are being formed at one time, distribution can be accomplished by initially compiling a list of all students who accept the invitation to participate and then sorting the list. Of course, recruitment will have to target those less likely to feel welcome. In some cases, the highest-functioning students may be the most reluctant to join, fearing that the groups are geared only to "problems" and "counseling" and that participation will somehow stigmatize them. These students might also feel some anxiety about the focus on nonacademic areas. Underachieving students and those with other risk factors may think that they will be the only ones in the group with stresses, vulnerabilities, fears, and problematic

performance or attitudes. The latter can benefit from realizing that everyone has developmental concerns. That reality should be included in any recruitment material. For example, stress from high expectations can be mentioned as a common denominator among many gifted teens.

All social, cultural, and socioeconomic groups have a great deal to learn from each other, and the group setting can be an ideal learning environment. Gifted teens may not feel comfortable talking about developmental concerns in intellectually diverse groups, but they are apt to open up when a group is composed entirely of gifted teens, including those with various levels of *achievement*. In fact, such group composition can foster highly productive discussions. Often, underachievers are amazed that achievers have social and emotional problems; some achievers are equally amazed that underachievers can be highly intelligent and extremely articulate. Discovery of common ground is a good overarching goal. Gifted students with behavior problems, difficulty with authority, or poor social skills are usually well served when group membership is mixed (for example, at least half of them with good interpersonal skills, behavior, and achievement). The group may be a rare opportunity for them to communicate with those who don't struggle with these developmental issues.

If mixing is not possible in your setting, or if your group has been brought together because members share a common concern or have a specific purpose and agenda, you can still use these guided discussions with confidence, since they deal with common developmental issues. In fact, I often recommend to my counseling students that talking about developmental challenges can help even the most angry or disruptive students. In other words, the topic does not have to be anger or behavior, per se, even though it might be helpful to brainstorm strategies for improving behavior at some point. Simply having a chance to connect with others, express concerns, and feel more comfortable with themselves and with the school environment can help to reduce problematic behaviors. Talking and being heard are important in helping students feel that school is an accommodating and comfortable place.

When forming a group, you also need to consider whether to have a mixed-gender or same-gender composition. With gifted teens in high school, I prefer mixed-gender groups. It is important for teens this age to learn about each other in a safe and nonjudgmental environment, outside of the regular classroom and apart from usual social settings. It is also important for both genders to learn how to communicate with, and in the presence of, each other.

Especially for gifted teens who are shy or who lack social contact, a discussion group can provide a chance to have contact with the other gender. But even for the highly social, a group can raise awareness of gender issues and enhance the ability of boys and girls to function effectively with each other in relationships now and in the future, including in marriage and other partnerships, in employment, and in board rooms.

At the middle school level, sometimes same-gender groups work best, probably because of the typical social and emotional developmental gap between boys and girls at that time, a gap which tends to diminish during high school. Boys generally talk as well as the girls, as a group, when separate. Girls often appreciate the safety of talking with other girls. However, I have indeed had successful mixed-gender groups in middle schools.

When students understand the purpose of the groups, and after they move beyond initial discomfort with the nonacademic emphasis, they can relax, invest, and appreciate the opportunity to talk with others at their intellectual level about growing up. For gifted teens, one key ingredient in trust and feeling understood is relatively equal ability.

Forming groups where students are of the same age is another key ingredient. Because the sessions are geared to social and emotional development, not to cognitive and academic concerns, it is best to set up age-based groups—especially when gifted students have skipped grades and are in a grade with older students. A twelve-year-old in eighth grade is developmentally different and has different concerns from eighth-graders who are fourteen, for instance, and even thirteen- and fourteen-year-olds can have difficulty connecting with each other about social and emotional concerns. Gifted seniors are likely looking ahead in ways that even juniors are not, so seniors of any age might have common career-development and college concerns. However, socially and emotionally, a thirteen-year-old senior probably would connect better with gifted age peers. Relationship issues differ along the age continuum, and it is best when students can communicate with others in their own age group about these concerns. Intellectually, and in regard to interests, even very young gifted children might feel most comfortable talking with gifted teens or adults. But socially and emotionally their developmental needs and challenges are likely to be similar to those of age-mates.

Inviting Students to Join a Group

In a school, the best way to encourage students to join your group, if membership is voluntary, is to invite them personally. In any event, I recommend that you not call it a *counseling* group when describing it to prospective group members, even if you are indeed a counselor, but certainly if you are not, since then there are liability concerns. Some students are automatically turned off and turned away by the counseling label. Later on, if someone asks if it is a counseling group, explain that counseling is basically talking and listening with someone trained in that process. In that regard, if you are a trained counselor,

your group could be called a counseling group. *Support group* is appropriate when there is a common, specific agenda, or a shared problem area. However, if the group is largely preventive, with self-awareness and personal growth as goals, then *support* probably is too problem-oriented for many students. *Discussion group* is always my preference in school settings.

In schools, I have contacted students individually to explain a proposed group, and I have also called in small groups and full-size discussion groups to hear the plan. In either case, you need to assure the students that joining the group is not a high-risk thing to do. That message is important for gifted teens, especially those who are not used to venturing into the unknown with confidence that they can adapt to whatever transpires. The advantage of calling in the group as a whole is that the students can see who else will be attending. On the other hand, some might decide against joining for that very reason, hanging on to stereotypes, without giving unfamiliar or unknown gifted peers a chance. When meeting with students individually, you might give them the names of a few prospective members—but only if they ask, and if it is possible to share names in advance. If a student wants to ensure that friends will be in a group, I prefer to say, simply, "I encourage you to come and be surprised. It's good to get to know new people, and sometimes it's good *not* to know anyone else well at the outset. If you decide later that you are not comfortable with the group, you have the option of not continuing." If you decide to meet with all prospective members together, be prepared to do at least a typical, brief activity to demonstrate what the group will be like.

Be sure to emphasize the social, as well as the emotional, purposes of the group. Gifted kids may be surprised and intrigued by that information, since elsewhere in their lives the emphasis may be largely on academics and talent. Tell them that it will be a rare opportunity to connect with gifted peers about nonacademic life—even those they interact with regularly otherwise. I routinely mention stress and stereotypes as sample topics for discussion, and these seem to resonate. Explain that, beyond pursuing general goals, the group will determine its own unique atmosphere. That much of an explanation usually suffices. If students want to know more, show them the contents of this book. The session titles are varied, and students usually find them interesting—and unexpected.

If you use this book with gifted high school students, it helps to tell them, in addition to other potential benefits, that once you get to know them better through the group experience, you will be able to write more complete job, college, or scholarship recommendations for them. Explain that you will also be a better and more informed advocate for them if they ever need assistance.

Students Who Have Significant Risk Factors

If, as a professional counselor, you want to form groups for gifted teens around a major concern, a variety of developmental topics in this volume are appropriate for generating discussion. A common concern related specifically to giftedness might be any of these:

- lack of family affirmation of high ability
- anxiety
- perfectionism
- profound giftedness
- dual-exceptionality (learning disability and giftedness)
- bullies and those who are bullied

Other life events and circumstances are certainly possible concerns as well:

- family disruption
- parental or student substance abuse
- physical or sexual abuse
- family tragedy
- lack of family support for school attendance or achievement
- a potential for dropping out of school
- terminal illness in a family member
- frequent family moves
- poverty
- bereavement
- parental military deployment
- school crisis
- pregnancy
- being new in school

For several of the above concerns, faithfully applying the guidelines of this book and focusing on development can provide sufficient support and helpful interaction. However, unless you have counseling training, facilitating groups with the others (for example, abuse, tragedy, and bereavement), and forming groups composed solely of individuals who struggle with depression, hyperactivity, or behavioral or emotional disability is unwise, unethical, and potentially unproductive. There are also significant privacy issues related to grouping kids together with a stated concern. Even for trained professionals, such grouping often is not recommended. One common guideline is not to have the same pathology in all group

members. In this regard, however, underachievement should not be seen as pathology; grouping gifted underachievers together can indeed be productive.

Students may not be eager to join a group. If attendance is voluntary, I recommend that you meet first with these students individually. Explain that you will be leading a discussion group for gifted students, and you are inviting them to participate. If the student has difficulty with authority, is an underachieving student, or is known as a "joker" or a "rebel," for example, state that you are looking for interesting, complex students who can help to make a good group. Say that you are looking specifically for students who express their abilities in unusual ways because you do not want a group that is afraid to challenge each other and think, and you do not want only students who always do what is expected of them. Reframing characteristics usually considered troublesome in this positive way often takes students by surprise and encourages them to participate.

However, no matter what a particular student's behavior might be, always present the group's purpose honestly: to give gifted students a chance to talk about issues that are important to teens. Be sincere, accepting, and supportive in your invitation. With students in distress, as with all prospective group members, take care not to frighten them away by sounding invasive or therapy oriented. Give them time to warm up to the idea of interacting with others about growing up.

Primary and Secondary Prevention

The Essential Guide to Talking with Gifted Teens is appropriate for primary prevention in the form of focused, development-oriented discussion meant to prevent problems and enhance development. It is also appropriate for secondary prevention, for use when there appears to be potential for problems. For such purposes, the sessions are potentially beneficial for groups composed of a variety of gifted populations. Gifted students need attention to social and emotional development as much as other students, and their giftedness might even put them at unique risk for poor emotional and/or educational outcomes. Circumstances can also put them at risk.

Teens experiencing family transitions can benefit from the sessions in the Stress section. They might also find affirmation and be able to express uncomfortable feelings in some of the sessions in the Identity section. Some of the family-oriented sessions in the Relationships section might also be helpful during transitions, as well as some sessions in the Feelings and Family sections.

Gifted teens at risk for poor personal or educational outcomes might benefit from these sessions:

- "Façade, Image, and Stereotype"
- "More Than Test Scores and Grades?"

- "Learning Styles"
- "Intensity, Compulsivity, and Control"
- "Influencers"
- "Authority"
- "Getting What We Need"

Group members who are feeling sad or depressed often find some of the sessions on stress to be helpful. In addition, the following can be valuable:

- "Self in Perspective"
- "Intensity, Compulsivity, and Control"
- "Playing"
- "Lonely at the Top"
- "Getting What We Need"

Gifted students returning from, or currently in, treatment for substance abuse or eating disorders might also find these sessions helpful, including when they are quietly integrated or re-integrated into a "regular group" (that is, without a common concern). The prevention- and development-oriented sessions specifically focused on substance use or eating disorders are not necessarily appropriate for these students, although they might be. But basic developmental topics are appropriate regardless of situation. Gifted teens can indeed be using substances and/or involved with potentially life-threatening behaviors. They do not fit the stereotype of "gifted kids," but do certainly exist, whether identified for special programs or not.

Leading the Sessions

Facilitators

These sessions are designed to be used in a variety of settings with gifted teens. Group facilitators may include the following:

- school counselors
- counselors and advisors at residential or other programs/schools for gifted teens
- teachers in school programs for gifted students
- counselors and social workers in community agencies, treatment centers, or private practice
- group builders and wellness advocates at retreats for gifted youth
- parents or primary caregivers (in informal one-on-one or family interaction)

Are You Ready to Lead a Discussion Group?

Especially if you are not used to dealing with large or small groups in an informal discussion setting, you may find the following suggestions and observations helpful:

- Discussion related to social and emotional areas involves more personal risk and is much less "controllable" than that related to the intellectual realm. Such loss of control can feel frightening for anyone (facilitator or group member) accustomed to using cognitive and verbal strengths to control situations.

- It is important to recognize that some members may be more intellectually nimble than you are (a common admonition during training of teachers for education of gifted kids). A group member may be, literally, 1 in 100,000 or 1 in 1,000,000 in terms of intellectual ability. Do your best to make this a nonissue, regardless of how you perceive your own ability. Acknowledging it overtly calls attention to something that might always be a distancer for the gifted teen. Instead, keep the attention on emotional, not cognitive, development. Group members all are developing socially and emotionally, probably not easily.

- If you are careful to keep the focus on social and emotional issues, there will be little opportunity for group members to play competitive, "one-up" verbal games with you or with each other.

- Significant adults in gifted teens' lives might have focused more on behavior than on feelings, more on academic than on social and emotional needs, or more on performance than on personal development. Some teens will be eager and immediately grateful for the emphasis on the social and emotional, but some might be uncomfortable or even frightened by the developmental focus initially, especially those whose families guard privacy at extreme levels and view emotional expression as problematic. Regardless, your concentrated attention on social and emotional concerns will probably be a new experience for them. Discomfort may even generate problematic behavior at first. Social and emotional concerns are not likely to be debatable, but, because of anxiety, some "debaters" might want to deflect attention onto political or other issues initially—until you rein them in.

You might also want to consider your own motives for establishing groups for gifted teens, as well as your sense of security around them. When I train counselors and teachers to work with gifted individuals, I advise them to carefully consider the following questions:

- Can you avoid feeling competitive with gifted teens, or needing to assert control over them?

- Can you be confident around them, not threatened by their abilities?

- Can you stay focused on the social and emotional, no matter what comes up?

- Can you deal with gifted students simply as human beings with frailties, insecurities, sensitivities, and vulnerabilities, regardless of their school performance and/or behavior?

- Can you avoid needing to "put them in their place"?

- Can you accept their defenses, including arrogance and bravado, and give them time to let themselves be socially and emotionally vulnerable?

- Can you recognize that they may not be accomplished risk-takers socially, academically, and/or emotionally, and that they might need to be encouraged to take appropriate risks?

- Can you look honestly at some of your own stereotypes or negative feelings about gifted kids that might interfere in your work with them, and can you put these aside for the duration of the group experience?

- Can you let group members teach you about themselves without judging them?

- Can you avoid voyeurism (being preoccupied with ferreting out details about families and personal lives)? That is not what these groups are about.

- Can you resist the urge to psychoanalyze members and to interpret behavior?

- If you are a teacher, can you indeed move away from an evaluative mode and adopt a supportive posture?

- Can you leave an adult-expert position and accept that teens know themselves and their world better than you do—and that you need to learn from them?

- Can you enter their world respectfully?

- Can you keep in mind that gifted teens may have no other place to talk that is noncompetitive, nonjudgmental, nonevaluative, nonperformance-oriented, and nonacademic—so that you don't slip into any of these modes?

If you can answer yes to all or most of these questions, don't worry. You're ready to take on a roomful or small group of gifted teens. If your answers were mostly negative or unsure, perhaps you should consider other ways to work with gifted teens or should (if you are not a counselor) consider co-facilitating a group with a counselor at least initially. Such co-facilitation may help you develop listening and responding skills and move toward an objective, nonjudgmental posture.

General Guidelines

The following general guidelines are designed to help you lead successful and meaningful discussion groups with gifted teens. You may want to review these guidelines from time to time over the life of a group.

1. The function of the group leader is to facilitate discussion. The best posture is "learner," not "teacher," with the group members doing the teaching—about themselves. Adolescents talk when adults step back and apply active-listening skills.

2. Be prepared to learn how to lead a group by doing it. Let the group know that this is your attitude. If you are a trained counselor, you may need to become comfortable with *focused* discussion. In addition, even if you lead groups regularly, reviewing basic tenets of group process might be beneficial. If you are not a trained counselor and are not able to co-facilitate a group with a counselor, as mentioned above, ask a counselor for information on group process and listening and responding.

3. Don't think that you have to be an expert on every topic covered. Tell the group at the outset that you want to learn with them and from them, and you want them to learn from each other as well. It is better to be "one-down" (unknowing) than "one-up" (expert) in your relationship with gifted teens. That is an appropriate place to start, and they will respond. For most sessions, having information is not the key to success. Trust your adult wisdom. That is one thing you have that your group members do not. But, again, recognize that your job is largely to facilitate discussion, not to teach.

4. Monitor group interaction and work toward contribution from everyone without making that an issue. Remember that shy students can gain a great deal just by listening and observing. You can encourage everyone to participate, yet not insist on that.

5. Keep the session focus in mind, but be flexible about direction. Your group may lead you in new directions that are as worthwhile as the stated focus and suggestions. However, if they veer too far off track, with only one or two students dominating, use the focus as an excuse to rein in the group.

6. It is probably best to go into each session with two related session ideas in mind, since the one you have planned might not generate as much response as

expected. You can always unobtrusively guide the group into a new direction. Try several approaches to a topic before dropping it, however. It might simply require some "baking time."

7. Be willing to model how to do an activity, even though it is usually not necessary. The activity sheets are fairly self-explanatory, but on occasion, you may need to demonstrate an appropriate response. If you are not willing to share your thoughts and feelings, your group may wonder why they should be expected to do so. However, your doing only one small, discreet, carefully selected self-disclosure early in the life of the group may suffice—for an entire series of meetings. The modeling you do should be only for the purpose of facilitating student responses. Too much can actually inhibit response. Attention should be focused on group members, not on you.

8. Every now and then, especially after the group has established a rhythm (perhaps after five or six meetings), check out how group members are feeling about the group. Is there anything they would like to do differently or change? Are they comfortable sharing their feelings and concerns? What has been helpful? Have they noticed any problems that need addressing, such as discussions being dominated by a few, not enough flexibility in direction, a personality conflict within the group, or too much leader direction? Processing group dynamics (*process* is an important verb in the counseling profession) provides an opportunity for members to practice tact in addressing group issues (see #10).

   Incorporate student suggestions that fit the overall purpose of the group. If you do not yet feel comfortable as a facilitator, and if the students are being negatively critical, tell them that you are still learning about groups, and they are as well. Be aware that some may press for "no focus" for a long time. You should review the rationale for focus outlined on page 15 prior to your first request for feedback. Depending on group composition, you may choose to delay questions about format until the benefits have become fairly clear. Or simply be prepared to explain the purpose of the format while emphasizing that the format is flexible. Support the group and give guidance as they make progress in overcoming group problems. Above all, try to be secure in using a focus. If you seem unsure and ask too frequently about the format, you may experience "mutiny," especially if there has not been sufficient time for the group to bond and appreciate the benefits of some structure. I often ask for feedback midway and also late in the life of a group, otherwise relying on members' level of cooperation to tell me

how the group is functioning. If lack of cooperation is a problem, I process that (see #10 below).

9. If group energy consistently or increasingly lags, discuss that in the group. Let the members help you figure out how to energize the discussions and/or deal with group inhibitions. However, do not readily reject the idea of maintaining a focus for each session. Perhaps you need to alter your questioning style (see page 18), or more deftly follow some directions that come up spontaneously. Or perhaps you need to be more selective when choosing topics. The written exercises and activity sheets often help to encourage sharing. Thoughtfully creating your own activities related to the focus, or incorporating various media into the meetings, can also energize a group.

10. Anything can be processed in the group—crying, interrupting, disclosing something unexpected, being rude, being sad, belching, challenging the facilitator, group negativity. That is, group members can discuss what just happened—in the present. A facilitator can say, "What was it like for you to challenge me just now?" or "How did the rest of you feel when she challenged me?" or "How are you feeling right now, after she disclosed that?" or "That comment was a surprise. How is it affecting us?" Processing what happens in a group gives members a chance to reflect on their own feelings and on the group's interaction and to learn skills in articulating emotions.

Choosing and Adapting Session Topics

Group facilitators are often reluctant to adapt the format to their particular groups. Yet it's important to approach the topics creatively, responding to the uniqueness of each group. At the very least, time constraints may mean that some written exercises need to be shortened. Depending on the age level or language ability of your group, some vocabulary might need to be changed. In addition, some of the suggestions provided for each session might not fit your setting. In that case, ignore them or devise your own unique approach to the focus. Examine the sessions to determine which ones might be most helpful, enjoyable, and appropriate for your group. Finally, be aware that intellectually precocious teens may be only average, or even *below* average, in social and emotional development; take that into consideration when selecting topics. Too often, adults forget that gifted kids are "just kids." However, beware of underestimating group members' awareness of the world or need for information just because they are chronologically young.

   Two additional cautions are in order here. Even though it is likely understandable to gifted teens, the background material at the beginning of most sessions is intended for teachers and counselors (and parents who use this book for family discussion), not to be read to the group. It is meant to provoke thought, raise awareness, and provide a perspective. In addition, always be aware of, and respect, community sensitivities. For example, parents and other members of the community might object to discussions related to sexual orientation, sexuality and sexual behavior, gender roles, and family roles. Even discussions about depression might not be deemed appropriate.

Ethical Behavior: Confidentiality

Counseling codes of ethics provide behavioral guidelines for counselors, in order to protect those who are counseled. Your behaving ethically as a group leader is crucial to the success of your group work. For instance, sharing group information in the teachers' lounge, with parents, or in the community will not only be hurtful, but may also ultimately destroy the possibility of small-group activity in your school. When trust is lost, it is difficult and sometimes impossible to re-establish.

If you plan to conduct groups in a school setting but are not a counselor and are unfamiliar with ethical guidelines for counselors (including those specifically related to group work), get a copy of such guidelines from your school counselor and read them carefully. Be especially aware of your responsibilities regarding confidentiality. These include familiarizing yourself with situations in which confidentiality must be breached, such as when abuse is suspected, when someone is in danger or may be a danger to others, or when someone is planning to disrupt or damage school mission, personnel, or structure (the last item is specifically stated in the school counseling code). The "informed consent" aspect of group work can be addressed by discussing format, content, confidentiality, limits of confidentiality, and purpose at the first meeting.

Confidentiality cannot be guaranteed in a group. Explain what actions you will take to protect confidentiality, but emphasize that you can guarantee the behavior of only yourself, not of group members. However, since trust is so essential for comfortable group discussion, strongly encourage group members not to share what is said in the group outside of the group. Tell them that not keeping comments "inside the group" can destroy the group and even prevent *any* groups from existing in the school or organization in the future because of lack of trust. Facilitators should not use the word *secrets,* however, because it may raise unwarranted concerns and because it may be frightening to students whose families direct them not to share personal information. Discussion about confidentiality should not be threatening or overblown.

You may wish to address these issues in a letter to parents asking their permission for their children to attend the group. For a sample letter, see page 21. Please note that this letter is appropriate for groups not designed for specific problem areas. Feel free to adapt it.

Group Members Who Betray Trust

If you or a group member learns that confidentiality has been breached, processing the experience will be crucial. Barring the betrayer(s) of trust from continuing in the group is not the only appropriate response and may not be appropriate at all. Since these groups are focused on development, the situation is an opportunity to discuss trust ("What are your thoughts about the trust level of the group?"), feelings in the group ("What are you feeling right now?"), prospects for regaining trust ("What would we need to do to regain trust?" "How long do you think it might take?"), what the breacher(s) can/will do in the future ("What would ___ need to do to regain your trust?"). Maintaining poise and objectivity as you conduct the discussion models that difficult feelings and situations can indeed be discussed, shame and guilt can be "worked through," and repair of trust is possible, though not likely to be quick. These are important revelations to teens, who otherwise may not know that such a discussion and such outcomes are possible. Teens can be empowered by the discussion, take ownership of their future, and decide what to do about the situation. Betrayal of trust, in itself, is not a crime and does not automatically warrant expulsion from the group, but the ripple effect can be significant.

Group Members Who Are Quiet or Shy

Groups can actually help to affirm quiet personal styles by overtly recognizing quiet members' listening and observation skills, which gregarious members may not have. However, although listening can be as valuable as speaking in finding commonalities and gaining self-awareness, it is important for reticent individuals to be heard by their peers, even if only at modest levels. Earnest efforts to ask students who are quiet or shy for at least one or two comments each meeting can help them to feel included and gradually increase their courage and willingness to share. The written exercises and activity sheets can be used to provide them with a comfortable opening for sharing. Even uttering a simple phrase from a sheet can feel huge for a shy teen and may represent significant risk-taking. Small talk between a leader and a shy student while everyone is getting settled may also contribute to comfort and ease, which eventually might generate spontaneous comments. However, the value of communication with peers, in contrast to communication with the group facilitator, should not be underestimated. Gifted students with little social contact or verbal interaction with peers may feel poorly informed. Post-group feedback in my group work has indicated that quiet group members gain as much or more than assertive members from the group experience.

Group Members Who Dominate

One strategy for dealing with verbal dominators is to revisit the group guidelines (page 22) as a group, with no one the target. Processing group discussion, after the fact, can also be used to raise awareness (for example, "How does it feel to be in the group at this point? How are we doing in making sure that everyone gets a chance to talk and that no one dominates?"). If you notice someone rolling eyes when a dominant group member talks, call attention to that (for example, "I was just noticing a facial expression in the group. _____, would you be willing to share with the group what is on your mind? It might be important for helping us to be a better group.")

Counseling Individual Group Members

When a level of trust has been established within a group and between members and facilitator, individuals with pressing needs sometimes, understandably and appropriately, seek consultation outside of the group if the leader is accessible. A trusted facilitator, sought out during a crisis, may indeed play a crucial role in ensuring the well-being of a group member. The following are general guidelines related to such situations, but if you are not a counselor, refer to "Handling the Unexpected" below for additional information.

If you will not be on the premises every day, it is important to tell the group, at least at the outset of the group series, about times when you will be available. I do not recommend giving out your phone number or email, since it is easy for particularly dependent students, and those with poor boundaries, to abuse access. On the other hand, it may be possible (even though not easy) for you to model boundary-setting if the email or phone calls become invasive. Anyone can usually find contact information on the Internet if persistent enough—another reason for not giving it out to the group. As in everything, moderation is the key—and caution as well.

It is important to note that too much emphasis at group sessions on outside conferencing can turn off members who do not want to connect the groups to "counseling" and might also encourage some to steer their communication away from the group in order to have a special relationship with the facilitator. Facilitators should certainly not refer to outside conversations in group meetings. In addition, if members complain about the group to the facilitator between sessions, they should be encouraged to bring their concerns to the group, putting responsibility on the group for improvement and giving the group an opportunity to gain skills in resolving conflict.

Handling the Unexpected

Most gifted students are appropriately discreet in what they share in small- and large-group meetings, especially when the facilitator does not pry for private information,

does not appear to "need" it, and does not unduly reward those who share it. However, you can probably expect a highly charged moment to occur once in a while.

What happens when something shocking comes out, when someone breaks down and cries, or when intense conflict arises within the group? No one can predict these events, since every group has unique dynamics, and groups are full of surprises. However, keeping basic cautions in mind, you will learn to trust your instincts. With experience, you will become increasingly ready and able to handle whatever comes up.

Have tissues handy for the student who cries, and simply convey a silent request to a nearby group member to pass the box to the member who needs it. It is important to affirm the expressed emotion in your facial expression and body language and accept the tears with poise. In fact, your empathetic composure will model for group members that it is all right to cry and express emotions genuinely, that others do not have to rush in to "fix" the situation, and that it is important not to be hyper-reactive to others' discomfort, since objectivity and ability to help may then be lost. When appropriate, ask the individual if he or she would like anything from the group. Overt support? Just listening? No attention, for the moment? It may be helpful to process an outburst, after the fact, asking the group questions like "How did it feel to have someone express emotion through crying?" or "Is there anything you would like to say to (student who cried)?" Then ask the latter, "What was it like for you to hear that?"

If a student makes a dramatic revelation, immediately remind the group about the importance of confidentiality. You might say, "It probably took courage for (name of student) to share that. She/he trusted you as a group. What was said should stay in the group. If you are tempted to share this with someone outside of the group, keep quiet. That's very important. We want to protect our group." Beware of exaggerated responses, nonverbal and verbal, which can promote the idea that a particular revelation is "too much to handle." The sharer might, in fact, have been testing that belief.

If you work in a school and are not a counselor, consult with a school counselor or administrator to learn what to do in specific situations. For example, if a student drops a "bomb" (or even just a hint) about abuse or suicidal thoughts, you should know how to follow up (see the session "Dark Thoughts, Dark Times," pages 208–213, for some guidelines). Your school or organization likely has guidelines specific to these issues. It is best to know them ahead of time. If students seek you out independently about a personal concern, remind them that you are not a counselor, but that you will certainly listen and that you may subsequently encourage them to see a counselor (or accompany them there), depending on what the concern is.

If you are a counselor, it is of course important to follow up a revelation about abuse or neglect with a one-on-one meeting with the student to determine if the revelation was made genuinely, and, if so, to validate the experience through supportive comments and call a child protection agency.

Groups are ideal settings for practicing conflict resolution. You can help those in disagreement to talk it out and listen carefully to each other. If you're a counselor, you might gather material on conflict resolution to share with the students or simply apply your expertise. If you are not a counselor, ask your school counselor for strategies to help your group deal with disagreements and perhaps even consider having the counselor conduct mediation. Be aware that your own fears, discomfort, or emotionality about conflict might actually prevent members from handling contentious situations in a healthy manner.

Announcing the Session Topic

If your group is voluntary and a session topic is announced in advance, some teens may decide not to come if the topic does not sound interesting or relevant. You want group attendance to be consistent, and it is distracting and detrimental when all students show up one week and only two the next. Therefore, I recommend that you use a "trust me" response when students ask about the next session's topic. Suggest that they show up and be surprised. Remind them that one can never anticipate the interesting directions a particular topic might take. Besides, many topics are more complex than they first appear.

Journal-Writing

Depending on the purpose of your group, group members' class and activity loads, the level of access members have to you outside of group meetings, and time available for group meetings and for you to respond to the journals carefully and briefly in writing, you might consider including journal-writing in your group's experience.

In general, I prefer to use the entire group time for open, semistructured discussion, with or without activity sheets. Adding discussion related to journals diverts time and attention away from the new focus, since journal entries are probably related to preceding, not present, topics. While I am a proponent of using journals to respond to literature, I do not recommend personal journals in classrooms or during group work in schools and summer institutes because of the potential for voyeurism and for other reasons detailed below. I have known language arts teachers who faced difficulty when parents found students' personal journals and challenged the teachers for not informing them about the activity and for infringing on family privacy. For group facilitators who are not trained counselors, a great amount of personal information may be shared, placing a burden on them regarding what should be revealed and how to respond.

Keep the following points in mind if you consider using journaling as a strategy:

- Fundamentally, the emphasis in this group approach is on *oral* expression.

- Some gifted teens eagerly write about their feelings. Through writing, they can articulate, clarify, expand on, and sort ideas and issues that are important to them. They may be more likely to remember ideas and issues they want to bring up in the group, and shy group members, especially, may feel more confident about expressing them.

- However, other gifted teens have a strong aversion to writing. Some highly talented visual artists, musicians, and kinesthetic learners, for example, find it difficult or bothersome to write. Regardless of impressive strengths in other areas, gifted teens may also struggle with poor small-motor skills or have learning disabilities that affect their ability to write. Some simply may not be highly verbal. For these reasons, adding journal-writing to a group experience might not be wise. If you do incorporate it, reassure the group that it will not be graded or edited, since this kind of group work is meant to be nonjudgmental. What is important is what they have to say. Your saying this might be a relief for both achievers and underachievers, certainly for those who do not enjoy writing. But it may not be enough to encourage reluctant writers.

- In schools where there is considerable journal-writing in language arts classes, students are less likely to welcome journals in the discussion groups, regardless of their writing skills. There can definitely be journal burnout. If you do use journals, explain that this experience will differ from journal-writing in regular classes. Here, they can explore feelings and issues related to discussion topics. However, journal-writing is not a good idea if it is part of one or more of members' classes otherwise.

- Teens sometimes need strong enticement to join groups, especially when groups are first being established in a school. Students are most receptive when the group experience does not seem like work. Journal-writing can easily be perceived as just one more classroom assignment, amid many, in high-pressured academic environments and might actually discourage group attendance. In addition, though gifted immigrant students with low English proficiency can gain both receptive and expressive language in a group, writing may be especially challenging for them and may create enough discomfort that they will drop out of the group, thus losing an opportunity to make connections with other gifted students.

- Journals can give group members a chance to communicate privately with you about important concerns. Facilitators can then carry on a dialogue with members who may not feel comfortable talking about their thoughts and feelings in the group. Conscientious, well-considered feedback is essential. However, journals should not take the place of talking. Remind reluctant talkers that while you appreciate their sharing their thoughts with you, it is important that they contribute to the group.

- Recognize that if members share journals with you privately, you will need to mentally keep track of which information has been presented in the group and which in the journals. That can be a difficult dance. There is already a great deal to keep track of. Do not share journal information with the group, even if the writer encourages you to do that. Journals should be considered private communication, and group members should share thoughts orally.

- You might simply encourage group members to keep a private journal at home, written only for themselves as a way to process group meeting.

- English/language arts teachers might use suggestions in sessions as pre-writing exercises or questions as writing prompts.

About the Sessions

Focus

Why have a focus for each session? Development is the common denominator for the sessions—not a particular issue, behavior, need, or goal, as is common in group therapy. Nevertheless, working with an explicit focus, or theme, is indeed worthwhile, as it provides a starting point for discussion and an excuse to rein in group behaviors, including dominance. It also insists on addressing topics that might be somewhat uncomfortable but important and developmentally appropriate. In addition, all gifted teens are not as flexible as they might appear, and product-oriented members may quickly tire of "not really doing anything." Some need structure to contain their anxiety and impulsivity. On the other hand, some teens are quite flexible, and, especially if they are verbal and spontaneous, they may prefer a looser format. In fact, they might say, "Just let us come in here and talk about whatever we want to talk about." The structure recommended here can benefit a wide range of personalities and meet many needs. Even teens who resist structure often find the variety of semistructured approaches interesting and worthwhile. Consider carefully how much structure is warranted. Complaints

may initially reflect only apprehension about addressing developmental concerns.

Individuals who like order and structure and are uncomfortable when there is no "map" or clear purpose usually want group time to be worthwhile in specific terms. Linear thinkers, sequential planners, and perfectionist group members, in particular, may object to meetings with little structure. Lack of focus, if the group is a voluntary activity, may mean that students do not attend when something else seems preferable—including reviewing for an exam or eating with friends in the lunchroom. They may also object when assertive members set the pace and topic each time. Teens with new and dramatic needs each week can quickly dominate, and others may then either defer and listen or leave, frustrated that their own issues or interests are not being addressed. Discussion groups should not be just for natural talkers.

On the other hand, group discussions need not be rigidly programmed. Although *The Essential Guide to Talking with Gifted Teens* proposes a focus for each session, sometimes with several sessions building on a theme, there is great potential for nimbly changing direction during discussion. A flexible facilitator can adapt the session to themes that emerge, yet still gently steer the group to closure, overtly acknowledging that the focus inspired unexpected directions. Especially with topics that members view as intimidating and difficult, the focus is an excuse to persist with tough questions and issues, not just gripes and frustrations, gossip and banter.

Having a focus also helps group facilitators to communicate with administrators, parents, and other faculty about the group and its activities, an important consideration in today's educational climate. Many outsiders assume that discussion groups are for teacher bashing, airing family secrets, or simply "hanging out"—the first and third of these being of particular concern when key gifted students have a reputation of being critical of teachers or for acting "entitled." Being able to say, "We've been dealing with stress the past four weeks, a problem for most gifted teens" or "We're focusing on self-awareness this semester," or, more specifically, "We've been talking about bullying" helps to lessen anxiety or suspicion. Listing even a few topics underscores that groups deal with significant issues and are worth the time and energy that the logistical challenges of group work often require.

The sessions that focus on self-esteem and friendship in this volume look at those concepts from several angles, including developmental. I have found that focusing on self-esteem, motivation, or friendship more narrowly is often not productive in small-group work. That is not to say that enhancing these is not a worthy goal. However, meaningful discussion, connections with peers, new social skills, and information about development can all potentially enhance how gifted teens view themselves, peers, and schoolwork. Both self-esteem and motivation are probably related to developmental challenges, and friendship skills can be improved through making connections *about* development. Therefore, focusing on development-related topics makes sense if general goals include increased self-esteem, motivation, and friendship. I also believe that focusing on strengths (a hallmark of counseling), rather than on limitations, deficits, or problems, is key to helping gifted teens stay on, or move to, solid ground during adolescence—including socially and academically.

Background Information

The background information at the beginning of most sessions is designed to help you prepare for the session and think broadly about the topic at hand; to provide basic information that might be useful during the session; to inspire further reading; to anticipate student concerns; and to assist you in determining a possible direction for the discussion, according to the needs of your group. It is not appropriate to read this information to the group unless directed to do so, since that might inhibit some teens from thoroughly exploring the topic. A resource section in the back of the book provides trusted sources for additional information on some topics as well as resources that are appropriate to recommend to teens who request information.

Objectives and Suggestions

The objectives listed for each session tell you what to work toward and what to expect if the general suggestions are followed. They may also help you communicate content to administrators, parents, and teachers who wonder what your group is doing. You may want to prepare a list for parent conferences, for example. The objectives are not meant to be read to group members.

The suggestions are just that—suggestions. Use all, some, or none of them, and adapt those you use to meet the needs of your group. Time limits, group temperament, and group history are three of many factors you should consider when choosing which suggestions to follow. For most sessions, there are more suggestions than you will have time for. Teachers and counselors have told me that they appreciate having several suggestions to choose from.

Activity Sheets

Several of the sessions include activity sheets that may be reproduced for group use. They can also be downloaded using the instructions on page v for easy printing and copying. In my experience, these written exercises do not make discussions too structured, and most teens do not resist them. However, receptivity depends on how the sheets are used.

Especially when activity sheets are not used too often, groups of gifted teens have told me that they appreciate the handouts for giving them a chance to think quietly and focus at the outset of a meeting; to write, objectify, and edit their thoughts; and to ponder complex issues. Even highly verbal group members like being able to see expressive vocabulary on the sheets, terms they then can use during discussion about feelings and concerns. It is a new vocabulary for them, in some cases. Perhaps having time to pause helps them to feel a sense of control, especially if they are not used to taking social risks. The sheets also give everyone a chance to be heard. Introversion, common among gifted individuals, is less of a problem when activity sheets are used, since shy members can share responses on the sheets without having to compete with assertive peers. Discussion can involve only a few or all of the questions or items on a sheet, and group members can be polled efficiently for categories of responses or asked for specific answers to a few or all of the items. Even with those choices and limits, group members may communicate more with the sheets, more complexly and more openly about their social and emotional development than elsewhere in their lives.

Activities using paper, pencils, index cards, or other items that can be manipulated provide opportunities to consider thoughts and may help teens express their feelings and opinions. On the other hand, with some teens, those items easily become paper airplanes, something to "rattle," and a distraction. If group members can contain impulses to throw them, soft balls, bendable plastic sticks, and small stuffed animals can give them something to "fiddle with" and to provide safe distraction when topics evoke uncomfortable emotions. However, if your groups can handle discussion without these items, I recommend that you not make them available. I actually have never used them with groups of gifted kids, but I know that some facilitators regularly use them, especially at the middle school level. Manipulatives can indeed be helpful.

You may want to keep file folders for all group members in a secure place and have students file their folders at the close of each session, ensuring that personal information does not end up on the classroom floor or circulating through the halls. (When activity sheets contain questions about family or sensitive issues, I recommend collecting and disposing of the sheets after a cursory glance to check for serious concerns or notes written intentionally for you to see. Out of respect for family and individual privacy, I believe it best not to store these.) At the final group meeting, I recommend that members simply take time to look over the accumulated stash, consider the variety of developmental issues addressed, and then shred the sheets. The *process* of glancing over them, rather than the content, is the key—and is sufficient. Shredding them reinforces their right to privacy, affirms the developmental challenge of establishing a separate identity, and confirms the respect of the group leader for both of these elements. Another option is for you to simply dispose of all sheets at the end of each session, ideally by shredding them.

Under no circumstances should the sheets be shown to any school personnel. However, because you have been clear at the outset that abuse, neglect, and danger to self and others must be reported (see page 12), group members who share that kind of information on the sheets will be aware of your responsibility. Meet individually with students who indicate a threat to safety, remind them of your responsibility, check out the seriousness of the situation, encourage contact with an available counselor (if you are not one), accompany them to the counselor's office, and follow through, if appropriate, with a report to child protection services. In the case of suicidal ideation, make sure that you or a counselor contacts the student's parents and provides appropriate guidance or, if parents are not available, ensures the safety of the teen.

Session Closure

Each session includes a suggestion for closure. It is always a good idea to end a session with a summary activity, whether you provide it yourself or solicit it from the group. Attending to closure reminds the group that the discussions are purposeful, that members share common concerns, and that they have been heard. If an important new thought or issue is introduced in the closing minutes, it is still good to have some kind of deliberate closure, even if it includes suggesting that the group continue with the new idea next time or expressing regret that there won't be time to pursue it. Normally I recommend that session topics not be continued into the next session. Each is meant to stand alone or be combined with another topic for one session. The purpose is to learn through the process, not to cover content. It is fine to conclude discussion on a topic before it feels "done." You will have provoked thought and provided an opportunity for skill-building in that session, and that is the value. The topic may actually "run dry" after just a few minutes at the next meeting, if continued.

If you complete the session and closure and still have time left over, you might use it to begin the next writing activity or to ask questions that will encourage thinking about the next session or focus.

Getting Started

How to Begin

Begin the first meeting by letting students know how pleased you are that they will be part of the group. Remind them that the purpose of the group is to "just talk"—about various topics related to growing up. Their contribution will be to share feelings and concerns and to support each other.

Explain your role in the group. If you are a teacher or other professional without counselor training, tell the students that during group meetings you will not be a "teacher" in the usual sense of the word. Instead, you will be a discussion leader or facilitator, and the focus will be on them. It will be *their* group, developing uniquely. You will be their guide, listening carefully, sharing insights when appropriate, and helping them to connect with each other. Emphasize that you will all learn from each other.

Move next to introductions and a get-acquainted activity, such as the "Warm-Up" (pages 23–24). Tell the group to read through the sentence stems silently and slowly and then provide entire thoughts, when possible, rather than one-word answers. Then invite responses—either to one sentence at a time across the group or with each member, in turn, reading the entire sheet all at once. Or, if you prefer, go directly to another session you have chosen to begin the group experience. During your first meeting, since it is important that group members learn what being in the group will be like, avoid becoming bogged down with rule-setting and warnings. Instead, conduct an activity that generates interaction and helps them become acquainted in a new way. Explain that at each meeting they will similarly talk and do things together.

At some point during your first or second meeting, distribute copies of "Group Guidelines" (page 22). Go over the guidelines one at a time, with volunteers reading them. Ask if anyone has questions or if there is anything they do not understand. Tell the group that everyone—including you—is expected to follow these guidelines for as long as the group exists. Explain that they will be learning and practicing these skills over the life of the group. Stay positive, indicating that the guidelines are simply common sense.

How to Proceed

First-year groups, particularly at younger ages, often need more structure than more experienced groups. First-year groups of older teens usually attain depth more quickly than younger groups. It does take any group a while, though, to establish ease and fluidity in discussion, especially when members are not acquainted outside of the group. When experienced, teens are able to deal with personal topics readily, and they are likely to be patient and tolerant when new formats are experimented with.

Follow the suggestions in each session description for introducing the topic, generating discussion, and managing the activities. You may find it difficult to follow the printed text while leading the discussions. Rather than reading anything word for word to your group, familiarize yourself thoroughly with the content of a session before your meeting. Then you will have a general direction in mind and some ideas for other discussion directions, while keeping an eye on the session materials, if necessary. Be prepared for the possibility that your group may generate a good discussion for the entire session on only the first suggestion. This is not unusual. Be flexible. Never feel you need to finish all suggestions. Then move to another session focus for the next meeting.

Be aware that even when students in a school enjoy a group, they can forget to come to meetings—in spite of their exceptional abilities. If your group is voluntary, you may need to remind them for several weeks about meeting times and places. Eventually attendance may become a habit for most. However, in schools I have found it worthwhile and beneficial to the group to send reminders to everyone (usually a classroom "pass") for every meeting. Students can even fill out their pass for the next time at the outset of a meeting. Reminders for meetings held at school outside of school hours might be able to be filled out and distributed similarly. Email and other technology might also be used.

Tips to Keep in Mind

1. Remind the group that anything said in the group stays in the group. Confidentiality is important whether or not sensitive information is shared. Gifted teens usually take this "rule" quite seriously, given their rare place on the bell curve and their consequent sensitivities and concerns about trust and safety.

2. Ask open-ended questions, not "yes" and "no" questions, to generate discussion. Questions beginning with *How, What, When,* and *Where* are preferable to closed questions beginning with *Do, Does, Is, Are, Have,* and *Has,* since they require more than a yes or no response. However, for reluctant contributors, closed questions such as "Was it a sad time?" offer low risk and are also appropriate in conjunction with open-ended questions when a point of information is needed. In general, entire discussions can be facilitated without using any questions at all. Statements can actually be more facilitative than questions (for example, responding to a group member's comments with "School can be challenging," "You've had a rough week," or "I can hear that it was very upsetting"). When someone feels validated, more ease and information often follow.

3. When a member offers a cryptic comment, which gifted teens are quite capable of offering, respond with "Tell us more about . . . ," "Put words on that feeling . . . ," "Help us understand . . . ," "Can you give an example of . . . ?" or "What do you mean by . . . ?"

4. Always allow group members to pass if they prefer not to speak during any group activity, whether activity sheets, checklists, or discussions. Be clear from the beginning that nobody ever *has* to speak, even though you hope you can all become acquainted through the discussions. Being able to say, "I'd rather not" may represent a new ability to set a boundary in a life where others normally invade personal space and privacy.

5. Don't preach or moralize. Teens probably hear enough of that already. This experience should be different.

6. Don't judge. Let your group "just talk," and accept what they say. Feel free to say, "That's an interesting view" or "Pretty risky, huh?" if they share experiences related to unwise decisions or behaviors, make comments that are not convincing, or say something inflammatory. In responding calmly, without judgment, you are establishing a rare context where teens can feel free to explore thoughts and developmental challenges with an adult present.

7. Take them seriously and validate their feelings. For some gifted teens, this might be a new experience. Paraphrasing ("You felt she didn't understand" or "You had a long, difficult day"), checking for accuracy ("Did I hear you correctly? This happened a week ago?"), asking for more information ("Tell us more about that"), acknowledging feelings ("I can see how disappointing that was" or "It makes sense that you would feel that way"), or simply offering an "Mmmm" in response to a comment shows that you are listening and want to understand.

8. Relax and let the group be more about process than product—more about trip than destination. It may not always be apparent that something specific has been accomplished, but as long as members keep talking thoughtfully, you're on the right track.

9. Beware of sharing your own personal experiences too often and in too much detail. Always remember that the group is about the group members, not about you. Every time you self-disclose, you take the attention away from them. They will feel that and may quickly tire of hearing about your family or your adolescence. Your personal experiences are also often not as helpful or pertinent as you might think. I rarely fill out the activity sheets myself, and therefore I do not participate in a "go-around" with the sheets. Having a posture of limited self-disclosure from the outset establishes an appropriate facilitator role. If someone asks you a personal question, consider saying something like, "This group is for you, not for me. Discussions in groups like this should be among peers. I'm just the leader. I want to be careful to do my part well."

10. Be prepared to protect members from each other and themselves. For example, pertinent to a situation already alluded to in "Handling the Unexpected," if a group member begins with something like, "I've never said this to anybody—it's about something pretty bad that happened to me," you may want to encourage the individual to pause before continuing. To do that, reach out one hand toward the speaker, palm away, and ask, "Are you comfortable about sharing this with the group?" Then ask the group, "Are you ready to be trusted? Remember what we said about confidentiality." Then go back to the speaker: "Do you still want to share this with the group?" In doing this, you give the student time to reconsider (especially if the student prematurely assumed group trustworthiness), and you also remind the group about their responsibilities. After the speaker finishes, you might process the telling with the group: "What did that feel like to be trusted with that information?" The focus remains on feelings and support.

11. In situations where members of the group verbally attack each other, you need to intervene (for example, removing the students from the room or calling for assistance, if the situation is dangerous, or perhaps simply holding up your hand, palm out, and saying firmly, "Whoa!"). The group can also process what has happened by sharing their feelings about the conflict. In fact, processing the experience can in itself defuse conflict. When there is conflict, process it. ("What is/was that like for us to have conflict in the group?" "What did/does it feel like?" "What would you need to hear to help your anger fade?" "Is anyone able and willing to say that—from the heart?"). This is an excellent opportunity to practice talking honestly about feelings and to experience conflict resolution.

12. If anyone expresses emotion with obvious discomfort or tears, offer verbal support, a tissue (which should be handy), or touch (a pat on the arm, perhaps, if in proximity). Group members may follow your lead. However, be aware that some may not want to be touched at all. In fact, beware of assuming that a hug is "best." Even a hug may meet the facilitator or other group members' needs more than the sad teen's needs. For some, touch understandably means danger and discomfort. You might say, "It's okay to express emotion. Let us know if you need something. We'll continue."

13. Listen carefully to whoever is speaking, but also monitor the nonverbal behavior of those who are not speaking. Are they showing discomfort (averted eyes, moving back, facial tics), frustration (agitation, head-shaking, mumbled negatives), or anxiety (uneasy eyes, unsteady hands, tense face), impatience, boredom, judgment? Depending on the situation and the student, you might want to ask sensitively about what you are noticing.

14. Be genuine in your comments and compliments. Watch for opportunities to tell group members that they articulated complex feelings and situations well ("You put words on a very complex feeling" or "You explained that very well"). Avoid insincere, noncredible comments about members' strengths. Instead, be on the lookout for courage, compassion, kindness, wisdom, common sense, responsibility, and problem-solving abilities, for example. Gifted teens are as hungry as anyone for feedback about their personal strengths, and whatever positive support you give them will be taken seriously. Elsewhere, for them, academic performance or nonperformance may be the main focus.

15. If you are in a school, you might want to update parents periodically on topics to be discussed in an upcoming series of group meetings. If you are in a summer program, a list of general topics might be included in orientation information for parents. They will probably appreciate that communication. If parents ask about what their child has said in the group, assure them that you would/will contact them if there is cause for alarm (such as suicidal or homicidal thoughts or a plan to commit a crime). However, in general, confidentiality will be honored, in order to protect trust in the group. Reassure them that the discussions are focused on growing up in a teen world, not on private family concerns, and also that the focus is on discussion, not on your presenting information as a teacher.

Endings

How to end a series of group meetings should be carefully considered, since members might have become quite attached to the group. It is wise to wind down purposefully. "Ending" (pages 266–269) can be used to conclude a series of meetings.

Important in any final session, and possibly in the last two sessions, is the need for teens to talk about what they have experienced in the group. I have found that asking them to write a few paragraphs during a final session is helpful. Sometimes, when group attendance was voluntary, I have asked, "Why did you keep coming to the group?" At other times, I have simply invited members to talk about what they have gained in personal insights, what they have appreciated, what they regret, what they have learned about adolescence, what common ground they have discovered, and if and how they have changed since the group began.

All groups, whatever their size and duration, need to prepare for the time when the group will no longer meet.

Members will likely miss the group and feel a sense of loss. Especially if they have grown to depend on the group for support, they may feel anxious about being without the group in the future. If they have made friends in the group, they may wonder if they will lose touch once the group disbands.

A few sessions prior to ending, mention casually that there are only a few meetings remaining. Continue to do that until the next-to-last session. At that time, tell the group what you have in mind for the final session, or ask the group for suggestions. You might plan a party, have food brought in, and/or take a group photo. Be aware, though, that changing the "mode" of the group might create discomfort at a time already stressful because of the ending. After all, the focus until then has been on discussion. Even the addition of food or music changes group dynamics. Everyone must interact in a new way, with little time to become comfortable with it. With that said, however, use your own judgment. You know your group.

Be sure to leave time at the final session for the teens and you to say good-bye. If they will likely not have much future contact with each other, provide a way for them to share home and email addresses and phone numbers and wish each other well. Be aware that you will be modeling strategies for ending something that has likely been a profound experience. For many people—adults and teens—that is a difficult process.

Evaluation

It is not always easy to "read" a group of gifted teens and to know whether they are moving in a positive direction. Individuals who readily and frequently give feedback cannot speak for everyone. Quiet members may be gaining insights that they simply are not sharing. A session that seemed to generate an indifferent or poor response might, in fact, have made an impact, but the effect may not be readily apparent. Groups are complex, and members differ in their needs and what they respond to. Therefore, it is wise periodically to have group members fill out an evaluation, particularly at the end of the group experience.

On page 269, you will find an evaluation form to copy and use. Or you may choose to create your own form, tailored to your group and to what you hope to learn. Feedback provided on such evaluations can be invaluable when assessing current groups and planning for future groups. To administrators, teachers, or funders, evaluations can also help to defend group work as part of a curriculum for gifted youth, as part of a school counseling program, or as a program at some other facility focusing on gifted students.

A Note for Parents

The Essential Guide to Talking with Gifted Teens can help parents know their adolescents in new and important ways. It can help parents to access what their teens are thinking and feeling; the issues that are important to them; their current concerns; and their hopes and plans for the future.

Parents and teens sometimes have difficulty sustaining conversations. Teens may become increasingly private and reluctant to talk at home. Sometimes parents don't know what to talk about beyond schoolwork, family members, video games or other technology, chores, and food. They initiate conversations unsure about which subjects are "safe" and which are not. Sometimes all topics seem to be off limits. *The Essential Guide to Talking with Gifted Teens* provides a potentially intriguing way for teens and parents to break down barriers.

By scanning the background information and suggestions, parents can find possible topics and conversation-starters. They can also discover insights into developmental issues that they and their children may be wrestling with. It is easy to forget what adolescence felt like, and the background information can help parents understand the complexities of life for a gifted teen today.

Most of the sessions—especially those in the Identity, Relationships, and Family sections—can help to generate family discussion. Some teens ask for extra activity sheets to take home for their parents to fill out. Since many personal issues persist into adulthood, they are good to discuss even with young adolescents, who are beginning to be aware that some of their parents' issues are theirs, too. Such sharing can be helpful to gifted teens as they forge a separate identity and prepare to be launched into the next developmental stage.

Several of the sessions in the Stress section are also worth discussing as a family. Coping strategies, procrastination, and sorting out stress are particularly good topics for family sharing. Adults themselves are never done with such concerns, and it is good for them to acknowledge their humanness and ongoing development to growing children. Nonauthoritarian "realness" can help create dialogue, especially if adults do not dominate the conversation and if they communicate genuine interest (without judgment) in the teen world.

Permission for Student Participation

Dear Parent/Guardian/Caregiver,

I have invited your son or daughter to participate in a discussion group for gifted teens at school, and he/she has expressed interest in attending. The purpose of the group is to provide an opportunity to talk about growing up and to improve skills in talking and listening. Such skills are important to students now in relationships with peers, teachers, and parents—and later with spouses, coworkers, and children. In general, the group will offer support for gifted teens as they deal with the challenges of adolescence and prepare for the future. Format and content will be based on *The Essential Guide to Talking with Gifted Teens* by Dr. Jean Peterson.

Adolescence can be stressful in even the best of situations. Not only are there physical changes, but also new emotions and new expectations. There are new activities, academic choices, and the future to think about. Social relationships are probably also changing. Stress levels may increase. Gifted teens face developmental challenges like anyone else their age. However, because of their exceptional abilities, their experience of development may be somewhat different from the experience of others. They usually appreciate being able to discuss developmental challenges with peers with similar ability, who can understand.

Our discussion group will focus on development. Even though we may discuss academic concerns now and then, the group will be different from the often competitive school world. Students will relax with each other and find out what they have in common, including the challenges of adolescence. They will learn how to support each other. They will become acquainted with classmates—for the first time or simply better than before.

If your teen participates, you may soon notice positive changes both at school and at home. Communication may improve. Talking about stress, developing strategies for problem-solving, gaining a clearer sense of self, feeling the support of trusted peers—all of these group experiences may improve your teen's self-esteem and overall well-being.

The group will begin very soon. If you give permission for your teen to be involved, and if he/she decides to participate, please sign below and return the form to me as soon as possible. If you have any questions, please contact me at _____ .

(email and phone)

_____
(Signature of facilitator)

_____ has my permission to participate in the discussion group.
(Name of student)

_____   _____
(Parent/Guardian/Caregiver signature)   (Date)

Group Guidelines

The purpose of this group is to "just talk"—to share thoughts, feelings, and concerns with each other in an atmosphere of trust, respect, caring, and understanding. To make this group successful and meaningful, we agree to the following terms and guidelines.

1. Anything that is said in the group stays in the group. We agree to keep our conversations confidential. This means we don't share information outside of the group. We agree to do our part, individually and together, to make this group a safe place to talk.

2. We respect what other group members say. We agree not to use put-downs of any kind, including words, body language, facial expressions, and sighs. We agree to control our own behavior so that everyone feels valued and accepted.

3. We respect everyone's need and right to be heard. We agree that no one will dominate the group. We also understand that listening and keen observation are valuable skills. Someone who is shy may be quite aware of what is going on in our group.

4. We listen to each other. When someone is speaking, we look at him or her and pay attention. We use supportive and encouraging body language and facial expressions.

5. We realize that feelings are not "bad" or "good." They just are. They make sense, under the circumstances. Therefore, we don't say, "You shouldn't feel that way."

6. We are willing to take risks, explore new ideas, and explain our feelings as well as we can. However, we agree that someone who doesn't want to talk doesn't have to talk. We don't force people to share when they don't feel comfortable sharing.

7. We are willing to let others know us. We agree that talking and listening are ways for people to get to know each other.

8. We realize that sometimes people may feel misunderstood, or may feel that someone has hurt them accidentally or on purpose. We agree that the best way to handle those times is through talking and listening—to the individuals involved. We encourage assertiveness, not aggression.

9. We agree to be sincere and to do our best to speak from the heart.

10. We don't talk about group members who aren't present. We don't criticize group members who aren't here to defend themselves.

11. When we do need to talk about other people, we don't refer to them by name. For example, we may ask the group to help us solve a problem we are having with someone, but we won't name the person.

12. We agree to attend group meetings regularly. We don't want to miss information that might be referred to later. Most of all, we know that we are important to the group. If we can't attend a meeting, we will try to let our leader know ahead of time.

Warm-Up

Name: _____

Complete these sentences:

1. I think being in a group will _____

_____

2. Something interesting about me is _____

_____

3. When I have free time, I like to _____

_____

4. Something I have that is very special to me is _____

_____

5. You might be surprised that I'm good at _____

_____

6. What am I not good at? I'm not good at _____

_____

7. Probably the most exciting thing I've ever done is _____

_____

8. I'm glad that I can _____

_____

9. I like people who _____

_____

(continued)

Warm-Up (continued)

10. I'm probably most relaxed when I _____

_____

11. I'm probably most tense when I _____

_____

12. If I could, I'd always get up in the morning at _____

_____

13. What is going well so far at school this year is _____

_____

14. Someday I probably will _____

_____

FOCUS Identity

FOCUS Identity

General Background

Developing a personal identity is an important developmental task, and it may be a particular challenge for teens with exceptional talents and/or intellect. High achievers may have an identity as a stellar student, athlete, or musician, for instance, but may not feel the need or freedom to explore identity further. I have known high achievers who wondered, as they finished high school, who they were—besides an achiever. Gifted teens who have negative parental models may feel an urgency to be separate from family, therefore contemplating identity earlier than those with nurturing, competent parents. Similarly, for better or for worse, underachieving gifted teens—at least those for whom nonperformance is a choice (and not a paralysis of will)—may already have moved toward differentiating themselves from achieving parents, siblings, or friends, if, in fact, that is their situation.

In general, teens develop an identity through hearing what others say about them, identifying what they feel and value, and thinking about themselves in relationship with others. The messages they receive may be positive and helpful. However, even when performing well, some gifted teens receive mostly negative, critical messages as their "definition." In addition, parents may not be positive models for relating to others, and the behavior of bright, capable teens in turn may preclude their receiving positive messages about themselves. They also may have little opportunity to talk about their doubts and fears related to identity.

During identity formation, confusion and doubt can lead to tension, sadness, acting out, underachievement, hyperachievement, perfectionism, and relationship problems. In contrast, knowing and being comfortable with the self may help gifted teens to accomplish other developmental tasks, including finding career direction, establishing a mature relationship, developing autonomy, and resolving conflict with parents.

In group discussions, members can gain skill in articulating thoughts and feelings. Discreetly talking about what is "inside" is practice for friendships and relationships in the workplace and at home. Sharing thoughts and feelings can also help teens discover what they have in common, learn that they are not as different as they might believe, get feedback from peers and the facilitator, and answer a vital question: "Who am I?"

General Objectives

- Gifted teens affirm that they face universal developmental challenges.
- They make progress in defining themselves as unique individuals.
- They discover what they think and feel by sharing thoughts and feelings with the group and receiving and evaluating feedback.
- They apply what others share to their own self-assessment.
- They recognize and accept their comparative learning differences.

FOCUS Identity

Developing—Similarly and Uniquely

Objectives

- Gifted teens recognize and affirm that they and others are continuously developing.
- They recognize and affirm how they are similar to and different from age peers who are not identified as gifted.
- They feel connected to others with similar intellectual ability.
- They learn that their giftedness may make their experience of "normal development" different from the experiences of others their age.

Suggestions

1. To introduce the topic (and the group experience, if this is the first session), explain that the focus will be on development—figuring out who they are, where they are going, how to get along with others, how to manage conflict, how to move toward autonomy, and how to find satisfaction in life.

   Ask the group to define *developing*, as it applies to what you just said. They might mention "growing up." Ask what kinds of development they are currently experiencing.

   You might mention four general areas: physical, cognitive, social, emotional. Ask for examples of each area, including how they think they have changed since last year. You might give a quick example of how you are different from a decade ago—to emphasize that adults continue to develop. (Then immediately refocus group attention on them.)

2. Ask how they know that everyone else in their extended family is, like themselves, continuing to develop (oldest children leaving home, youngest entering school, teen with a new driver's license, grandparents retiring, mom starting a new business, dad promoted).

3. Ask them how they are the same as all others in their grade level at school. (All are facing similar developmental challenges, tasks, and changes.) Then ask how they might differ from others in their grade level. If they mention giftedness, explore whether intellectual or creative gifts affect the experience of growing up. If no one mentions differences, accept that. Accepting what they share will set the tone for the group experience—that is, you will not be judgmental and evaluative, and their opinions and thoughts will be received and affirmed.

Scholars who have written about characteristics of people with high capability have suggested that giftedness is connected to certain kinds of sensitivity; to a strong sense of fairness; to a drive to accomplish things; and to intensity. Explain that you probably will discuss characteristics like these at a future meeting. However, ask here if they think that these perceptions are accurate. Some gifted teens may resist the idea that they are different from others their age, depending on how much they have incorporated giftedness into their identity.

4. In order to explore similarities and differences within their group, invite students to line up along one wall of the room (or form an angle where two walls meet). Tell them they have just formed a continuum. Designate one end as "10—to a great extent/a lot" and the other end as "0—not at all." Explain that you are going to read a series of statements. As you read each one, they should physically move to the point on the continuum that best represents where they think they belong.

   Read aloud each statement from "Uniquenesses and Similarities: A Continuum Activity" on page 30. After each statement, and after group members have found their places on the continuum, select only two to four teens to explain why they placed themselves where they did. Be sure not to ask the same few to report each time, and avoid spending too long considering individual statements. Their considering each statement and then moving physically on the continuum can enhance self-awareness even without discussion.

5. For closure, ask the group if they noticed any trends among themselves (similarly creative, flexible, impulsive, perfectionistic, organized, orderly?). Can anyone offer a general statement describing the group? Then, process the experience (see page 11 for guidance): "How was it to participate in this activity?" "What was the best part of it?" "What was the hardest?" If this is your group's first meeting, explain that at each future meeting they will be discussing aspects of development, sometimes with activities. Thank them for being willing to take some risks and for letting themselves be known a little to each other.

Uniquenesses and Similarities: A Continuum Activity

1. I like tough challenges and feel best when I am challenged.

2. I am cool in a crisis, and I can even lead others in a crisis.

3. I can change direction easily when I am doing something—for example, if suddenly someone wants/needs to do something different or do it in a new way.

4. I am organized in every part of my life.

5. I am a dreamer, spending a lot of time in fantasies.

6. I work rapidly in whatever I do.

7. I am a highly creative person.

8. I am a perfectionist in almost everything I do. I like things to be "just right."

9. I prefer to work alone, rather than with others, on most things.

10. I prefer to *be* alone, rather than with others, if I have a choice.

11. I am quick to respond to almost all situations.

12. I am impulsive, often wishing I had thought first before doing something.

13. I can work effectively without encouragement from someone else.

14. I like to work with my hands.

15. I am an avid reader.

16. I am quite critical of others.

17. I worry a lot.

FOCUS Identity

What Does Gifted Mean?

Background

I like to begin a group series with at least one other topic before addressing giftedness, per se. Since the focus of this book is on development, discussing development in general—without considering achievement, lack of achievement, or the "gifted" label—conveys that development is a universal phenomenon and that it deserves discussion apart from a person's place on a bell curve of ability. However, the label and the concept of giftedness are both worthy of discussion. The experience of development is likely to be qualitatively different for gifted teens than for others, and the gifted label may feel heavy. The concept and label are also controversial. This session is an opportunity to explore, in a safe setting, how giftedness is interpreted and experienced.

Objectives

- Gifted teens understand how giftedness is interpreted and identified in their school or other setting.
- They recognize that *giftedness* and *intelligence* are terms applied to abilities, characteristics, and skills that are valued in a particular culture.
- Through articulating personal strengths, they affirm capabilities and enhance self-esteem.
- They learn that it is all right to have limitations.
- They learn more about themselves and become better at assessing themselves realistically.
- They learn to value their own and others' strengths.

Suggestions

1. Ask the group what they understand about giftedness. Let them be the teachers. It is important that you find out what they know before offering new information. Some may not have thought much about the concept, may not consider themselves gifted, and may not embrace the term, even if they have been identified for a program. Some may wear the label as a badge of honor; others may reject it.

   Be prepared to explain the program philosophy and identification criteria used in the teens' school(s) or district(s) (if you are aware of those). Offering the following information may help establish a group climate that values genuine thoughts, feelings, and opinions and is not preoccupied with "right" and "wrong" responses.

Be aware that creating an atmosphere of unconditional respect and trust takes time. Receive whatever the students say without judgment or challenge.

Important

Cultures differ in what is deemed to be gifted. One of my own studies found that U.S.-dominant-culture classroom teachers, when nominating children for a special program, generally valued individual, competitive, conspicuous achievement—looking for verbal assertiveness, "standing out," and a strong work ethic in classroom work, for instance. These are the same values held by the U.S.-dominant culture as a whole, according to anthropologists. In contrast, representatives of a Latino community mentioned most often arts as a means of expression (not as performance) and humility when identifying "gifted" individuals. In an African American community, representatives mentioned selfless service to community and handiwork most. In an American Indian settlement, residents declined to identify anyone as gifted, since they did not believe in standing out, although they respected individuals who could be comfortable in both white and Indian cultures "without assimilating." Adaptability was most highly valued by recent Asian immigrants, who often mentioned the importance of education in the United States in that regard. In a low-income white community, both adults and high school students placed the highest value on nurturing of children and service to others. Overall, participants from the nonmainstream cultures valued "nonbookish" wisdom, not knowledge. It is important to recognize that the cultural values of one group are not better or worse than others, just different. Your group might find it interesting that all cultures do not necessarily value, and thrive in, a highly competitive school culture that demands intelligence and talents be demonstrated.

2. Have the students list on paper their personal strengths—what they can count on, have confidence in, or trust about themselves, both as they interact with others and when they are alone (read the following list, if needed). You might ask, "What do other people value in you?" Encourage them to share their lists. Tell the students they will need to speak or write about themselves with confidence during job interviews, on scholarship applications, and in college-application essays. Students whose cultures value humility, rather than self-promotion, may find this exercise difficult. Acknowledge potential cultural differences, but without making assumptions. U.S.-dominant-culture teens may not have considered that some cultures do not value standing out.

organized	a good listener
responsible	kind
compassionate	energetic
personable	even-tempered
patient	an eager learner
athletic	a good dancer
helpful	not moody
intelligent	good sense of humor
witty	verbal or mathematical skills

mechanical gifts   musical or other artistic talent
good with elderly people and/or young children

Important Teens usually are willing to share their lists, even when the group is just beginning. Contributions help build a group. However, remind the group that they always have the right to "pass" if uncomfortable about responding to a question or participating in an activity.

3. Have the students list on paper their characteristics, habits, and flaws that keep them from being how they'd like to be (read the following list, if needed). Encourage them to share their lists. If the students list more limitations than strengths, don't be surprised. If time permits, ask the group for opinions about why this might happen.

unmotivated	bad-tempered	trouble with authority
spreads gossip	disorganized	not a team player
impatient	irresponsible	bossy
messy	mean	easily distracted
trouble listening to others	critical	self-critical
naive	easily depressed	impulsive

4. Some theorists believe that intelligence is a general quality. Others believe there are different kinds of intelligence. In *Frames of Mind: The Theory of Multiple Intelligences* (New York: Basic Books, 2004), Howard Gardner identifies several intelligences, most of which are reflected in the first nine items on the "Thirteen Intelligence Types" activity sheet (page 34). Group members can rank the items, according to the directions, or simply identify three they feel quite strong in, as well as at least one that is relatively less strong. (NOTE: The activity sheet lists more intelligences than Gardner has identified because the goal here is to generate discussion of strengths and limitations related to effective living, not necessarily intelligences, per se.)

5. In addition to #4, or as an alternative activity promoting active listening, divide the group into pairs and ask them to tell each other about something they enjoy or are good at. You might want to write prompts on a wallboard (for example, What do you know a lot about? How long have you been into it? Could it turn into a career? Do others share the interest? Has someone mentored you?). Then each student tells the group about his or her partner's strength or strong interest. Finally, ask students how they showed they were interested and how their partner showed interest—even without talking.

6. For closure, ask the students which strengths and limitations were common in the group. Then ask, "How did it feel to talk about your strengths and limitations?" If you included the partnering activity, ask the group how they felt during it. If you used activity sheets, dispose of them or add them to group folders.

Thirteen Intelligence Types

Name: _____

Rank the following types of intelligence, from 1 (lowest) to 13 (highest), according to how you see your strengths and limitations.

_____ Verbal (you are sensitive to the nuances of written and oral language)

_____ Mathematical, scientific (you enjoy working with numbers and symbols, readily recognize patterns, and are good in math and science)

_____ Social (you have good interpersonal skills, can read social cues, and find it easy to be around people)

_____ Artistic (you appreciate color/hue, shape, line, spaces, and arrangement in many areas of schoolwork and elsewhere, including in science, and/or are good in art)

_____ Physical (you are athletic, coordinated, and have a good sense of how your body moves)

_____ Mechanical (you like to tinker with machines; you have a curiosity about how machines work)

_____ Self-aware (you know yourself well; you interpret your emotions accurately)

_____ Musical (you are attuned to rhythm, tone, counterpoint, and musical forms and/or perform music impressively)

_____ Influential (classmates observe and admire you; they follow your example, whether it is negative or positive)

_____ Creative (you think outside of the box, have unusual ideas, and create unique things)

_____ Insightful (you are perceptive and can make sense of complex matters, seeing them in new ways)

_____ Practical (you make good decisions, solve problems, use common sense, are tuned in to the real world)

_____ Resilient (you show inner strength, no matter what you have to deal with)

FOCUS Identity

Self in Perspective

Background

Depending on what is generated in discussion, this session might be divided into two sessions. Part 2 and/or 3 of the activity sheet might be discussed at the second session.

Objectives

- In the presence of supportive peers, gifted teens thoughtfully compare their real, their disliked, and their ideal selves and assess how different or similar these three selves are.
- They learn how members of the group perceive them.
- They compare others' perceptions of them to their perceptions of themselves.
- They explore the role of appearance in creating impressions.

Suggestions

1. Have the group complete the activity sheet (pages 37–38) with single words or phrases. Tell them they will be invited to share whatever they are willing to share.

   Encourage them to share their responses from Part 1. Afterward, ask the group if they were surprised about anything listed and/or if they want to say something supportive. Then ask the following:

   ~ How similar or different are your "The Way I Really Am" and "How I'd Like to Be" lists?
   ~ How comfortable are you with the parts of yourself you don't like (on a scale of 1 to 10, with 10 being "very comfortable")? What would you like to change? How might the changes affect your life?
   ~ Which traits listed under "How I'd Like to Be" would be possible for you? What can you do to move in those directions?
   ~ On a scale of 1 to 10, with 10 being "totally," to what extent do you accept your "real self"?

   Then move to Part 2. Ask these questions when they are finished reading their responses:

   ~ How do people send messages about themselves nonverbally?
   ~ (NOTE: Ask the following one at a time.) What nonverbal messages suggest that someone is arrogant? nervous? critical? uptight? content? tired? secure?

insecure? confident? self-conscious? sad? angry? irritated? frustrated?
a risk-taker? popular? serious? shy? mean? a perfectionist?

2. Direct the group to look at what they wrote in Part 3 of the activity sheet. Focusing on one person at a time, invite volunteers to share what they wrote about that person. A few minutes might be devoted to that individual. Then ask that student if there is anything he or she would like to ask the others. (Examples: "Do I seem arrogant?" "Am I too talkative?" "Do you see me as a friendly person?" "Am I okay to be around?")

This can be a powerful activity. In the safety of the group, each student has an opportunity to hear others' perceptions and to ask important questions.

If your group is not yet comfortable sharing, working in pairs may be a better approach for this activity. For later use, write the descriptors listed at the end of #1 on one section of a wallboard before the group arrives. First, pair the students and then ask either-or questions, with partners making assumptions about each other on paper (for example, prefers water or soda? left a neat or messy bed this morning? has all assignments for today done or not? has an orderly or messy closet? prefers in-line skating or a roller-coaster? prefers spaghetti or lasagna?).

Next ask a volunteer to sit in front of the words on the board. As others offer adjectives to describe the volunteer (sometimes from the list on the board), write them on another area of the board. The volunteer cannot say anything during this time. After a minute, have the volunteer look at the words and circle any he or she disagrees with or wants more information about from the group. Last, divide the group into subgroups to read children's books and describe a character's image, based on behavior or dialogue.

Important	Teens are usually sensitive to others' feelings. With that said, however, it is always the facilitator's responsibility to protect group members from psychological harm. Be alert to inappropriate or insensitive comments. If they occur, say something like, "Let me ask you as a group how you just felt when he/she said that to her/him. Do you have any comments for (the speaker who made the insensitive comment) or (the target of the insensitive comment)?"

3. For closure, ask the group to comment on what was interesting and/or valuable about this session. If appropriate, commend the group for their honesty and supportive comments. Dispose of the sheets or add them to the group folders.

How Others See Me, How I See Myself and Others

Name: _____

PART 1: List adjectives or phrases under each heading.

THE WAY I REALLY AM

1. _____

2. _____

3. _____

THE SELF I DON'T LIKE

1. _____

2. _____

3. _____

HOW I'D LIKE TO BE

1. _____

2. _____

3. _____

The two lists that are most alike for me are _____

If I could "try on" a new image, I think I would like to be _____

PART 2
Complete each sentence with at least three descriptive words.

My mother thinks I am _____

My father thinks I am _____

My teachers think I am _____

My friends think I am _____

People who don't know me and have never heard me talk but just see me in the halls at school probably think I am _____

People who know me usually appreciate my _____

I think I am _____

(continued)

How Others See Me, How I See Myself and Others (continued)

PART 3

List the names of all the people in this group. Leave some space after each person's name. Use the space to write your *first* impression of him or her, no matter how long ago it was. If you can't recall your first impression, describe what is communicated by the person's facial expression and the way he or she stands, walks, sits, talks, gestures, and dresses.

_____

_____

_____

_____

_____

_____

_____

_____

FOCUS Identity

Façade, Image, and Stereotype

Background

Gifted teens often speak negatively of "hypocrites." They are quick to judge others as insincere. They are disgusted by fake smiles, and they gossip about others' status-seeking behavior. They sneer at teachers and administrators who claim to be interested in individual students but cannot remember their names. Yet, in spite of their judging, they probably wear a façade of some kind themselves. We all do. They might act their way into the right social circle or feign interest in a topic to impress a teacher. A no-worry demeanor might hide anxiety. Smiles and congeniality might hide sadness, anger, and important needs because they know that displaying such feelings would not draw people to them. With a blank, cold, or negative façade, they may say, "Leave me alone" or "Don't mess with me."

Regardless of whether he or she is perceived accurately, a teen who's seen as a rebel, risk-taker, joker, or member of the popular crowd may feel stuck in that role. A bubbly, energetic student may feel constrained from expressing sadness. A nice guy may be tired of being nice. The class comedian may yearn to be taken seriously. A bad reputation can be difficult to escape. The "brainy" student may not feel able to ask a "stupid" question. It's possible to be a prisoner of image. Both stellar gifted achievers and rebellious gifted underachievers may be reluctant to take risks with their respective images.

Here is an opportunity to discuss how image and stereotypes affect gifted teens. Common stereotypes may prevent gifted underachievers from being affirmed for their intellect, and stereotypes may also narrow others' perceptions of high achievers, for instance. Gifted kids usually appreciate a chance to delve into this complex topic.

Objectives

- Gifted teens explore the idea of the "social face."
- They consider how they do and do not fit stereotypes that are applied to them.
- They learn that sharing doubts and other feelings enhances trust in the group.

Suggestions

1. Begin with general questions such as the following:

   ~ What is a façade? (If students have never heard the word, explain that it means a "front," like a storefront. It may be deceptive, or it may put a new "face" on something.)

~ How can the word *façade* relate to people?

~ What social purpose might a façade serve? (Possibilities: It can help people to fit in, not cause conflict, have comfortable social relationships, and protect the self.)

2. Move the discussion from the general to the specific. Ask, "If it's normal to wear a façade, what kind of social faces might we be wearing here now?" You might tell the group what kind of "face" you assume you are wearing at the moment, showing that you are interested, warm, compassionate, and alert. Then ask questions like the following.

~ What is your social façade? Do you have more than one—for various places?

~ What purpose does it serve?

~ Does it ever cause problems for you or the people around you?

3. Direct the discussion to consideration of places where students feel comfortable enough not to wear a façade. (For the last two questions, invite only voluntary responses.)

~ Where can you take off your façade?

~ What are you like when it is off?

~ Are people who know the real you more, or less, respectful than those who don't?

4. Invite the group to consider how and when façades begin to develop.

~ How do we respond to young children's spontaneous, innocent, direct comments?

~ When do children start to become more socially aware and less spontaneous? Why might this happen?

~ How might the façades of adults and teenagers differ?

~ A social face has advantages. What might be a downside? (Perhaps: A façade could keep others from knowing when someone needs support and help. My own research of gifted kids has repeatedly shown that they often do not ask for help even when highly distressed.)

5. Depending on whether your group used the preceding session topic, "Self in Perspective," and how much "image" was discussed, you might ask the group if they ever have had an image they thought they had to live up to. If they need help, read aloud some of the images that follow. Ask, "Can anyone identify with these?" "What part of your image would you like to erase?"

class clown	winner	jock
high achiever	loser	nerd
underachiever	responsible and conscientious	in control
leader/organizer	irresponsible	good girl/boy
decision-maker	someone who can handle anything	bad/mean girl/boy
anti-school	cool	rich kid
cynical	skateboarder	

After group members reveal their images, ask questions like the following, being careful not to imply judgment about what is said or about image in general.

~ What might be the cost of always living up to an image? What might be the benefit?
~ What might happen if you didn't live up to your image?
~ Does anyone in the group not fit the image you had of them prior to knowing them in the group?

6. Ask for a definition of *stereotype*. If necessary, say, "A stereotype is an idea that many people share about a particular group of people. It is a way of describing the people in that group without knowing or noticing anything about them as individuals." Ask the group, "What is the stereotype of a gifted student?" "How do you fit that stereotype? How not?"

7. Continue by asking one or more of the following questions. Make sure that each member has a chance to be heard.

~ What do you wish your classmates understood about you?
~ What do you wish your teachers understood about you?
~ What do you wish your parents understood about you?

8. For closure, ask for a volunteer to share one or two thoughts about the session— either the content of the session or the process of discussing it. Were these comfortable topics to discuss?

FOCUS Identity

Intensity, Compulsivity, and Control

Background

Many gifted teens like to compare notes on interests and passions, especially those who don't have anyone to share an interest with otherwise. They learn that they're not alone, and that their intensity and drivenness aren't "weird." Giftedness and intensity often go hand in hand, and, whatever the interest, gifted students may take it to the limit. They might read, think, and talk about it continually, trying the patience of their parents and teachers—until moving on to something else. Passions can last a lifetime, perhaps even being a career. Compulsivity, however, is another matter. Students (and adults, of course) sometimes become so involved in an interest or activity that it takes over their lives, resembling (or being) an addiction. People can also become compulsive workers, eaters, neatniks, runners, shoppers, exercisers, cleaners, and savers. Parents sometimes worry about video games in this regard. A discussion can help students take stock of behaviors that affect quality of life and move toward moderation.

Highly able teens are probably used to being in control, even if that means withdrawing from uncomfortable situations. They are likely to be intellectually nimble and/or have exceptional talents, often including verbal agility. Underlying this session is the assumption that there are times when even these well-endowed individuals feel out of control. Control is the third dimension of this session. Depending on time, you might need to choose just one or two of the suggestions.

Objectives

- Gifted teens learn that others are, or have been, passionate about a particular interest or activity.
- They consider aspects of intensity, compulsivity, and moderation. They learn that even those who seem secure are concerned about being *too* something.
- They learn to articulate their concerns about being *too* something.
- They think about control as it relates to their lives.

Suggestions

1. Ask the group if they can recall a passion—a topic or activity they were intensely interested in and spent a lot of time pursuing at some earlier time. Present the idea that such intensity has probably contributed to discoveries in science and to social progress. Ask questions like these:

~ Who did you share this passion with?

~ How did your parents feel about your passion?

~ How much was your passion expressed or demonstrated in school?

~ When did your passion diminish (if it has)? What do you think contributed to that?

~ If intense involvement is typical for you, how long does a passionate interest usually last?

2. Explore extreme characteristics. Mention a *too* characteristic of your own. Invite the group to share their self-perceptions regarding *being* too much or too little in some way, or *doing* too much or too little in some area. Examples follow:

shy	talkative	active
loud	clumsy	busy
lazy	easily distracted	worried
lonely	people-pleasing	social
"driven"	nervous	critical
rebellious	depressed	

3. Ask how these characteristics might, in fact, have some advantages. Give the group several seconds to ponder that possibility. If you asked them to write their qualities on paper, direct them to exchange their lists with a partner. Have each comment on possible advantages of the other's extremes. You might first provide an example of a "reframe" (putting a negative inside a positive frame).

For example, shyness might be a mysterious, intriguing trait that some people find attractive. Shy people might be more comfortable alone than extroverts are. They might be able to work more effectively on a long-term project than a highly social person. They probably think before acting. They may be better at finding strength from within, instead of relying on others to help them. Reframing shyness can affirm quiet group members.

4. Ask what they associate with being "in control." (Examples: Academics, leadership, sports, having a room of one's own, music, conversation, cleaning.) Then ask the group what they associate with feeling "out of control." Give them time to consider this. If needed, mention the following. Especially with a large group, volunteers could make lists on a wallboard.

strong emotions	feeling intimidated	sibling rivalry
being "outclassed"	fears	bullying
depression	anxiety	high stress level
abuse	family rules	perfectionism
dating	food	conflict
anger	arguments	alcohol and other drugs

being around the other gender

being in a group of peers doing something dangerous

Invite the group to shares incidents from their lives when they felt out of control. Modeling discretion, share an experience from your life. You might say, "I feel comfortable sharing this. There are some other situations I wouldn't be comfortable sharing. Share whatever feels comfortable to you." It is important to offer such guidance about setting boundaries, although group members of all ages usually share discreetly, according to level of trust in the group.

5. Move the discussion toward what it means to have a sense of control in one's life by asking these questions:

   ~ What do you think contributes to feeling in control in life?
   ~ On a scale of 1 to 10, with 10 being "total control," to what extent do you feel that you have control in your life?
   ~ Without giving a name, do you know anyone who seems to have a good amount of control in life? What has given you this impression?
   ~ What are your thoughts about people who seem to be in control?
   ~ How might adults and teens differ in feeling in control?
   ~ What are some examples of being "in control" in a negative way? (Possibilities: Using threats and other kinds of bullying, being abusive, intimidating others, or manipulating others.)
   ~ What are some things in life that people do not have 100 percent control over? (Possibilities: Health, environmental changes, feelings, other people, taxes, death, safety.)

6. Invite the group to share what they could do to have more control now and in the future. They might mention some of the following:

counting to ten before responding when angered	having a good relationship
using relaxation techniques	paying more attention to health
talking about feelings	being more careful with money
getting a good education	getting a good job
being independent, on one's own	attaining financial security

7. For closure, ask, "What did you learn from each other today? What are some things you have in common with others in the group? How did this discussion feel?"

FOCUS Identity

Learning Styles

Background

Depending on how a school identifies giftedness, especially if high achievement is not the only factor considered, group members may vary considerably in learning style, some preferring to learn by listening, some by seeing, some by doing. Gifted teens collectively probably vary as much as the rest of the population in learning style. However, many may feel frustrated and uncomfortable in classrooms because of sensitivities and priorities related to learning and relationships.

When teaching style and learning style are at odds, problems may result. However, both the teacher and the student may be unaware that some of the problems may be related to their differing styles. Similarly, when teaching and learning styles are a match, good progress is likely. Teachers are encouraged to teach to different learning styles. Nevertheless, some teachers teach largely in their own preferred style, and students may resist teaching styles that don't match their own preferences. Both teachers and students need to be encouraged to teach and learn in their unpreferred modes, as well, in order to accommodate styles that differ from their own.

In contrast to stereotypes, some gifted students do not learn best by listening or reading or working in sequential steps. Some prefer hands-on and/or collaborative-learning activities. Some start writing assignments "in the middle," with good results. Yet programs for gifted kids and advanced classes may have only more-and-faster curriculum, involving reading, writing, lecture, and long-term projects—with little room or support for creativity or ingenuity. Long-term projects and written work are often difficult for kinesthetic learners, including those with impressive capabilities. Yet these same "troublesome," bright students might nevertheless enjoy school and do well as adults in a work environment that fits them.

Achievers are not necessarily strong in all academic areas and may be much stronger in nonverbal than verbal areas. You may want to keep a record of the various learning styles that become apparent through the continuum exercise used in this session. Such information can be valuable when advocating for changes in the classroom for underachieving students in particular (for example, beginning with, "In our groups, I've noticed that many of the underachieving gifted teens don't have a stereotypical gifted student learning style"). This session can help students understand why they appreciate some teachers more than others, why they are having trouble in some classes, and how they could ask teachers to alter teaching methods.

- Gifted teens learn about various teaching and learning styles.
- They become more aware of their own preferred learning styles.
- They understand why students may experience learning difficulties.

1. Introduce the topic by summarizing the background information. Explain that learning style can affect which courses students choose, which teachers are preferred, which kinds of assignments are easiest to accomplish, which class activities are enjoyed, and student success.

2. Direct the group to line up along one wall of the room (or form an angle at one corner, with the walls being the two sides) for an activity similar to the one described (with cautionary statements about tempo and procedure) in suggestion #4 on page 29. Designate one end of the continuum as 10, "a lot," and the other end as 0, "not at all." Explain that you are going to read a series of statements about learning styles. As you read each statement, students should physically move to the point on the continuum that best represents where they feel they belong.

   Read aloud each statement from "Learning Styles: A Continuum Activity" (page 47). After each statement, and after group members have found their places on the continuum, select two to four members to explain why they placed themselves where they did.

   When finished, ask the students to make summary statements about themselves as a group. If they need help, ask if there were learning preferences where most were bunched together. Do most of them like orderly teachers and classes? Are most of them easily distracted? Do most like to work in groups or alone? What learning preferences might cause learning problems in most classrooms?

   You might encourage group members to strengthen their unpreferred modes by engaging in those ways of learning. The more flexible they are, the easier it will be for them to learn in all types of educational situations now and in the future.

3. For closure, compliment them (if appropriate) for their participation and serious thought. Wish them well regarding being able to ask, tactfully and effectively, for what they need in teaching style and being flexible and adaptable in the classroom.

Learning Styles: A Continuum Activity

1. I prefer to learn by doing—building, measuring, drawing, mixing, or fixing—instead of by listening or viewing.

2. I prefer to learn by listening—teacher presentations, speakers, or CDs or tapes.

3. I prefer to learn by viewing or seeing—reading, overhead projector, DVDs or videos, chalk/dry-erase board information.

4. I need to write something down to remember it.

5. I like to know what to expect in a class before it begins.

6. I like to know the purpose of what I am doing in a class.

7. I prefer classes that are highly structured and highly organized.

8. I like classrooms that have many interesting and colorful things on the walls.

9. I like to work in groups.

10. I like to argue and debate about things in class.

11. I can stand having information coming at me from many directions at once.

12. I like to have my teachers know me well.

13. I like to have teachers call on me and give me attention in class.

14. I learn best when I like the teacher. I don't do as well when I don't.

15. I easily accept a teacher's authority.

16. I am easily distracted.

17. I like to sit in the front of a class.

18. I feel anxious and agitated when a class is disorderly.

19. I like to show what I know in class.

20. I prefer to work alone.

21. I can work and concentrate in the midst of a lot of noise or activity.

22. I try to do well in school because I don't like to be criticized.

23. Most of my teachers like me.

FOCUS Identity

Perfectionism

Background

A drive toward excellence can be a positive trait, inspiring people to do a good job, set high standards, receive awards and praise, and be consistent and dependable. However, when this drive moves "out of bounds," the result is perfectionism, and the list of negatives is long.

Perfectionism might not encourage academic, personal, or social risk-taking. It may be hard for perfectionists to enjoy the present moment, the process, or a job well done because of a preoccupation with "product" and the burdens associated with needing to produce a fine product or performance "next time." Perfectionists may be self-critical, competitive, and critical of others, with perfectionism interfering with relationships. We probably want our surgeon, dentist, banker, highway construction crew, and auto mechanic to be perfectionists in their work, but we might find it challenging to live with, be friends with, or be taught by a perfectionist.

Because perfectionism has been linked with giftedness, it is worthy of discussion. Some gifted teens are debilitated by it both in their school lives and in their personal lives. Underachievers may not achieve because they have anxiety about being able to perform at the level they envision, refuse to be involved in a situation that is not ideal, or fear evaluation. Perfectionism can interfere with high achievers' ability to enjoy life and learn simply for the sake of learning. They may fear error and see self-acceptance and love as conditional, dependent on excellent performance.

This discussion will be especially important to gifted teens who are beginning to recognize that their perfectionism and anxiety are interfering with their well-being. For those who are predisposed to anxiety disorders, being able to talk about feelings, struggles, anxieties, perfectionism, and mistakes may be crucial to their emotional health.

Objectives

- Gifted teens consider whether perfectionism affects them.
- They think about what contributes to perfectionism.
- They practice articulating feelings and thoughts about perfectionism.
- They explore strategies for combating perfectionism.
- They consider their attitudes about making mistakes.

Suggestions

1. Ask, "What is perfectionism?" Discuss striving to excel versus striving to be perfect. Then ask, "When might perfectionism be bad?" If students don't contribute the following ideas, offer some of the following to the discussion. Perfectionists sometimes or often . . .

  ~ set unreasonable, impossible goals for themselves
  ~ are chronically dissatisfied with even excellent work
  ~ can't enjoy the present, because they are preoccupied with the next hurdle
  ~ avoid taking risks (academically and/or socially) because they fear "failing"
  ~ have an all-or-nothing view: "If I can't do it perfectly, I won't do it at all"
  ~ are highly self-critical and preoccupied with their own and/or others' expectations
  ~ are critical of others
  ~ are highly competitive and constantly compare themselves to others
  ~ experience stress and anxiety
  ~ are afraid of making mistakes
  ~ are afraid of revealing weaknesses or imperfections
  ~ procrastinate because of their need to do something perfectly
  ~ spend time and energy doing something over and over until it is "perfect"
  ~ are prone to depression
  ~ have relationship problems because they expect so much of themselves and others
  ~ connect self-worth to performance and are sensitive to criticism
  ~ cannot imagine unconditional love
  ~ are compulsive planners and may not tolerate ambiguity well
  ~ see situations or performances as (all) good/right or (all) bad/wrong
  ~ are dissatisfied with situations that are not ideal

2. Ask, "In what areas might you be a perfectionist?" Then, "catastrophize" about some responses: "What's the worst thing that could happen if you didn't _____ perfectly?" If they mention what someone would think, disappointing someone, or having someone comment on their imperfect performance, encourage them to elaborate on their fears. Ask, "Then what would happen?" "And then?"

3. Ask, "If you're a perfectionist, does that come from within you or from others? If from within, what do you say to yourself when doing something? If from others, what do they say—or what do you assume?" (NOTE: Expectations might be assumed, not actually stated, although they can indeed be vocalized by parents, coaches, and others. Fear of error may also actually *invite* criticism.) Introduce the following ideas if they do not emerge. Ask the students to raise their hands if these statements fit their situations:

  ~ People (parents, teachers, other adults, friends) expect me to be perfect.
  ~ I'm supposed to be the "perfect child" in my family. (NOTE: You might explore this issue further, asking questions like these: "How long have you played that role?" "Who in your family is allowed to make mistakes?" "Who tells you that

you must be the perfect child?" "What would happen if you suddenly weren't the perfect child? Who would notice first? What would they notice?")

~ I worry about letting other people down.
~ If I'm not perfect, I get criticized.
~ Everything around me is in chaos. Being perfect is the only way I feel in control.
~ I have to be perfect for people to like me and accept me.

4. Invite students to brainstorm strategies for combating perfectionism. Some suggestions follow.

~ Be average for a day. Give yourself permission to be messy, late, incomplete, imperfect.
~ Become involved in activities that are not graded—and focus on process, not product. (NOTE: Discuss a "process" approach to life—that is, life as a journey. People and skills are forever being made. It's possible to be involved in something with no end or product in mind.)
~ Take a risk. Sign up for a course that has a reputation for being a challenge. Smile and start a conversation with someone you don't know. Do an assignment or study for a test without overdoing it. Alter your morning routine. Start a day without a plan.
~ Give yourself permission to make at least three mistakes a day. Smile at them.
~ Plan less compulsively.
~ Stop using the words *should* or *I have to.*
~ Share a weakness or limitation with a friend. He or she will not think less of you.
~ Acknowledge that your self-expectations might be unrealistic and unreasonable.
~ Find out more about perfectionism.
~ Explore possible contributors to perfectionism. Comments heard at home or school? Wanting approval? Fearing disapproval? Hard-wired temperament?
~ Savor your past accomplishments. Savor the present moment.
~ Ask friends to help you overcome your perfectionism by giving you a sign when they notice it.
~ Tell yourself repeatedly that it's okay to be less than perfect.
~ Laugh at yourself—and at your perfectionism.

5. As an extension of this session, or as a separate session, turn the focus to the mistakes aspect of perfectionism. Say, "Close your eyes and think about the last significant mistake you made in the presence of someone. . . . Imagine that you have just made the mistake. . . . What are you feeling? . . . What are you expecting? . . . Does something happen? . . . What is your response? . . . How do you feel? . . . How long does this feeling last?"

Encourage the group to share experiences related to mistakes. Invite them to respond to each other. If that does not occur spontaneously, model acknowledging what is shared, without treating it like a catastrophe (Say, "Oops!"). It is important to give eye contact to whoever shares, to reflect the speaker's tone (lighthearted? serious?), and to show that you have paid attention by reflecting a feeling

("I can hear your embarrassment" or "That must have been scary"). If an error had dangerous or disruptive repercussions, you might say, "I'm sorry you had to experience that. That must have been difficult." In general (but not when a serious or tragic error is recounted), you might ask, "Has anyone had a similar experience?" Then ask how they felt during the exchange, how they would describe the group atmosphere, and if the sharing affected their perceptions of anyone.

6. Initiate a general discussion about mistakes with some of the following:

   ~ On a scale of 1 to 10, with 10 being "no problem," how do you usually feel about your mistakes?
   ~ How much time do you spend around people who routinely point out others' mistakes?
   ~ What happens at home when you make a mistake?
   ~ What happens when you make a mistake around your friends?
   ~ Do you know any people who typically laugh at their own mistakes?
   ~ What is a healthy attitude about making mistakes, in your opinion? (If not mentioned in the group, comment that we can forgive ourselves, apologize when our mistakes hurt others, laugh at our errors, not think of them as catastrophes, and put them behind us.)

7. For closure, have everyone choose an anti-perfectionism task for the next week from the list of strategies brainstormed in #4. Invite them to create a motto about mistakes. (Examples: "I have the right to make mistakes," "Nobody's perfect," and/or "I'm human.") Thank the group for their contributions and ask how they felt during the discussion.

FOCUS Identity

More Than Test Scores and Grades?

Background

Most schools are understandably preoccupied with achievement measures. However, sometimes parents of gifted kids become so absorbed in test scores and grades that they bring them up even in social situations. Sometimes gifted teens themselves get caught up in this kind of competition socially. Academic data may indeed be a major chunk of personal definition. Highly able students need to be aware that their calling attention to grades and scores can seem arrogant, insensitive, and socially unsmooth, and these also lose much of their currency after high school. College students quickly realize that earlier grades are related to context, and at some universities everyone was probably an impressive student in high school. For some, it is a major adjustment to no longer be able to use test scores as personal definition.

Regardless of the place of grades and scores in the competitive world of academics, scholarships, and college acceptances, no single test can assess the broad range of traits and abilities that helps a person to be successful, good company, or even professionally respected. Fundamentally, all tests are imperfect measurers.

Scores on group-administered tests (often used initially to screen for special programs) may be affected by any number of factors, including test anxiety, fatigue, stress, verbal deficiencies, problems with reading, room temperature, attitude, and cultural values that don't embrace competitively displaying one's knowledge. Scores on individually administered ability tests may also be affected by the gender, manner, and experience of the examiner, health and fatigue, and even cautious responses (when timed) because of perfectionism. And, scores may not reflect strengths important to success as adults.

However, test scores can indeed be valuable indicators of who might benefit by special programs. Great discrepancies among subtests might indicate a need for curriculum modifications. Ability tests (often generically referred to as IQ tests) may identify gifted students who otherwise would be missed because of poor grades or because high intelligence helps them to compensate for a learning disability, which may be revealed when results on subtests are compared. Scores on achievement tests (for example, standardized tests used by states or nationally to measure mastery of curriculum) might identify gifted individuals who are not absorbing the curriculum because of attendance problems, disability, or lack of family support for homework. Over time, there may be high scores one year, and average the next because of changing life circumstances, the latter potentially when students are identified for gifted education programs. Gifted students can indeed be "found" by scrutinizing cumulative student records, including test scores. Low scores might not accurately reflect ability; however, high scores aren't achieved by accident. When there are uneven scores, the high scores should be respected. A child doesn't become "ungifted" during an off year.

Then there are grades. It is important to acknowledge that grading is at least somewhat subjective when quantitative measures are not possible. In spite of the current emphasis on standards, performance criteria may also differ. Some teachers reward creativity; some discourage it. Lack of organization can lead to low grades for a highly gifted teen where completed homework is crucial. When gifted teens' circumstances change, academic performance can change in response.

Tests and grades have their place, and both are here to stay. Whether or not academic achievement is a high priority, each gifted teen is more complex than test scores and grades reflect. Tests and other student data need to be kept in perspective. Whether achiever or underachiever, rebel or conformist, artist or musician, or athlete or computer whiz—all gifted teens can benefit from examining the sources of their personal definition. Peers and a leader listening without judgment can help gifted teens embrace an appropriately broad, complex personal definition.

Objectives

- Gifted teens consider self-definition.
- They put grades and test scores into proper perspective.

Suggestions

1. To introduce the idea of personal definition, invite the students to think about individuals who have made either positive or negative comments about them that have had an impact—mother, father, sister, brother, other relatives, teacher, coach, friend, enemy, competitor.

    Ask the students to write down the most powerfully positive message anyone has given them—and then the most powerfully negative message. Encourage them to share these. Respect the wishes of those who prefer not to share the negative messages. Acknowledge their messages with a nod, smile, wince, or remark (for example, "Yes, that's positive!" or "That must have hurt!"). Then ask if and how these messages have affected them. Acknowledge that others' views become feedback that we can accept or dismiss.

2. Ask them how they define themselves.

3. Turn their attention to other sources of definition by exploring grades.

    ~ What are grades for?
    ~ If your school decided not to give grades, how would that affect your performance?
    ~ How accurately do grades reflect what students know? level of intelligence? conscientiousness? wisdom? motivation?

~ What else might grades reflect? (Some might mention teacher-pleasing, attendance, class participation, problem-solving. Keep the focus on *their* perspectives.)

4. Ask how they feel about large-group achievement tests that are given once or twice a year, as well as tests to gauge college aptitude.

   ~ What are standardized achievement tests supposed to measure? (What has been learned in the curriculum.)
   ~ What might affect a gifted teen's ability to do well on them?
   ~ What abilities and skills do achievement tests *not* measure?

5. Initiate a discussion about intelligence and testing in general. Read one or more of the following statements, or pass them out on slips of paper and have students read them.

   ~ "Brilliance" isn't necessary for life success. Those who are "comfortably bright" can do almost anything if they have motivation, perseverance, stability, and can figure out how the work world functions.
   ~ No test can determine exactly *how* one thinks.
   ~ Working slowly on a test does not reflect a "slow mind." A student with high capability might, in fact, consider a question more deeply than most other students do. Some highly intelligent individuals may read slowly because of anxiety, a reading disability, or even visual sensitivity.
   ~ Most tests rely heavily on verbal ability. A student's strengths might be in other areas.
   ~ Intelligence and achievement tests usually do not measure creativity, leadership, mechanical skills, artistic talent, ability to communicate, sensitivity to others, common sense, everyday problem-solving, motivation, perseverance, or the likelihood of having a satisfying life in the future.
   ~ Test anxiety, illness, the testing environment, and other factors can affect test scores.
   ~ Intelligence does not stay at a fixed level throughout a person's life. Although genetic factors play a role in determining potential *range* of intelligence, environment is key to its development.
   ~ Most ability tests measure three kinds of intelligence: verbal, logical-mathematical, and spatial. Some cultures might value other intelligences more highly than the ones that are usually tested for.
   ~ Depending on a person's culture, family, and peer group, working rapidly may not be valued or practiced. Most standardized tests are timed.
   ~ No single test should define anyone.
   ~ Tests may be reliable, but all have a margin of error (one reason a single score should not be a cut-off for program eligibility).
   ~ Many abilities are important in maintaining a healthy, well-functioning society.

6. For closure, ask for a volunteer to summarize the main point(s) of this session. Is there anything they might continue to think about in the days and weeks ahead? What were some feelings they had during the session?

FOCUS Identity

Understanding Underachievement

Background

Despite its title, this session is appropriate for both achievers and underachievers. The two groups have much in common developmentally, and many gifted underachievers were once achievers. A mixed-achievement group usually finds this topic interesting.

The chief criteria for identifying students for gifted programs are often classroom performance and scores on standardized tests. Students who do not achieve set benchmarks in these areas are often overlooked for gifted programs. Teachers may or may not be aware of such students' intellectual ability, and parents, relying on report cards to point out excellence or having too much faith in school processes, may not call teachers' attention to their child's ability.

Gifted students whose grades and test scores are lower than expected may be struggling with a learning disability, a difficult personal situation, peer pressure, bullying, depression, drug use, or difficulty accepting their own ability. For others, underachievement may be a choice. In either case, little is known about such students, because they are difficult for researchers to identify in large number. It is impossible to know how many gifted underachievers are not identified for special programs.

My own research has shown that some gifted underachievers become academic achievers late in high school, late in college, or in graduate school. In one study, 87 percent went on to college, and 51 percent of those had completed four years of college four years later. Some students who were extreme underachievers in high school had received degrees from well-known universities. Two other studies showed that when multiple adolescent developmental tasks were accomplished—finding career direction, forming mature relationships, becoming autonomous, and resolving conflict with parents, for example—motivation for academic work followed. Healing from trauma was also shown in a study to be related to a move toward achievement. And in yet another study of successful adults who once were considered adolescent underachievers, "rebellious" girls, with the help of an achieving mentor and peer milieu, did well after leaving home. In summary, we simply cannot predict the future of any student, based on only one stage of development. In fact, underachievement might be mostly developmental "stuckness."

The abilities of gifted students may even fly under teachers' radar if those students don't contribute to class discussion. For many, problems at both home and school may interact to create an underachievement habit and lifestyle. Sometimes responsibilities or conflict at home require so much energy that there is simply little left for schoolwork. For other students, creativity or personality factors make them a poor fit in the traditional school system.

Sometimes school and family can work together to help a student achieve academically. Family counseling can examine the function and effects of underachievement within the family. Individual counseling about anger and control can address passive-aggressive behavior. Teens from highly controlling families may gain power by not performing. For them and for those in conflict-ridden, chaotic homes, achievement may be the one controllable dimension. However, in group sessions, facilitators should usually avoid focusing stridently on underachievement, since it might not be the most important issue. Building a nonjudgmental relationship with gifted underachievers may be crucial to well-being and to movement forward. The goal is effective living, not necessarily high achievement.

Underachievement probably took some time to develop, and it may take just as long to change, if in fact academic achievement is the goal. Small, incremental improvements can be quietly noted. Many factors likely contribute to chronic underachievement in gifted students. It makes sense then that no single group session will have a significant impact to change this behavior. However, working continually to increase students' self-awareness and thinking about family, relationships, and feelings often leads to positive change, as does a stress-free, noncompetitive, nonjudgmental environment for discussion with intellectual peers.

Through this session, underachievers may learn something about themselves. Achievers will learn something about underachievement, become more sensitive to underachieving students, and even respect the courage of some not to do the expected. You might remind the group that success and satisfaction in life are not necessarily connected with school performance. The die is not necessarily cast during the school years. Keep the background information in mind, but avoid presenting it, per se. Many gifted underachievers resist anyone telling them who they are. Participating in a group for gifted kids affirms their intelligence. That in itself might be important for some underachievers.

Important	Avoid preaching or cheerleading when dealing with gifted underachievers. Quietly affirm intelligence and worth. Acknowledge that they may be in control of their achievement—unless there is a learning disability, depression, or another factor not controllable by will. Avoid implying that they could do better if they tried. They have heard that before, and it might not be true. If achievement is within their control, one approach is to encourage them to be pragmatic—and use the school to get what they need for later life: academic credentials.

Objectives	• Gifted teens consider and confront stereotypes of achievers and underachievers. • They become more aware of issues that affect motivation and achievement. • Underachievers consider strategies for doing better in school—for their own sake. • Group members explore how they define *success* and *failure*.

Suggestions

1. As an introduction, mention that many students with high capability are not academic achievers. Some experts have estimated that half of those with high ability do not perform well in school. Although many educators are pessimistic about the future of gifted underachievers, success and satisfaction are indeed possible.

   Ask students to define *underachievement* (usually defined as a student who scores high on achievement or ability tests, but doesn't perform as expected academically).

2. Ask, "How do achievers usually feel about underachievers?" Allow for responses before asking, "And how do underachievers usually feel about achievers?" Then ask, "Do you think achievers and underachievers have anything in common?" (Possible shared characteristics: Feeling stress from expectations, sensitivity, family situations, social difficulties, and concern about the future.)

3. Ask the group what they think contributes to underachievement. Ask if any underachievers are willing to talk about when their school performance began to decline. What was going on in school or elsewhere for them at the time? Did they get good grades earlier in school? If not already mentioned, point out that some or all of the following can contribute to underachievement:

   ~ moving often, getting behind/ahead in curriculum
   ~ death or serious illness within the family, or student illness
   ~ emotional problems, including depression
   ~ changing one's group of friends
   ~ problems with siblings
   ~ trouble at school, including being bullied
   ~ parents' attitudes toward school
   ~ deciding that school isn't important or challenging enough to work at
   ~ hostility toward parents and teachers

4. Depending on the level of trust and honesty in the group and whether you think it is appropriate, ask members to identify whether they think they are perceived by teachers as achievers or underachievers. Then invite them to consider some of the following questions. You may want to have achievers and underachievers respond to the questions separately, with the achievers answering first. Underachievers might be surprised by the achievers' responses.

Important

Choose questions carefully. Respect any and all responses. Especially for the underachievers in your group, it is important that you listen to their comments without challenging them.

~ Everyone in this group is quite intelligent. Where do you let it show?
~ Who in your life believes you are an intelligent person?
~ On a scale of 1 to 10, with 10 being "high level," how much do you focus on academics?
~ What is the most comfortable part of school for you? The most uncomfortable?
~ How would you rate your "social savvy" and "street smarts"?
~ What would you gain if you started (under)achieving in school?

~ How would family members react if you started (under)achieving?

~ When you achieve or underachieve, who gives you attention?

~ How many gifted (under)achievers are in your family? In your circle of friends?

~ How much of your school achievement (grades) is in your control?

~ What is your attitude about life in general? What is your level of self-confidence, well-being, physical health, or energy?

~ On a scale of 1 to 10, with 10 being "a lot," how satisfied are you with your career direction right now?

~ What concerns do you have about life after high school?

~ How much influence might you have over the achievement of others?

~ How do you respond to competition, especially in school?

~ What affects your school achievement the most?

5. Ask the underachievers how they could use the system to their advantage without sacrificing themselves to it. Although all underachievers are not rebels, this kind of question may raise new possibilities in their minds. (However, they might not yet be comfortable talking about actual changes they could make.)

6. Depending on interest, make a brief detour and examine the terms *success* and *failure*, which are part of the school and broader cultures. Ask the group to define the terms. Then ask them some of the following:

~ How much do success and failure depend on other people knowing about them?

~ Can successful people feel like failures?

~ How might success in academics and activities affect adult life—if at all?

~ How might poor performance in these areas affect adult life—if at all?

~ When have you experienced success? failure?

~ Who and/or what has influenced how you think about these?

~ Who do you want to tell when you feel successful?

~ How much do you worry about failure?

~ A popular view is that it is important to learn how to fail. Do you agree?

~ Do males and females define *success* and *failure* differently? Do adults and teens?

~ What will help you feel successful when you are thirty, fifty, retired? (Possibilities: Being respected; using talents; feeling content; having a successful relationship; having lots of money; being healthy.)

~ What could contribute to feeling failure at those ages?

~ How does society, in general, view success?

7. If group members are all underachievers, and if they seemed comfortable and honest earlier, ask if they are interested in trying an activity for a few weeks. Hand out the activity sheet (page 59). Explain that each week they will write one small goal on their sheet. At the end of the week, they will use the sheet to report progress to the group (or individually with you). You may want to keep separate file folders for UNAN. While it is a contradiction (to the anonymous aspect) to have names on their sheets, you need to file them.

8. For closure, ask one or more students what they learned or felt during the discussion.

Underachievers Anonymous (UNAN)

Name: _____

- I will work conscientiously on the goals stated below.
- I will check in weekly, track my progress, and stay committed to my goals.
- I will not brag about any lack of effort, lateness, and/or any other underachieving behavior that implies the system is beneath me.
- I will remember that effort is the key, and I will try to work hard to meet the goals I set.
- I am doing this activity in my own self-interest.
- I will keep in mind that this is good practice for what I will face later in life.
- I will support others involved in UNAN, knowing that my attitudes and behaviors influence others.

WEEK	GOAL	REACHING MY GOAL (1 to 10 scale, 1 = no success; 10 = great success)
1.		
2.		
3.		
4.		
5.		
6.		
7.		
8.		

Signature: _____

FOCUS Identity

Giving Ourselves Permission

Background

Bright, capable people sometimes censor, constrain, or otherwise protect themselves—and miss some life experiences. They do not give themselves permission to say something that needs to be said or to do something that might be beneficial (or interesting) to them. This session usually helps a group become more open, since it is quite thorough, and many aspects of a person are revealed in just a few moments—safely. It is also a potentially empowering exercise, since it clearly focuses on a teen's own power to grant (or not grant) permission to the self. If your opportunity to lead a particular group is limited to only a few sessions, this one should definitely be among them, since it promotes group bonding.

Objectives

- Gifted teens recognize that they are in charge of how they respond to their various environments.
- They become aware that they could perhaps enhance their lives by giving themselves permission to do, say, or experience more.
- They learn that individuals may limit themselves in a variety of ways.

Suggestions

1. Introduce the topic with whatever seems pertinent from the background information, perhaps reading the first sentence to begin. Hand out "Giving Myself Permission" (page 62). Explain to the group that they may interpret each item however they wish. However, some gifted teens may see being selfish or being angry or making mistakes in only negative terms. You may want to point out that being selfish can mean taking care of important personal needs; being angry is better than stuffing anger and feeling sad; making mistakes is a way to learn.

   In this exercise, it is important for you to model for the group. Fill out the activity sheet yourself and read down your list, prefacing all or many of your items with, "I would like to give myself permission to . . ." in order to impress on them that it would be possible for you to make a change if you had the necessary courage and will. Limit your checked items to ten, in order not to take up too much group time. Checking ten will also give students permission to check more than just one or two. Pause for a second or two after each item so that the group has a chance to register it. Throughout, it is important that you model honesty and vulnerability, thereby giving them permission to be open and genuine. (I typically include "feel good about my body," not only because that is true for me, but also because it gives permission to group members to check that common and significant teen concern.)

Give the group a few minutes to complete the activity sheet. Remind them that they will mark what they are *not* doing. Invite them to add items if something they want to give themselves permission to do is not included.

2. Encourage the group to share their lists. If you go around the circle, begin with a volunteer and then move in whatever direction will allow shy or unsure teens to wait before sharing. As you modeled in #1, they should simply read down their lists, prefacing perhaps every fourth item with "I would like to give myself permission to" and pausing briefly between items. Encourage the group to listen carefully to each other. You may want to tally their responses in the margins of your own sheet. Tell the group you will do that and that you will ask them, in the end, what items were checked most often.

After each person shares, ask the group if there is anything they would like to know more about or if they heard anything that surprised them. For example, it's probably news if a star athlete wants to "feel good about my body," or if a high achiever wants to "be intelligent." If there is a dramatic insight or revelation, encourage the group to respond and offer support. You may also want to ask for elaboration on one reported item per student, if appropriate. (Examples: What kinds of risks would you like to take—social, academic, emotional? What kind of fun would you like to have? What part of your life would you like to take charge of?) Model respect for any reluctance to elaborate. Encourage them to say, "I'd rather not." Many individuals may have difficulty setting boundaries socially, so compliment anyone who is able to do so.

Before closure, ask which items were reported most often. Verify their responses with your tally.

3. For closure, ask for a volunteer to summarize the activity, including referring to common elements and surprises. Ask each group member to name one item they could give themselves permission to start working on today. Compliment them as a group: "It's good to see you becoming a group," if that is appropriate. Dispose of the sheets or file them.

Giving Myself Permission

Name: _____

I would like to give myself permission to . . .

____ have fun
____ take risks
____ focus on *now,* instead of focusing so much on the future
____ be angry
____ be talkative
____ be quiet
____ be kind
____ love
____ be loved
____ feel good about my body
____ be intelligent
____ take care of my needs first
____ make mistakes
____ achieve
____ follow my own path
____ show others I am upset
____ be happy
____ be sad
____ be free to "just *be*"—and not worry about others' expectations of me
____ accept authority in others
____ be okay in a less-than-perfect situation
____ be comfortable when alone
____ stop a bad behavior or a harmful habit
____ be imperfect
____ relax
____ be "bad"
____ be "good"
____ say difficult things to someone
____ take charge of my life
____ admit that I have conflicting and opposite (good and bad) feelings about someone in my family

____ _____
____ _____
____ _____

FOCUS Identity

Self-Esteem

Background

Many teens, especially those with high intellectual or other kinds of ability, do not express their lack of confidence or their doubts about themselves. Yet appearance alone does not tell us what they think of themselves. They may be highly self-critical, agonize over mistakes, and feel uncomfortably different. Many (perhaps most) do not seek out trusted adults to talk with. This session gives students a chance to talk in a supportive group about what they think of themselves. Group members can give feedback.

Low self-esteem affects relationships with peers and family. It may play a role in level of classroom participation; cruel gossiping, bullying, and intimidation of peers and siblings (even though those aggressive behaviors do not necessarily reflect poor self-esteem); sexual risk-taking; or eating disorders, for example. It can contribute to abusive relationships, as well as to alcohol and other drug abuse and other dangerous behaviors. Even highly successful students who appear self-composed may have low self-esteem. Their stellar achievement may mask personal struggles, fears, and doubts. Their social, emotional, and/or physical development may lag behind intellectual development. They may feel like an imposter, with the gifted label, concerned that they will be found out. If they are struggling with a deficit in focus and concentration in class, they may have difficulties academically and socially. Intellectually gifted teens may even have reading problems or problems with sequential learning or organization. Regardless of who is in your group, they all can benefit from this discussion.

Important

It is best to place this session far enough into the group experience that positive comments have credibility. When such comments are made early in the life of the group, they may not be believed, since group members have not had enough opportunity to become well acquainted.

Objectives

- Gifted teens consider the sources of self-esteem and how self-esteem affects them.
- They brainstorm ways to improve their sense of self.
- They practice giving and receiving positive feedback.

Suggestions

1. Introduce the topic by asking group members to define *self-esteem* (perhaps "how people see or value themselves"). After a brief discussion, hand out "Rating My Self-Esteem" (page 66). Give students a few minutes to complete it.

2. Have them report their various self-esteem ratings and explain how they determined their ratings. Then ask one or more of the following:

   ~ What standards have you set for yourself physically, academically, socially, and emotionally?
   ~ What are the physical, academic, social, and emotional standards of your peer group?
   ~ What are your family's physical, intellectual, social, and emotional standards?
   ~ What do you tell yourself, about yourself, in each of the four areas?

3. Invite the group to consider where self-esteem comes from with these questions:

   ~ How much do you think positive self-esteem is the result of praise, gifts, and attention? How much might low self-esteem come from these things?
   ~ How do we develop positive self-esteem? (If group members do not mention the following, contribute them to the discussion: learning how to do things for ourselves; gaining skills through meeting challenges. Invite them to comment on these ideas.)
   ~ How are self-esteem and self-sufficiency related—or aren't they?
   ~ What kind of parenting do you think helps children develop positive self-esteem?
   ~ How much choice do we have in how we respond to others' messages about us?
   ~ How do you know you're okay and that you're valued? (Be aware that some teens may indicate that they do not know they are valued. If that occurs, encourage the group to offer support—especially if group members have previously demonstrated that capacity.)

4. Ask whether and how adult life might be affected by low self-esteem. Introduce the following ideas if they do not come up in discussion and if they seem appropriate for your group:

   ~ marriage and partnership (feeling inadequate; being abused or abusive; being competitive, critical)
   ~ parenting (feeling inadequate; being abused or abusive; inability to be close to one's children; alienation; fearfulness; isolation; pessimism; needing constant affirmation)
   ~ social relationships (feeling inadequate; having a tendency to dominate or be dominated by others)
   ~ relationships at work (being unable to compliment and support others; gossiping; being unassertive; being self-absorbed)
   ~ career direction and success (feeling inadequate; feeling unable to make necessary career moves; lacking focus)
   ~ productivity (being preoccupied with one's flaws and inadequacies; lacking a can-do attitude)
   ~ contentment and satisfaction with life (low or nonexistent)

5. Have the group brainstorm ways to start improving their self-esteem. Here are some suggestions:

   ~ Give yourself compliments and praise instead of relying on others to do it.
   ~ Accept approval instead of rejecting it. "Parent" yourself. Do for yourself what others have been unable to do for you. (This is especially important for teenagers who have grown up in homes with depressed, neglectful, abusive, or substance-dependent parents.)
   ~ Do something you know you're good at, and then congratulate yourself on a job well done.
   ~ Try something new. If you fail, congratulate yourself for taking a risk.
   ~ Accept and acknowledge all of your feelings, even the "bad" ones: anger, guilt, inadequacy, disappointment. (Doing that takes courage.)

6. Ask students to write down at least one positive comment about everyone else in the group. Then, focusing on one person at a time, invite all other members to share their positive comments about him or her. If time is short, move this activity along fairly quickly. Let the comments be heard, but do not discuss them. You might suggest that each person wait to hear all comments from the group before saying a simple "Thank you."

7. For closure, thank the group for sharing, for articulating their concerns in personally sensitive areas, and for being generous and thoughtful in their comments. Dispose of the sheets or add them to the group folders.

Rating My Self-Esteem

Name: _____

In each of the following four areas, rate how you view yourself on a scale of 1 to 10, with 1 being "very low" and 10 being "very high."

PHYSICAL

    1   2   3   4   5   6   7   8   9   10

INTELLECTUAL

    1   2   3   4   5   6   7   8   9   10

SOCIAL

    1   2   3   4   5   6   7   8   9   10

EMOTIONAL

    1   2   3   4   5   6   7   8   9   10

Now give yourself an overall rating:

    1   2   3   4   5   6   7   8   9   10

FOCUS Identity

Conformity

Background

A question worth discussing is whether gifted teens are more or less conforming than others their age. Teens with high ability have greatly differing personality styles. They also vary greatly in interests, attitudes, and values. There is undoubtedly a wide range of conforming and nonconforming behaviors among them as well, perhaps an important revelation in itself.

Objectives

- Gifted teens recognize that conformity is part of their social and academic worlds.
- They examine how they are responding to the pressures to conform and not to conform, and they consider possible sources of these pressures.
- They reflect on the price and value of both conformity and nonconformity.

Suggestions

1. Begin by explaining that conformity can exist both in the majority, or mainstream culture, and in a minority, or counterculture. Ask the group how much they generally conform to the majority in the following situations. Then ask them how much they conform to a minority. Their choices may be about hair and clothing styles, behavior, social activity, attitude, music tastes, technology, food or drink choices, or lifestyle. Their level of conformity might differ from context to context, depending on their situation or environment.

    socially at school   socially outside of school
    at work (for older teens)   at home
    academically at school

2. Ask how they show their uniqueness in the above situations. Then pursue some of these directions (as always, letting the group teach, without your evaluation):

    ~ What encourages you to conform? Not to conform?
    ~ How easy or difficult is it for you to resist negative peer influences when being social?
    ~ Who sets standards of behavior or appearance in school, at work, out of school, at home?
    ~ Is there a right way to behave in each of these worlds?
    ~ When might conformity be bad? (Example: When it means doing things that are dangerous to ourselves, others, public safety, or property.)

~ When might conformity be good? (Examples: When it means acting in someone's best interests; when it is necessary for survival.)

~ What price might we pay for conformity? (Examples: Loss of individuality; anger at ourselves for caving in to pressure; loss of creativity; loss of valuable ideas; personal harm, if conformity means putting ourselves in dangerous situations.)

~ What price might we pay for nonconformity? (Examples: Losing out on what schools or other institutions offer; loss of opportunity; disruption and hassle; loneliness; ostracism; abuse; ridicule.)

~ How do you feel about conformists generally? about nonconformists?

~ Are you mostly a conformist or mostly a nonconformist? How do you feel about that?

~ What does your family value most, conformity or nonconformity?

~ Are gifted teens more conforming than other kids their age? less?

3. If your group likes to think abstractly, brainstorm nonconforming behaviors and ideas that have made big and small changes in society by challenging the norm. Ask them for their ideas first. Then offer these:

civil rights activism

feminist activism

women voting

nose rings and other body piercings

tattoos

fast food

mixing animation with live actors in film

the three-point shot in basketball

the theory of relativity

drive-through—and then electronic—banking and bill-paying

organ transplants

mixing different types of music (religious/rock; country/pop)

airplane flight

movies on videotape, DVD, and other media

shopping malls

telemarketing

infomercials

laptop computers

email

Internet

cell phones and portable media players

4. For closure, invite the students to share some of the feelings and thoughts they had during the session. Ask, "How did you feel during the discussion—uneasy, proud, comfortable, critical, discouraged?"

FOCUS Identity

Influencers

Background

Sorting out how others influence their lives and learning how to deal with others' expectations are important tasks for gifted teens, whose antennae are often hyperalert. Regardless of their home situations or social comfort, reflecting on the role of people who influence their lives can be interesting and beneficial.

This session is a chance to chuckle over the warnings teens repeatedly hear—and consider their effects. As always, the purpose is to articulate thoughts and feelings, not to receive advice. During discussion, the group may have feelings about what they share and hear, but they will not have to spend emotional energy resisting or weighing admonitions from you. This session can be particularly valuable for at-risk gifted teens.

Objectives

- Gifted teens consider the effects of encouragement and discouragement on identity.
- They explore influences on their values, direction, behaviors, and attitudes.
- Gifted teens who are at risk for poor educational and personal outcomes consider people who have influenced them to respond to school, to other people, or to life in negative ways.
- Group members acknowledge individuals who have influenced them positively.

Suggestions

1. Introduce the topic. Direct the group to list on paper those people who encourage them and, in a separate column, those who discourage them.

   Invite the group to share their lists and describe the encouragement or discouragement. Afterward, focus on a particular encourager: "Who seems to give you unconditional support—no strings attached, no conditions to meet, no tests to pass?" (Pose this question to the entire group, waiting to see if anyone volunteers a response. Some may not know such a person. If so, ask how they encourage themselves.)

2. Ask the group to list on paper people (real people; any age) who have had a positive influence on their values and direction. Then ask them to list people who have had a negative influence on their values and direction. (Some individuals might be on both lists—and were on the list in #1.) They might make a separate column for people they have promised themselves *never* to be like. As always, focus

on *their* world. Be prepared to hear that high-profile sports figures and pop-culture idols are significant influencers.

Encourage the group to share their lists. Invite them to give a reason for listing each person. Generate discussion by asking questions like the following:

~ Have your positive influencers mostly influenced your beliefs, skills, or direction for the future? What about your negative influencers?

~ How would you describe the group of people you have listed? (Mostly family members or people outside of your family? Males or females? People who are similar to each other or many different types of people? People you know personally or people you have heard about? Rebels or conformists? Achievers or laid-back types? Optimists or pessimists?)

~ Is there one key individual on your positive list who has influenced you more than anyone else? If so, what would that person wish for you? Does that person know how much you have been influenced by him or her? Are you in contact with that person?

Important
....

Some gifted teens may have had few or no positive influencers. If you notice some group members are struggling with that category, encourage them to describe the kind of person they would listen to for guidance. They may be willing to tell how the absence of positive influencers has affected them. If they become angry or sad while exploring this sensitive topic, support their feelings and invite them to help the group understand their experience. Remind the group of confidentiality.

Before the group series ends, you might try to match these teens with adults who were in difficult circumstances as teenagers but have since grown up to be contributing members of the community. Local service clubs may be helpful in setting up such arrangements.

3. Invite the group to write a note of thanks to someone on their list of positive influencers. Mention that such messages are usually appreciated, but are often never communicated or thought of too late. Tell the group that they may choose to send their notes or not.

4. Ask the group to brainstorm areas they have received advice about in their lives. If the areas listed below are not mentioned, ask what they've been told about these:

careers	chores	women
food	manners	men
health	personal appearance	friendship
alcohol and other drugs	cleanliness	dating
safety	fitness	sex
strangers	hair	Internet use
hitchhiking	clothing	cell phones
driving	body decoration	text messaging

Then ask these questions:

~ What do you think about the advice you've received?
~ What advice have you followed, if any? How has it affected you?
~ What is the worst piece of advice you have ever been given?
~ What is the best piece of advice you have ever been given?

5. For closure, invite the group to note the most interesting or most thought-provoking advice they heard in the meeting.

FOCUS Identity

Playing

Background

Although this session title may seem odd, fun is a topic that merits attention—especially for high-achieving students. In one informal survey of gifted teens, 11 percent said they didn't play well at all. One of my other studies showed that gifted teens feel overcommitted and highly stressed, with little time to be social and to play.

High-achieving, heavily committed students may not know where to start for fun, but underachievers may be similarly unable to just enjoy the moment.

On the other hand, some students in your group may genuinely have fun doing schoolwork, being involved in activities, learning via the Internet, and/or working at a part-time job. These students may not separate work and play; they are able to enjoy and feel satisfied with whatever they are doing—taking a test, practicing an instrument, writing an essay, mowing the lawn, serving hamburgers. They may not set aside time to relax, but they are able to lose themselves in the moment, without anxiety. Perhaps they will approach their future career as play, too.

Boredom is a topic pertinent to a discussion of enjoyment. Gifted students, especially in their early teen years, may indeed complain about classes being boring, but the term deserves scrutiny. Teens in middle school face a difficult adjustment challenge: Reading assignments are longer, anthologies are thicker, advanced classes aren't yet available in some areas, and teachers have many more students to pay attention to. Underachievement may become a pattern during this period, but not just because of lack of challenge. Underachievement may occur even when content and instruction are highly differentiated. Gifted teens may call everything "boring," but that term might reflect lack of teacher attention, not having friends in class, having a strict disciplinarian for a teacher, or sitting in a class that lacks variety. Adults should ask for details: "Help me understand *boring*." If nothing else, that request shows interest in the student's world. If indeed lack of challenge is an issue, gifted teens might be guided to approach a teacher about working independently or collaboratively designing a differentiated curriculum. In addition, artists can draw, readers might be allowed to read, and thinkers can think in a slow-paced classroom, especially when no differentiation is possible. At home, gifted kids can be encouraged to create their own safe and stimulating diversion.

Objectives

- Gifted teens explore the concepts of play, boredom, and fun.
- They consider that playing is part of a healthy, balanced life.
- They become more aware of whether and how they have fun.
- They recognize that it is possible to play as an adult—even at work.

Suggestions

1. Ask the group to define *fun* and *play*. (Accept their responses without comment but show respect and receptivity with your facial expression and other nonverbals.)

2. Encourage them to share what they normally do for fun. Where do they go? With whom? How long do they spend on it? How often do they do these activities? To provoke thought, ask if *fun* and *enjoyment* are synonymous.

   Then ask questions like the following:

   ~ Some studies have found that gifted teens often feel overcommitted, overscheduled, and overinvolved. How much of a problem is that for you?
   ~ How much do you include fun and relaxation in your life? (On a scale of 1 to 10, with 10 being "a lot.")
   ~ (For those who include it a lot) How are you able to find time for fun?
   ~ (For those who don't) Are the barriers internal (from you) or external (from others)?
   ~ How do you feel after having fun?
   ~ How did you learn to have fun? Who has modeled "having fun" for you?
   ~ Do the adults in your life have fun? Do they play?
   ~ On a scale of 1 to 10, with 10 being "a lot," how much of your fun is unhealthy, destructive, or dangerous?
   ~ How much is the word *boring* part of your daily vocabulary?
   ~ How often do you feel restless and bored? What do you usually do about that?
   ~ In your opinion, whose responsibility is it to alleviate boredom?

3. Introduce the concept of *creative* fun. Make the connection between having fun and being childlike. You might say, "Some people think that having fun is just for kids. Think of things you did as a child that were fun. Are you still doing any of them today? How could you make it appropriate for your age group?" Brainstorm ideas that meet the following criteria:

   ~ It's something I can do with a friend or in a group.
   ~ People talk and laugh together.
   ~ It doesn't hurt anyone, including me.
   ~ It helps people get to know each other better, maybe even become friends.
   ~ It doesn't involve alcohol or other drugs.
   ~ It brings out the best in everyone involved.

4. Invite the group to look ahead to the future. Ask questions such as these:

~ Can work be fun? Do you know anyone for whom work seems like play?

~ When you picture yourself as a young or even as an older adult having fun, what do you see yourself doing? (NOTE: Encourage the group to imagine activities other than drinking and sex, if initial responses are centered on these.)

~ How will you balance work and play as an adult? Will your work be enjoyable for you?

5. For closure, either summarize the session yourself or ask the group to tell what they heard. Compliment them for taking the topic seriously, and wish for them balanced lives that include fun, relaxation, and laughter.

FOCUS Identity

Being an Interesting Story

Background

This session can help gifted teens sort through the various threads of their personal history at arm's length, affirm the texture of their lives, and appreciate that all experiences—pleasant or painful, delightful or difficult—combine to make each of us unique and interesting. What we experience leads to wisdom, strength, resiliency, vision, compassion, and complex emotions. Our life stories are quilt-like—complex, colorful, unique. This session can shed a different light on life situations, including those that are challenging, difficult, or horrendous. It works best when a group has developed a sense of trust, respect, and safety.

Since the "My Story" activity sheet requires at least ten minutes to fill out, and each student in the group should get the group's full attention when presenting his or her story, you may want to divide this session into two, depending on time available. If you do, be sure to collect the activity sheets after the first session for use during the following session.

Objectives

- Gifted teens learn that each of them is a story.
- They consider that sharing parts of their personal stories may help build bridges to others.

Suggestions

1. Introduce the topic with ideas from the background information. Hand out the activity sheet (page 77) and instruct group members to review it as you read the following:

   ~ Treat your life as a story. Pretend that you're writing a novel based on your life.
   ~ Don't worry about writing complete sentences. Brief notes are okay.
   ~ Be clever and creative, and use humor if you like, but take the activity seriously.
   ~ For #2, the chapter titles, you might divide your life story into time periods, important family events, major personal changes, or various family locations—or something else.
   ~ For #3, think of themes from books or stories you've read (such as change, survival, meeting challenges, problem-solving) or create something original.

Ask if anyone has questions about the "My Story" sheet. Be aware that some may finish quickly, and some may want time to write many details. Begin when perhaps one-third of the group seems done; tell the others they can continue writing during the discussion.

2. Invite the group to share their stories one at a time. Tell them that they may share all or part of what they have written, elaborating or omitting material according to what they are comfortable with. If group members share difficult situations, experiences, or facts, or if anyone becomes distressed while sharing, offer support with a validating statement (for example, "That sounds like a difficult time") and encourage the group to do likewise. Affirm all experiences—pleasant and unpleasant, positive and negative.

3. For closure, thank them for their stories. Affirm their rich, complex, varied, and interesting lives. Celebrate their uniqueness as individuals. Dispose of the sheets or file them.

My Story

Name: _____

1. Title:

2. *Chapter One:*

   Chapter Two:

   Chapter Three:

   Chapter Four:

   Chapter Five:

3. Basic themes:

   a.

   b.

   c.

4. Turning points: _____

5. Heroes/saints/angels: _____

6. Villains/enemies/"evil ones": _____

7. Very dramatic scenes (clear, powerful memories): _____

   _____

   _____

8. Blank times (not much memory about them): _____

   _____

9. Punishments for the villains/evil ones: _____

10. Rewards for the heroes/saints/angels: _____

11. Most compassionate, most understanding character: _____

12. Best friend: _____

13. Healer: _____

14. Leader/mentor/guide: _____

15. A possible sequel to this story will tell about: _____

FOCUS Identity

When We Need Courage

Background

With the emphasis on gifted teens' academic performance (or lack thereof), there may be few opportunities for them to talk about personal victories in other areas of their lives. This session provides an opportunity for students to share an experience that required them to act with courage and to receive affirmation for the strengths they demonstrated. No matter how intellectually capable gifted kids are, they face situations in life that demand more than booksmarts and nimble minds. While discussing this topic, it is important to bear in mind that gifted individuals come from a range of social, economic, educational, cultural, and family backgrounds. Regardless of identification criteria for the "gifted" label, all of the following questions might apply to your group.

Objectives

- Gifted teens recall times when they were courageous.
- They consider that courage is also needed for honest self-assessment.

Suggestions

1. Introduce the topic with selected thoughts from the background information. Ask the group to think of times when they needed courage. You might ask the following questions. (Alternatively, the topics below can easily be made into a one-page questionnaire with sections on "when my family was in crisis," "a time I had to confront someone," and "a time I was in danger myself.)

    ~ Has your family ever been in danger because of problems within the family or threats from outside the family? (For example, a serious illness or injury, parents getting divorced, the loss of a job, financial problems, a natural disaster.) How did your family survive (if they did) the dangerous time?

    ~ Have you ever had to confront someone you were afraid of or intimidated by? (For example, a bully, someone who threatened you or a sibling, someone with a reputation for violent behavior.) How did you find courage to do that?

    ~ Have you ever faced a danger or threat alone? Would you be willing to share the experience with the group? (Remind them that they can say, "I'd rather not.")

    ~ Were you ever caring for a child or animal who needed help or protection? What did you do?

    ~ Have you ever had to stand up against intense peer pressure?

~ Have you ever stood up to a parent or other adult when that required courage?

~ Can you remember a time when it would have been easy to avoid doing something difficult, but you found the courage to get it done?

~ Have you ever set an important personal boundary by saying no (or another version of no) in a stressful situation?

Model affirmation in response to the sharing (for example, "That's so impressive" or "That must have been very difficult to do").

2. Turn the discussion to the relationship between courage and self-assessment. Ask questions like the following, respecting students' right to stay silent, as always.

~ Compared to responding to danger, how much courage does it take to look honestly at ourselves? Can you think of a time when you have done that? (For example, taking responsibility for actions, accepting consequences, admitting mistakes.)

~ What kinds of changes in someone's life require courage? (For example, getting out of an unhealthy relationship, saying no to unhealthy or risky behavior, leaving a high-risk peer group.)

~ How much courage does it take to allow yourself to feel unpleasant feelings?

~ How much courage does it take to put the past behind you and get on with life? Have you ever done that?

~ How much courage does it take to be appropriately angry at someone who has harmed you in some way—and to let that person know you are angry? Do you have an example?

3. Ask if anyone is in need of courage now or will be in the near future. If one or more students choose to share a situation, listen and reflect supportively (for example, "It makes sense that you are worried and frightened" or "We'll hope for the best for you") and encourage the other group members to show support with comments. Remind the group about confidentiality and trust.

4. For closure, commend the group for the courage they have demonstrated in the past—and in the present—and thank them for sharing their examples with the group. You might also say something like this: "You probably know each other better now than you did at the beginning of this session. That happens when people share some of themselves, as we did today. I appreciate your trust in the group. We will be trustworthy in response."

FOCUS Identity

A Question of Values

Background

We hear the word *values* a lot—values education, national values, moral values, family values, personal values. Generally, values are the unspoken rules supporting a culture or society. However, values can be somewhat controversial because people interpret and apply them differently. One person's personal values may be seen by others as old-fashioned. Another's may be condemned as weak and offensive. Some people do not identify with the values of other religious or cultural groups. Major wars have been fought over values (and perceptions of values).

Who passes along cultural values? The family? Schools? Media? Given the fact that so many families are breaking up and breaking down, can we still expect them to perform this vital function? Can unhealthy families pass on healthy values?

Depending on your group, you may address these and other important questions about values. Or you might simply let the group reflect on and compare their own values. Gifted teens usually appreciate being invited to explore this topic.

Objectives

- Gifted teens consider the values that are important to them and their families.
- They note the differences and similarities between their and their parents' values.
- They examine their values in light of their plans for the future.

Suggestions

1. Hand out "A Question of Values" (pages 82–83). Explain to students that the activity involves identifying values—beliefs that reflect what is important to them and what guides their actions. If they're unsure of their parents' values, they can focus only on their own.

   Encourage the group to share their responses through group polling (for example, "How many of you marked 'community service' as an important personal value for yourself? for your parents?"). When you have gone through the list, ask students to share which values they crossed out. Invite discussion of these, if appropriate. Then ask questions such as:

   ~ How do your own values differ from your family's values? How are they similar?

   ~ Have differences in values caused conflict within your family?

~ Might these differences cause family conflict when you are an adult?

~ Does there seem to be a generation gap in your family regarding values?

~ If your group is typical of your generation, can you identify any value trends?

~ How do your values fit in with your long-range career and lifestyle goals?

2. For closure, ask someone to summarize what has been discussed in the session. Ask the group how the discussion felt. Dispose of the sheets or file them.

A Question of Values

Name: _____

Under "Parent/Guardian #1," mark with an "X" the ten most significant values of one of your parents/guardians (such as mother, father, stepmother, stepfather, or other female or male family adult).

Under "Parent/Guardian #2," mark the ten most significant values of a second parent/guardian in your life, if applicable.

Under "Self," mark the ten values you feel will be most significant to you as an adult.

Underline any values you have changed your mind about over the past few years.

Cross out any values that neither you nor your parents/guardians consider important.

	PARENT/ GUARDIAN #1	PARENT/ GUARDIAN #2	SELF
marriage	_____	_____	_____
having children	_____	_____	_____
family closeness, loyalty	_____	_____	_____
financial security	_____	_____	_____
health and fitness	_____	_____	_____
respect for the environment	_____	_____	_____
tolerance for different lifestyles	_____	_____	_____
religious faith and/or spirituality	_____	_____	_____
involvement in an organized religion	_____	_____	_____
loyalty to friends	_____	_____	_____
freedom from physical pain	_____	_____	_____
hard work	_____	_____	_____
political activity	_____	_____	_____
high moral behavior	_____	_____	_____
community service	_____	_____	_____

(continued)

A Question of Values (continued)

	PARENT/ GUARDIAN #1	PARENT/ GUARDIAN #2	SELF
leisure activities	_____	_____	_____
material possessions	_____	_____	_____
beauty of home and surroundings	_____	_____	_____
change, variety, and adventure	_____	_____	_____
travel	_____	_____	_____
creative self-expression	_____	_____	_____
achievement	_____	_____	_____
being rational and reasonable	_____	_____	_____
introspection	_____	_____	_____
self-sacrifice	_____	_____	_____
self-discipline	_____	_____	_____
commitment to social justice	_____	_____	_____
a high level of activity	_____	_____	_____
inner peace	_____	_____	_____
love and affection	_____	_____	_____
a good reputation	_____	_____	_____
personal freedom, individuality	_____	_____	_____
education	_____	_____	_____
family honor, family name	_____	_____	_____
cultural or ethnic identity	_____	_____	_____

FOCUS Identity

Lonely at the Top

Background

Gifted teens may have few intellectual peers in their environment, especially in small schools and communities. Being at the top of a bell curve might be lonely, although being alone does not always mean being lonely.

Perhaps the differences in how people perceive being alone are related to predisposition toward introversion or extroversion. Research shows that gifted individuals are more likely to be introverts than the rest of the population; therefore, this topic might be particularly interesting to your group. Introverts tend to find sustenance from within and appreciate time alone to recoup their energy, while extroverts tend to prefer people contact for support and renewal. However, it is undoubtedly more complex than that. Some in both groups feel insecure and afraid when they are alone. Maybe those feelings urge them to be social.

You might want to prepare for this discussion by researching introversion and extroversion. However, as always, let the students teach you about their world, their perceptions about themselves in various environments, and their feelings, rather than focusing on informing them about the concepts here. Thoughtful discussion is sufficient.

Objectives

- Gifted teens learn more about themselves by considering how comfortable they are when alone.
- They practice articulating their feelings about being alone versus being lonely and discover similarities within the group.
- They explore possible benefits of being alone.
- They consider ways to alleviate loneliness.

Suggestions

1. Introduce the topic by asking the group to define *alone* and *lonely*. Then, generate discussion by asking questions like these:

   ~ How easy is it for you to be alone? (Perhaps on a scale of 1 to 10, with 10 being "very.") How often do you feel lonely?

~ Who are you when you are alone? (Encourage group members to describe themselves—for example, a worried, anxious eighth-grader who would rather be with friends; a calm, content girl who is social in school, but enjoys being alone and quiet at home.)

~ How comfortable are you when walking down the halls in school alone? shopping by yourself? attending an event alone? eating alone? (Perhaps on a scale of 1 to 10, with 10 being "very.")

~ How do you feel about being at home alone on a weekend night? On a weekday night? (If being alone is linked with feelings of insecurity and fear, what are the fears?)

~ How do you feel about silence? What do you do when you're home alone in a quiet house?

~ How would you describe your parents' attitudes about solitude and quietness? Your siblings'?

~ What are some potential benefits of being alone occasionally?

Important

As always, there are no right or wrong responses to any of these questions. Simply let group members respond, encourage them to be genuine, and actively listen to them.

2. Encourage the group to explore ways to alleviate loneliness, if it is a problem, and/or give themselves permission to be alone.

3. For closure, ask a volunteer to summarize the session. Thank them for contributing to the discussion and wish them well as they endeavor to become more and more comfortable with themselves, whether with people or alone.

FOCUS Stress

FOCUS Stress

General Background

Stress is part of life—growing up, growing old, facing change, being ill, working, and caring for family members, for example. Pessimism, multiple responsibilities, trying to respond to others' needs, and isolation all can heighten stress levels. Even at an early age, gifted children may be quite aware of the stress of living in an increasingly complex world. Their parents bring home the stress of the workplace or of job loss. In a mobile society, moves and dislocations cause stress. There may be illness, accidents, or other dramatic events that cause physical and emotional repercussions for months or years, and having a disability can contribute to stress. Being in a cultural minority can also be stressful in school and community. Highly able teens may even be stressed by having potential to do well in many possible life and career directions, a phenomenon called multipotentiality. They may have anxiety about needing to choose one career direction eventually, leaving the others behind—a type of loss. There are pressures at school, including social challenges. For gifted teens who are high achievers, high-intensity classes, competitive activities, and community service may collectively contribute to stress-filled lives.

In addition, significant adults can be quite invested in the performance of gifted teens and communicate great expectations about the present or the future. It can therefore be frightening not to have clear career direction, no idea what the future will bring (economically or in terms of specific careers), or a sense that it will be impossible to match their parents' successes. It is possible that teens' expectations for themselves might be higher than the expectations others have for them, or that the teens simply *imagine* lofty expectations from parents. In contrast, other gifted teens might hear or feel no expectations. Any of these scenarios can be stressful. Sometime during adolescence, teens may ask themselves, "What do I want and need? Whose life am I living? What are my own expectations?"

Probably unconsciously, parents model coping skills. From them, some gifted teens learn healthy and effective ways to cope with life's stressors. They talk about their stress, step back and gain perspective, and problem-solve. They release tension through exercise, socializing, relaxation, diversion, or a deliberate change of pace and pattern. Others learn and practice less healthy coping: using alcohol and other drugs, overeating or under-eating, harming themselves physically, workaholism, sleeping, watching too much television, tantrums, abusing others, blaming, scapegoating, punishing, or accepting a victim posture. Some experience anxiety or depression.

The sessions in this section give gifted teens a chance to dissect their stressors. Within a safe, supportive environment, they can discuss coping styles and perhaps begin to address stressful situations more effectively. Your primary responsibility is to listen carefully, hear what is said, communicate that you have heard, and commend the group for their openness and genuineness.

General Objectives

- Gifted teens learn about stress.
- They learn to talk about stress and stressors and to sort out stressful situations.
- They consider various ways to cope with stress.

FOCUS Stress

Sorting Out Stress

Objectives

- Gifted teens gain understanding of stress through discussing it.
- They consider how giftedness may affect *how* they experience stress.
- They hear about others' stressors and put their own into perspective.
- They consider that people respond differently to similar stressors.
- They distinguish short-term from long-term stressors.

Suggestions

1. Ask the group to define and explain *stress*. If necessary, provide a few synonyms: *anxiety, pressure, tension, worry, apprehension, burden*. You might say that businesses and educational institutions often offer stress-reduction programs to their employees because stress potentially affects productivity, attendance, health, and medical-insurance rates. Provide information from the following that was not brought up in the group discussion. You might have each group member read one of the ten sentences that follow.

   ~ Stress can be good and helpful. It can lead to high productivity, a good level of competitiveness and performances, and high alertness. Some people even seek out stress, loving the adrenaline rush and performing better when the pressure is on.

   ~ Excessive stress can cause problems if people do not cope with it effectively.

   ~ Physical responses to stress can include accelerated heartbeat (as the body prepares for fight or flight), cold extremities (as the capillaries constrict to make more blood available at the center of the body to protect the major organs), tight muscles, tense shoulders, a pressure headache, dry mouth, clammy hands, and/or stomach or intestinal distress, among several possibilities.

   ~ Prolonged periods of stress can lead to significant physical problems. Medical professionals see many illnesses that may have origins in stress. When they see patients with pain and distress but no apparent physical problems, they might conclude that the symptoms are related to stress.

   ~ Emotionally, stress can affect concentration, sleep, safety, and appetite. It can cause irritability, extreme reactions to normal problems, self-blame, tearfulness, anxiety, depression, panic attacks, and debilitating perfectionism. Sometimes it can lead to addictions.

~ Most people react to excessive stress in a particular way. They may develop colds, diarrhea, stomachaches, headaches, skin problems, or tense neck and shoulders, for instance.

~ Stress can result from having to do something new or do something differently from before—for example, move to a different home, change schools, adjust to a divorce or a new family, deal with a physical problem, adjust to a new baby in the home, use new and complex technology, start new kinds of school assignments, or adjust to a loss.

2. Invite the group to describe their physical and emotional responses to stress. Ask all of these at once: "What tells you that you are under stress? How do you behave? How do you feel? How does your body react?"

3. Instruct the group to take out a blank sheet of paper and write their name at the top. In a column along the left-hand side of the sheet, have them draw six boxes. Then, ask them to write the name or description of a specific stressor in each of the boxes. (Examples: "Third period math," "sister invades my privacy," "dogs barking at night.") Encourage them to consider a wide range of stressors—a messy bedroom, a big project, Mom in the hospital, an obnoxious peer or coworker, no privacy at home, family fights, college applications, Advanced Placement exams. You might also acknowledge that some of them might be working hard at a job; caring for siblings; cooking, cleaning, and doing laundry for the family; walking a long way to school; distracted by circumstances at home; contributing to family income; being a "parent" to someone in the family; meeting all personal expenses; or dealing with a chronic illness or a disability.

Next, ask the group to draw a single oval on the right-hand side of the sheet of paper, halfway down. The oval represents themselves. They can draw a face in it or make a cartoon out of it.

When they have finished, ask them to draw a lightning bolt connecting each box to the oval. The density and width of the bolt should indicate how much stress they associate with that stressor. (The more stress, the more jagged the line.) Then instruct them to write a large "X" through the boxes of short-term stressors (not likely to be a concern after a few weeks or months), an "O" around each box connected to a long-term stressor, and a large "+" in each box of stressors they could do something about if they chose to. Encourage the group to share their stressors by listing them in order of intensity, and then explaining which ones they could do something about, which are short-term, and which (if any) might be long-term.

Important Now and then, ask the group, "Does this sound familiar? Has anyone else experienced this?" Depending on the situation, respond with a statement such as "That does sound stressful" or "That's certainly a huge change for you." Be alert for group members who seem unable to discriminate among their stressors, drawing dense bolts to all of them. They may be feeling overwhelmed. However, rather than calling attention to them, make a general suggestion at the end like, "If you had a hard time sorting out your stressors, because they all feel huge right now, I encourage you to talk with a caring and trusted adult, including the school counselor (or with you, if you are a counselor), to sort through them and get a handle on them." If you sense that a student is in crisis, seek him or her out privately at your first opportunity and ask, "Should I be worried about you?" If the answer is yes, ask if the student would like you to call a parent and/or if he or she would be comfortable talking with the school counselor.

I do not encourage problem-solving here. Simply naming, describing, and sorting the stressors can be valuable. Moving into a "fix-it" mode may not be beneficial or equitable, given that there are several group members. Stressed members may also not want to be advised or fixed.

4. Ask scaling questions (1 to 10, with 10 being "a high level") like the following to poll the group:

   ~ How much stress do you feel socially?
   ~ How much pressure do you feel to do well in school or in athletics or in music? How much from others? How much from yourself?
   ~ How much pressure do you feel to please others?

5. Consider inviting an expert to speak with your group for this or a follow-up session. Someone from a stress clinic or an expert on biofeedback, meditation/relaxation, or yoga might be available and willing.

6. With the following, explore giftedness as related to stress:

   ~ Are gifted teens more, or less, stressed than others their age?
   ~ What do you believe are the biggest stressors for gifted kids in your school?
   ~ What do you wish teachers understood about gifted kids, related to this topic?

7. Some gifted teens might combat stress effectively by focusing on the present, particularly those who seem anxious about what comes *next* in their education, even though selecting classes and setting goals demand attention. If the group mentions stress related to others' expectations, turn the discussion to this common concern and ask them to help you understand what these expectations feel like.

8. Write questions on a large "stress ball," asking about various stressors and coping strategies. The group plays catch, answering the question that their right thumb is nearest to when they catch the ball. This activity is a nonthreatening approach to the subject, and it is also a physical activity. You might provide healthy snacks, to emphasize good nutrition, and bring jump ropes, hula hoops, and other equipment to encourage further physical movement.

9. For closure, invite volunteers to summarize what they have learned, felt, or thought about during this session. You might add, "We can't eliminate all stressors from our lives, but we can learn how to cope with them by altering how we respond to them. We can also make sure we take care of our health, so that during stressful times we are less likely to feel overwhelmed." Dispose of the sheets or file them.

FOCUS Stress

Coping with Stress

Background

Gifted teens often prefer to sort out complex situations cognitively. This session offers an opportunity to do that. When perfectionism, extreme compliance, and sensitivity are factors, being able to talk with trusted peers may help to lessen stress. In our fragmented, conflict-ridden world, it is important for individuals to stop frenetic behavior, tune in to the self, plant their feet solidly on the ground, relax, and affirm who they are.

Objectives

- Gifted teens recognize that responses to stress and coping strategies are learned.
- They consider learning new responses to stress and unlearning responses that have become bad habits.
- They consider that they often take their bodies for granted, living too much in their heads.
- They learn that their minds can benefit from physical calm.

Suggestions

1. Use the following thoughts to introduce the topic and review some of what might have been discussed in the preceding session, if the topic was stress. Perhaps print them for the students to read in turn.

   ~ We can't avoid all stress, but we can care for ourselves in the midst of stressful situations.
   ~ Learning to control our reactions to stress is the key to coping well. Gifted teens can use their good minds to accomplish this.
   ~ We can pause before reacting to stressful situations and think about what we might do and probable consequences.
   ~ We can respond creatively and see stressful situations as a chance to become smarter and to figure out ways to stay more in control in the midst of them.
   ~ We can remember that fears about catastrophes are usually unfounded.
   ~ We can talk to our family, friends, teachers, counselors, coaches, or coworkers about stress. A good listener can help us sort out our stress by just letting us talk. We can even tell our listeners that we do not want advice.
   ~ We can learn to relax, take time to rest, exercise, eat healthfully, avoid caffeinated drinks, and not use eating, drinking, stimulants, or sleep aids as a coping strategy. When we feel good physically, we can cope with stress better.

2. Introduce the idea that, when young, we learn from adults around us how to cope with stress. Ask the group to list on paper important adults in their lives and then briefly describe how each deals with stressful situations. Explain that these should be not only adults they like and respect, but *any* adult who plays a significant role in their lives. Encourage the group to share their lists and descriptions.

3. Invite comparisons between their coping styles and those of the adults mentioned:

    ~ How does your coping style compare to the style of the adults?
    ~ How well do your coping strategies work for you? (The key question is whether they are effective.) If they're not effective, what other strategies could you try (for various situations)?
    ~ Has your way of reacting to stress ever made things worse?

4. Turn the focus to some specifics of how group members respond to stress.

    ~ How do you express anger or frustration or other strong emotions? How good are you at "talking out" anger or frustration or sadness?
    ~ If group members reveal that they believe they must always stay in control, be rational, and stay even-tempered, ask them how that feels when they are stressed.
    ~ How many of you have someone to talk with about stress? Would you be willing to tell us who that is? (Perhaps tally the number of friends, parents, siblings, or other confidants mentioned.) How often do you do that? What is that like?
    ~ If your way of coping isn't working well, what different ways could you try? What might happen if you responded to stress in that new way? (If one or more individuals indicated earlier that they typically talk about their stress with others, invite them to describe what the benefits are. What is the most helpful thing their listeners do? You might remark that people who are upset usually do not want to be "fixed." Just listening can help them.)

5. Invite the group to share successful coping strategies. Ask, "When you find yourself in a stressful situation, how do you help yourself to feel okay? What do you do to stay clear-headed? How long do you usually feel stressed?"

6. Ask, "Do you think that sometimes you take your body for granted?" If some or all group members say yes, ask, "How much do you pay attention to fitness? nutrition? getting enough rest? eating regular meals? your posture?" They might refer to paying attention during illnesses, recovery after an accident, or excessive fatigue. Explain that proper physical self-care is crucial to coping with stress.

Lead the group in a relaxation exercise. Tell them you are going to relax together as a group. Students should be sitting squarely on comfortable chairs, feet on the floor, since it is best if they do not have to move once the exercise begins. "Unsolid" postures work less well. When everyone seems ready, read the following very slowly in a well-modulated voice:

Close your eyes and just relax. We will open our eyes together when we are finished. Keep them closed until I direct you to open them. Now move your lower back so that it touches the back of your chair squarely.... Wiggle your toes and then set your feet solidly on the floor.... Touch your thumbs to your fingertips several times and feel those extremities.... Now sit very quietly and think about your body...your physical space.... Mentally trace the outline of your body.... Relax and let your body occupy your space comfortably.... Mentally, without moving, check to see if you are relaxed.... Concentrate on your thighs...your arms...your hands...your shoulders...your face...your eyes...your jaw...your mouth.... Are they relaxed?... Let them be slack.... Let all of your muscles be loose.... Now I'm going to be silent for one whole minute while you tune in to your breathing. Don't be in a rush. Breathe in and out. If you think about other things, it's okay. If your mind wanders, gently bring it back. Then tune in to your relaxed body, your breathing.... Recheck one part of your body at a time...your thighs...your arms...your hands...your jaw...your eyes.... If you realize you're thinking about other things, gently come back.... Check your body again.... Tune in to it.... Now I'll be silent....

Wait about a minute before continuing:

How does your body feel?... Focus on the center of your body, at the center of yourself.... How have you been doing lately?... Are you taking care of yourself?... Your feet are on the ground.... You are unique and strong.... You're okay.... Now sit quietly for one more minute with your eyes still closed. Check out your body. It might be quite relaxed. Your breathing may be very quiet. I will tell you when it's time to finish.

Wait about a minute before continuing:

Now slowly open your eyes.... Take a deep breath without moving your body.... Your fingertips may tingle a bit.... How do you feel?... You can slowly begin to move now.

Encourage the group to talk about the relaxation experience. Were they comfortable? Did they relax? Were they distracted? How do they feel?

Tell them that such an exercise, even for five or ten minutes, can help them before a performance, before a test, if they are too tired to read an assignment, and even to start their day if they have not slept well. They may feel less groggy afterward than if they took a nap. Some people relax in such a way daily, more than once.

7. For closure, thank the students for their cooperation, if appropriate. Wish them a good day and a good week—and good coping. They might find it interesting to observe their own and others' responses to stress. Encourage them to take care of themselves.

FOCUS Stress

Sensitivity and Safe Havens

Background

Scholars have written about sensitivity as related to giftedness, some referring to it as "ultrasensitivity" and others as "hypersensitivity." There can be intense intra- and interpersonal awareness, as well as great awareness of emotion, body, and environment, including smells, tastes, sounds, textures, colors, and patterns. Discussion can normalize sensitivities that are seen as "weird" or "crazy."

My own research has explored the phenomenon of sensitivity as related to developmental transitions, trauma, and other difficult situations. My findings in one study of bullying among gifted youth included intense memories of single instances of bullying. Some recalled the horror of long stretches of harassment, trying to avoid mistakes in order not to be vulnerable, trying to understand why anyone would hurt another person, despairing silently, and assuming responsibility for "fixing" the situation alone. In other studies, gifted teens responded sensitively to parental criticism, family conflict, wondering about sexual orientation, and physical and sexual abuse. Sensitivity was reflected in the degree of cognitive effort to make sense of intense, unsettling feelings and others' actions. In particular, these teens worked hard to keep afloat during adolescence, when complex situations were overlaid with normal developmental hurdles.

Sensitivity can exacerbate the challenges of developmental transitions—such as puberty, sexual awareness, establishing a mature relationship, and leaving for college—and of family transitions—such as changes in family structure, death and other losses, serious accidents or illness, parental unemployment, or relocation. Sensitivity can also be a factor, even at a young age, in rebellion (or feeling no permission to challenge authority), response to others' expectations, concerns for social justice, anxiety about finding meaning in life, and uncertainty regarding whether a higher power exists. All children and teens are likely sensitive to tension in the home, but gifted teens seem to have hyperalert antennae to family dynamics. Their rapid processing of information probably means that they must deal with complex feelings, whether or not they are overtly displayed.

Sensitive perfectionists might wilt quickly in the face of criticism. Altruistic gifted kids, sensitive to fairness, may lie awake at night, disturbed by the news of wars, natural disasters, and student misbehavior at school. Romantic interest might be particularly intense in gifted teens, with response to rejection just as intense. When there is a tragedy at school, their concern might linger for weeks or months, perhaps because they perceive that everyone just wants to move ahead and forget.

Ideally, sensitive gifted teens have safe havens—places where they feel accepted unconditionally; are in control, comfortable, and peaceful; and can "take a load off." If there are group members who do not have such a place, perhaps they can feel appreciated unconditionally in your group.

Objectives

- Gifted teens learn that giftedness has been associated with sensitivity.
- They consider the extent to which they respond sensitively to experiences and situations.
- They consider sensitivity as an asset and as a burden.
- They ponder whether and where they have safe havens.

Suggestions

1. Introduce this session by stating that scholars who study gifted people have concluded that many have particular sensitivity to the environment, to people, to situations. Ask, "Do you think that view is accurate? Do gifted teens have particularly intense and sensitive awareness and reactions?" Group members may agree (and give personal examples) and disagree (arguing that everyone is the same). Receive whatever group members say without judgment or argument.

2. Invite students to fill out the "Sensitivity" sheet (page 98). Go around the group, one item at a time, asking for their number responses. Do a tally as they report, and when they finish, ask which sensitivities characterize their group. Then ask for the examples they listed.

3. Ask the group how sensitivity can be an asset—and then how it may be a burden.

4. Have the group think of a place where they feel peaceful, comfortable, and good— or of a person who helps them relax. Encourage them to share details and feelings so that the others can understand the importance of the place or person. Invite them to draw their safe haven for a few minutes, if they prefer, continuing to add to the picture during the subsequent discussion.

   If some can think of no such place or person, ask them to describe an ideal, supercomfortable situation. Then ask, "How have you coped with not having such a place or person in your life?" If someone describes a nonsupportive home environment, listen with receptive body language and reflect (for example, "That's certainly a tough situation. I admire your strength in dealing with it as well as you have"). Your responsibility is not to offer advice for improving the situation, but to acknowledge the teen's challenges genuinely and affirm strengths. That can be powerful and rare for someone.

5. Ask the group to list (or simply think of) and share situations where they feel dumb or inept. It may be comforting to hear that everyone feels like that in some situations. Students may learn that some who appear confident are not always at ease.

Then ask where they feel smart and confident. It is assumed that even those who do not do well academically feel smart in some situations (including at school). If some do not feel smart at school, then perhaps they do with friends, at home, or when involved with interests. If some cannot think of anything, ask what they do well (for example, baby-sitting, fishing, skateboarding, snowboarding, cooking, mechanics, singing, playing music, blogging, card games).

6. For closure, ask for a volunteer to summarize the discussion. Ask the group what they felt during the discussion about sensitivity and safe havens. Dispose of the sheets or file them.

Sensitivity

Name: _____

Rate the following, on a scale of 1 to 10, with 10 being "very intense and extreme."

My level of sensitivity/reactivity

_____ during transitions between stages of normal development (for example, going to kindergarten, moving up to middle school or high school, going through puberty, staying away from home for the first time, having a crush on someone)

_____ when I see peers behaving badly to others

_____ to difficult and upsetting family situations

_____ to family events (such as illness, death, marriage, births, other major changes)

_____ when tragedies are reported in the news

_____ when hearing about wars

_____ when teachers' actions seem wrong

_____ to the plight of animals

_____ to the plight of people who are poor and without advantages

_____ to noise

_____ to smells

_____ to textures (cloth, foods, other materials)

_____ to tastes

_____ to my environment (inside and outside of buildings)

_____ when around people

_____ to silence/solitude

I have seen examples of high sensitivity in other gifted kids, as listed below (without names):

_____

_____

Examples of times when I have responded very sensitively to situations:

_____

_____

FOCUS Stress

Procrastination

Background

Procrastination! Parents and teachers of gifted teens, and the teens themselves, may recognize it as a significant problem—perhaps related to cleaning their rooms, doing homework, calling Grandma, sending a thank-you note, completing college applications, applying for a job, turning in next year's registration form, taking out the garbage. Many highly capable students know they can delay and delay and then finish a project or paper at the eleventh hour. Those who do not function in a do-or-die mode also procrastinate, but they may or may not deliver in the end. Students may have difficult circumstances, which drain energy and affect concentration, but they also might simply procrastinate—like everyone else.

Procrastination may make little difference most of the time, but it has potential to cause stress during a final, intense effort—or in not getting something done. It can also generate concern and frustration in those who worry about, or are affected by, the behavior of, the procrastinator. It should be noted, however, that everyone has a somewhat unique style of getting things done, and some procrastinators are actually quite productive. While procrastinating about something large, for example, they may be getting smaller things done—happily distracted, yet moving ahead.

Objectives

• Gifted teens look objectively at procrastination and how it affects them personally.
• They consider what might contribute to procrastination and ways to combat it.

Suggestions

1. Ask the group to define *procrastination*. Then ask, "Are there any procrastinators in this group?" Follow that with "What kinds of things do you procrastinate about?" Then ask, "How much of a problem is procrastination for you (on a scale of 1 to 10)? For other people in your life? What kinds of problems do you associate with it? How much should parents and teachers be concerned about it?" (You might encourage creative drawing to measure procrastination. One of my counseling students drew a "procrastimeter" for a group, inviting them to draw a needle to their level of procrastination. Underneath the meter, they listed what they procrastinated about.)

2. To encourage further exploration of the topic, ask questions like the following:

~ Some theorists claim that behavior is purposeful. What payoff does procrastination have?
~ What do you do in other areas of your life while procrastinating (if anything)?
~ How efficient are you when you do things at the last minute, if you do that?
~ What feelings do you have when procrastinating?
~ On a scale of 1 to 10, how well can you concentrate on what you need to do when needed?
~ Have you changed, over time, in how much you procrastinate?

3. With polling questions, help the group to identify other areas of procrastination.

~ How many of you procrastinate only in schoolwork? Only with household chores? Only with tasks that involve planning for the future, such as college applications or course choices? Only when you need to ask for something or talk with someone?
~ How many of you procrastinate in almost every area of your life?
~ How many of you procrastinate, but with no bad effects from it for you or others?

4. Use questions like the following to help the group explore possible connections between procrastination and other issues. It is important here to recognize that levels of procrastination vary considerably, from mild to severe, from harmless to debilitating. These questions should be skipped if procrastination is not a significant problem for your group.

~ On a scale of 1 to 10, with 10 being "a lot," how much do other people remind you about the things you have to do? How does this affect your relationship with those people?
~ What do you think about the paradoxical idea that procrastinators have a certain power over others, or over situations?
~ Is procrastination connected to stress? Do non-procrastinators have more stress than procrastinators—or less? (No "correct" answer here.)

5. Ask procrastinators to consider what might happen if they suddenly stopped procrastinating and did everything early—or at least without a last-minute rush. Invite them to explore this idea by asking questions like the following.

~ Who would be affected?
~ How would your life change?
~ What would you lose?
~ What would you gain?
~ How would you feel?
~ Who would notice first?

6. For closure, ask the group to comment on what they heard and felt during this session.

FOCUS Stress

Substance Abuse

Background

Teens probably learn something about substance abuse in health classes and/or school assemblies—with the rest learned from peers, experiences, and maybe parents. This session offers gifted teens an opportunity to discuss this important subject in a small group of intellectual peers led by a nonjudgmental adult.

Important

Prior to this session, familiarize yourself with the topic through research and consultation (for example, talking with local police about inhalant, methamphetamine, or prescription drug use among youth and local trends regarding drug use; talking with the school counselor about school issues related to substance use or about children of substance abusers). Contact organizations that deal regularly with those issues, and check out the resource section (page 271). They likely have helpful materials for teens, including for those whose families are affected by substances.

Consider inviting a counselor or administrator from a local substance-abuse treatment facility to visit your group. Suggest that he or she explain what treatment involves (attending to family issues and personal problems), how an evaluator assesses for addiction, what is currently understood about addictions and neurological effects, how addiction can affect teens psychologically. Other related topics might be current trends regarding substance use (such as newly popular substances). Do not assume that students are well informed on this topic.

If you do not invite a guest, you will need a reasonably good understanding of various substances and their effects in order to avoid providing erroneous information. However, let the group teach you first. They will likely engage in discussion more readily if you avoid teaching or preaching. Even if you hear obvious misinformation, delay correcting it until students ask for information. Late in the discussion, you can gently ask if they'd be interested in hearing or reading pertinent information. Add that you realize that it's not easy for them to get accurate information about substances.

As with all topics in this book, the goals are connection, communication skills, confidence, and self-awareness. The value lies in the discussion. You can justifiably avoid being informational.

If your group has been created to deal specifically with substance-abuse problems (certainly a possibility for gifted teens), most or all of the sessions in this book are appropriate, since the challenges of adolescent development are often inextricably entwined with substance use, and developmental support and discussion may actually be the key to reduction of substance use. Don't assume that having a group of users/abusers means you must talk about substances much or at all.

Objectives

- Gifted teens learn how some of their peers feel about substance use and abuse.
- They articulate their feelings about substance use and abuse in their age group.

Suggestions

1. Begin by taking a one-down (in contrast to an expert-teacher one-up) posture and asking the group to teach you about substance use and abuse in their age group—available substances, numbers of peers and substances involved, parties, behavior (especially dangerous behavior), frequency of use, types or groups involved, and parental attitudes related to alcohol and other drug use. What do they know about particular substances currently popular among teens? Expect some bravado and claims of (and actual) expertise during this part of the discussion, but also expect that some group members may have very little knowledge in these areas. Remember that evaluative comments move you out of a one-down position.

Important

Remind the group of the need for confidentiality; some individuals may share information that could be damaging if shared outside of the group. Encourage them, at the outset, not to name names in the discussion or to describe anything that is planned, but rather to talk in general terms about substance use. Remind them that safety for sharing now and in the future depends on their own trust-worthiness outside of the group. If you are a counselor in a school, follow your codes of ethics, particularly as they relate to past actions. If you're not a counselor, check with the counselor for guidance about what does and does not need to be reported, and tell students what you are required to report. If you report something that does not fit with your initial informed-consent information, the group will lose trust in you and in group work, perhaps irrevocably.

2. Ask some process questions: "How does it feel to talk about this serious topic? How do you feel about what you have just shared or heard?" Then ask these questions:

~ On a scale of 1 to 10, with 10 being "a lot," how much pressure to use alcohol/other drugs is there in your social group?

~ If there is pressure, and you are not using, how are you able to do that?

~ (Raised hands suffice for these questions.) Without naming names, do you know peers whose substance abuse is interfering with schoolwork and life? Do you know anyone who left college because substance use interfered with academics? Do you know of anyone who has died, or almost died, from drug or alcohol abuse? Do you know anyone who has been in treatment for substance abuse?

~ Do all teens have the potential to become addicted to alcohol and other drugs?

~ What motivates someone to use alcohol or other drugs? (Be aware that people often "self-medicate" with drugs to deal with problems such as depression, even though some drugs, like alcohol, act as a depressant. Rebellion and the pressure to fit in will likely be mentioned, but you might suggest that reasons for drug use are probably complex—for example, insecurities, feeling overwhelmed, having substances available, adult models.

3. Instruct the group to consider how their families view the use of alcohol and other drugs. Remind them of confidentiality guidelines and permission to pass. Ask questions like these:

~ How does your family feel about alcohol use? Other drug use? (If parent and teen attitudes differ, ask, "How do you feel about that?") How much do you talk about this as a family? (On a scale of 1 to 10.)

~ What do you know about alcoholism? addiction?

~ When would you know that you had an addiction? (Evaluators usually look, for example, for preoccupation with finding and funding the substance and arranging for use; no memory of use; using more than planned; using alone; concerns expressed by family or friends; and effects on school, relationships, well-being, work.)

~ Do you make a distinction between alcohol and other drugs? Should society?

~ What are your personal rules regarding alcohol and other drugs?

~ What other kinds of addictions are there? (Examples: Eating, not eating, exercising, smoking, chewing tobacco, using inhalants, drinking caffeinated coffee or soft drinks.) How vulnerable to becoming addicted do you think you might be? (On a scale of 1 to 10.)

4. For closure, ask a volunteer to summarize the discussion, with special emphasis on the information shared in #1. Express your hope that group members will make wise choices with regard to substance use.

FOCUS Stress

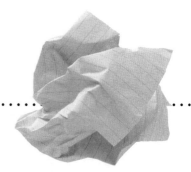

Cyber-Networking

Background

The purpose of social-networking sites on the Internet is to help people meet and communicate. That can be a boon for those who have difficulty socially, are isolated geographically, or simply enjoy communicating electronically. However, these sites can also contribute to high stress and even physical and psychological harm. No one can know for sure who their contacts are. Thus, the safety of people who cyber-network—particularly children and teens—is a concern. Parents, teachers, and government agencies are all aware of this safety issue, but it's not going to be fixed overnight. Currently steps are being taken to protect children and adolescents, such as MySpace.com and Facebook.com restricting usage.

However, bad things can and do happen, as news accounts attest. Users may be enticed to post more and more personal information, but they have little sense of how public that information is. The space feels safe and protected, but it is not. Users not careful about the image they portray, in print and through posted photos, are open to being stalked, bullied, harassed, seduced, and harmed physically. Predators know that sites designed for young people offer almost unlimited access. Gifted teens are just as vulnerable as anyone else, possibly more so. Having their own computers, writing easily and quickly, wanting to find a "mind mate," being fascinated with risk-taking in an otherwise contained life, being unquestioningly trusted by parents, or being naive might all contribute to vulnerability.

In chat rooms, teens and others meet and communicate in real time. But this communication can be with people who are not who they claim to be—even in chat rooms designed to draw only people with a certain hobby or interest, for instance. The communication is not one-on-one. Groups that evolve through chat-room contact may include voyeurs, some of them dangerous.

Chat-room users can exchange personal contact information, and at this point one-on-one instant messaging can occur or individuals may decide to meet, post photos, or talk on the phone. Teens, in general, are avid participants in all of these real-time activities. They are also frequent users of text messaging on cell phones, which, in contrast, is not in real time, and the messages are written. There is relatively less danger. However, safety in both of these forms of communication can be compromised through sharing personal information.

Students who use message boards—sites where people can post and view messages—may quickly or eventually feel that other users know them, and therefore share personal details, fight, get feelings hurt, form cliques, and even "flame" each other with cruel name-calling. Even though these are sites for people with common interests, participants may not be who they say they are. At best, perhaps, their lies may generate a great deal of attention for them when they post sad and dramatic stories. At worst, they may be ill-intentioned.

Blogs are public journals. Unfortunately, depending on content, predators and stalkers can learn a teen's daily routine and schedule. Friends' and relatives' names that are mentioned help to create complex understanding of a target. If photos have been posted, someone is easy to pick out of a crowd exiting school, for example. In addition, photos can be distributed to others. There is no way to control who sees them or reads the blog. If school peers are vindictive (and certainly both middle school and high school students can be), they can say anything about a peer on their blog, bullying viciously.

There is potential for positive connections through cyber-venues, of course. However, this discussion can raise group members' awareness of their vulnerability. Perhaps they have not considered how public their posted information is—and what the dangers are. Like many high-risk behaviors, cyber-networking may seem like something they can handle—and that others, not themselves, are at risk. This may especially be true for gifted teens, whose intellectual nimbleness usually allows them considerable social and technological control. Risk might even be an enticement. The realities that even email is not secure, that cyberfriends might replace "real" friends, and that huge amounts of time can be absorbed with cyber-networking are probably also worth discussing.

Important
....

Internet pornography, though not directly related to the cyber-networking just described, also deserves mention here. In the past, pornography was not so easy to obtain. Now it is accessible, affordable, anonymous, and more acceptable. It is important to note that teens, both males and females, can become addicted to Internet pornography—preoccupied, compulsive, despairing, shame-filled. Pornography can have drug-like effects; euphoric recall can occur even at school, interfering with concentration. As with any addiction, a great amount of time is spent thinking about and satisfying the addiction, taking time away from relationships and positive activities. The addicted have a pathological relationship with pornography. Porn addiction can also affect sexual development by distorting sex. Young and older teens addicted to pornography learn to "do sex" through porn—which often focuses on domination and depersonalizes men, women, and children. Problems associated with easy access to pornography will likely receive increasing attention in the media.

Objectives
....

- Group members learn about the benefits and risks of cyber-networking.
- They reflect on their own attitudes and behaviors related to using the Internet.

Suggestions

1. Ask group members what communication technology they are familiar with and use. Have them list on paper the various ways they communicate with others electronically. Encourage them to share what they wrote; they may also tell how much they use each form of communication and the various purposes of their use. Be prepared for the reality that some students may be frequent users of such technology and some will not be. Be sensitive to socioeconomic and other differences, and avoid mentioning your own expertise and use, since the students are the focus. In addition, allying too strongly with those who can afford sophisticated equipment, for example, might contribute to some members' feeling isolated and not valued by you.

2. Ask the students to teach you what they know about both the benefits and risks of cyber-networking on the Internet. Be nonjudgmental and receptive, taking a one-down posture (in contrast to an expert-teacher one-up) and letting them teach you about their world. You may find out that they are quite aware of the risks. You might ask them to share experiences that relate to being in danger as a result of Internet or other electronic communication. Respect their hesitation to share, if you see any. Remember that evaluative comments move you into a judgmental, one-up position.

3. At this point, if they have not mentioned some of the elements in the background information, including the section on Internet pornography, share some of those realities. You might even read some of the paragraphs to them. Ask the group for their reactions.

4. For closure, thank group members for their serious treatment of the topic, if appropriate, and ask for one or two summary statements. To guide them, ask what they thought about or felt during the discussion. Express a hope that they will be vigilant, careful, and wise when involved with cyber-networking. Dispose of the sheets they wrote on or add them to the group folders.

FOCUS Relationships

FOCUS Relationships

General Background

Relationships can affect whether and to what extent someone feels satisfaction, self-worth, and balance in life. For some or most gifted teens, positive and satisfying relationships seem to come easily. For others, relationships are hard both to establish and to sustain. Teens learn about themselves through relationships, including with adults. Some teens hear encouraging and supportive messages and may feel secure. Others hear mostly critical, shaming, or intimidating comments and, as a result, may have trouble relating to people in authority. If the adults in their world have not been reliable, teens may believe that if they lean on someone, they will find no support. In some cases, their families might look to them for critical support because of their capabilities, perhaps to an inappropriate degree. Gifted teens may be taking care of others' needs, but may not know how to get their own needs met.

A discussion group gives gifted teens an opportunity to discover what they have in common with others who have high ability. Their lives are complex at this age, but there can be comfort in knowing that others are experiencing social struggles, for instance. Being supported—in the context of a unique group relationship—can help some to establish important interpersonal connections. In this section students consider how they relate to others, including peers and significant adults, and how these relationships affect their behavior, choices, decision-making, and view of themselves. Having a safe place to talk about relationships can nurture confidence, patience, the ability to support and affirm others, and optimism.

General Objectives

- Gifted teens learn to articulate feelings about their relationships.
- They discover common relationship concerns.
- They help each other with problem-solving about relationships.
- They ponder how relationships contribute to attitudes, behaviors, goals, and sense of self.
- They learn about how others see them.
- They identify personal needs and consider ways to meet them.

FOCUS Relationships

Friends

Experiences with friendship affect how comfortable teens feel in social situations. Teens develop social skills through friendships—appropriate personal communication, conflict management, mutual support and assistance, and give-and-take about wishes and needs. Just as the home environment and family interaction help children learn how to empathize and be comfortable with others, so do experiences in friendship.

Friendships among young children are often formed because of proximity. A few years later, common interests play a part. Personality, abilities, or shared backgrounds might be the key at a later age. Perhaps all through life, one person has only one close friend at a time, while another person always has many, with varying degrees of closeness. Some gifted teens are at ease socially, with impressive interpersonal intelligence, close friends, and many acquaintances. However, in some settings, gifted students may have difficulty finding "mind mates"—not only for interests, but also for level of mental processing. Some gifted teens have close friends who are older or younger than they are, but with common interests and similar abilities.

Friendships also change—or end—as interests develop and new school activities are pursued, or simply because the social world at some grade levels is precarious and volatile. Some gifted teens have difficulty making and/or keeping friends. Others have experienced pain, betrayal, and loss in friendships. On the other hand, some seem to be content without much social interaction.

Here, students teach each other about friendship and about themselves as they share experiences. Friendships might grow out of such discussion. In any case, gifted students who have felt alienated or invisible have an opportunity to feel known in a positive way. Skills gained in articulating feelings and thoughts will be helpful in future relationships.

Objectives

- Gifted teens examine feelings and share concerns about friendship.
- They share experiences and articulate what they have learned through friendships.
- They gain confidence that they are worthy of friendship.

Suggestions

1. Ask the students to define *friendship*. Encourage several to contribute. Be alert to the words they use, and follow up with questions about those descriptors.

2. Hand out "Friendships" (pages 111–112) and ask the group to respond to the questions in writing. Use the responses to generate discussion. Or use the questionnaire as an oral exercise, moving down the list of questions or asking the students which questions they would like to discuss. Remind them that they can pass on any questions. Assess trust level carefully as you choose questions. If you do not insist on a response from everyone, you may be able to use all of the questions.

   Be aware that some students may not have friends to describe. Ask those in the group who make friends easily to describe what they like and look for in a friend. Even if they have never considered that there are friendship skills, ask some to share how they would teach others to make friends, using their responses for question #14 from the "Friendships" handout.

3. Ask the group, "What are some common struggles in friendships at your age?" (Perhaps changes because of moving, new activities, being chosen or not chosen for participation, personality differences, moodiness, or dating outside of a friendship group.) Then ask, "Have you ever 'dumbed yourself down' in order to fit in socially?" (If yes) "How much, or what, did you change?"

4. Focus on what each person in the group can offer to a friendship. All can offer statements about themselves or comment about the assets of others in the group.

5. Discuss how people differ in their need for friends (number of friends or comfort in being alone, for example). Affirm those in the group who are not as social as others—perhaps because they are more self-sufficient, because they feel exhausted by social contact, because they prefer to be close to only one person or a few, or because they have had negative experiences with friendships, for instance.

6. Focus on sharing confidences by asking questions like these:

   ~ If someone chooses you to confide in, how should you view this? (You might suggest that it is a compliment, and that it signifies trust.)
   ~ If you choose a particular person to confide in, how should the person view that?
   ~ What do you expect from people you confide in?

7. For closure, invite a few students to share how they felt during the discussion—at ease, thoughtful, uncomfortable, inspired, sad, relaxed, grateful? Be aware of, and validate, group members who did not find the discussion to be uplifting, but do not press anyone to comment. If nothing seems to need discussion, and time remains, ask the students what experiences with friendship were common in the group. Encourage them to be friendly and to at least say "Hi" when they see each other. Commend them for what they did well. Dispose of the sheets or file them.

Friendships

Name: _____

1. How have your friendships changed over the past year or two?

   _____

   _____

2. What do you appreciate in your best friend, if you have one? _____

   _____

   _____

3. What do your friends appreciate in you? _____

   _____

   _____

4. How easy is it for you to make friends? _____ (on a scale of 1 to 10, with 10 being "very easy") If difficult, what seems to make it difficult? _____

   _____

   _____

5. How easy is it for you to keep friendships going? _____ (on a scale of 1 to 10, with 10 being "very easy") If difficult, what seems to cause problems? _____

   _____

   _____

6. Do you have close friends of different ages? Yes ❑   No ❑ What ages? _____

7. What are some things you and your friends do and don't have in common?

   _____

   _____

(continued)

Friendships (continued)

8. What makes friendships different at your age than when you were a few years younger?

_____

_____

9. Do you have some friends your parents don't approve of? Yes ❑ No ❑

10. What have you learned through friendships? _____

_____

_____

11. Have you ever lost a friend because one of you moved away? Yes ❑ No ❑

    If yes, how difficult was it to adjust to that loss? _____ (on a scale of 1 to 10, with 10 being "very difficult")

12. Have you ever felt rejected by a friend? Yes ❑ No ❑

    If yes, how did you cope with the rejection? _____

    Do you still think about it? Yes ❑ No ❑

13. How quickly do you develop close friendships? _____ (on a scale of 1 to 10, with 10 being "very quickly")

14. What advice would you give to someone who has difficulty making friends?

_____

_____

FOCUS Relationships

Being Social

Background

It is easy to forget that teens with high ability deal with normal developmental issues. They explore the self, differentiate themselves from their families, become increasingly aware of their sexuality, and yearn for someone special to love and to love them. Although all teens face the same developmental tasks, gifted teens' *experience* of development might be different. Most manage developmental challenges well; some do not. Sometimes their level of intellect interferes with their social lives. Their interests, thinking style, and personal characteristics may set them apart. Skills such as giving and receiving compliments and initiating and sustaining conversations with peers may need to be developed.

It is important to keep in mind that many gifted teens have few problems socially. However, especially during early adolescence, gifted girls may feel the need to hide their intelligence to be socially accepted; gifted boys might have similar concerns. Both genders may feel uneasy in mainstream socializing and may have difficulty performing the behaviors and participating in the rituals that are part of typical social interaction during adolescence and beyond. Like other teens, gifted students may experience intense infatuation, yet shyness, self-criticism, or even rapid information-processing might hinder their ability to talk to or otherwise pursue someone they are attracted to. Highly verbal teens might maintain control and camouflage insecurity and vulnerability with words, but their verbal skills might actually work against them socially.

In general, some with high intellect may be so fearful of sounding stupid that they have trouble initiating or sustaining conversations. Giving and receiving compliments, an important social skill, may also not be easy for those who are highly competitive and critical of others. They may fear appearing arrogant or self-absorbed if they accept compliments too readily. Or they may feel unworthy of compliments they receive, regardless of their capabilities. Gifted teens may worry also about what to do or say when something proper is in order, as they may not have various social skills taught or modeled at home.

You can take this opportunity to reassure students who feel out of place socially that the school social climate changes as they grow older. Popularity becomes less important; more friendships become based on shared interests; and intellect is increasingly valued and supported. Girls learn to appreciate (and become interested in) boys they used to ignore, and vice versa. Teens who become socially active later than average may also have the advantage of possessing a better understanding of who they are as individuals *before* they enter into intimate relationships.

This session offers gifted teens a chance to talk openly about what they feel inept at and to practice some skills. Whether group members are academic, talent, or athletic superstars—or the most uninvolved or awkward teens in school—they will appreciate the non-superficial attention to their social comfort and a chance to discuss, with others who can understand, concerns about their emerging sexuality and general socializing.

Objectives

- Gifted teens learn that their social and emotional concerns resonate with others.
- They learn and practice important social skills.
- They feel affirmed as interesting.
- They practice giving and receiving compliments.

Suggestions

1. Hand out "Being Social" (page 117) and ask the group to write brief, anonymous responses. Or use the activity sheet as a discussion guide. Assure the students that they can pass on any question. Let the discussion move in relationship-related directions. If shy students are not participating, or if a few students are dominating, you might want to refocus on the questionnaire in order to involve more of them. It is possible that highly verbal students may dominate out of insecurity, talking to appear socially experienced and avoiding serious issues. They might also avoid talking about real concerns and talk only to appear socially experienced. However, rather than calling attention to that directly, steer the discussion toward feelings *about* this discussion of social concerns (for example, "How does it feel to talk about this topic?" or "Which questions have provoked some uneasiness or discomfort?"). You can also use the questionnaire in a polling manner to equalize contribution. (You might want to create a new questionnaire with only selected items for young teens.)

2. Encourage the group to consider popularity, per se. Ask these questions:

   ~ How do you define *popular*?
   ~ What are the advantages and disadvantages of popularity?
   ~ Who are the most interesting students in your school? Are they popular?

3. Comment that some teens are concerned about not being interesting to others. With that in mind, ask them to list on paper three somewhat unique things about themselves—which few group members, if any, know. (Maybe they have a significant scar, a family history of frequent moves, a musical talent not displayed in school, an eccentric relative, a penny collection, a weird recurring dream, an interest in classic movies, a love of chocolate, or…?) Have each person share his or her list with a partner, who will ask for elaboration on just one of the items. Re-form the group and have each person tell what he or she learned about his or her interesting partner, reporting on all three items and concentrating on one.

4. Explore with the group what kinds of social situations are uncomfortable for them. (If not mentioned, ask about starting a conversation, small talk, introductions, talking with people they don't know, formal situations, being around people from a culture different than their own, being with the other gender, being alone with someone versus being in a group.) For each of the following situations, ask what might be uncomfortable, what might make this type of situation easier for them, and what they think is appropriate behavior.

funerals	dances
weddings	job interviews
visiting someone in a hospital	receiving a gift
being introduced to your parents' friends	staying overnight at a friend's house
being introduced to parents of a friend	eating at a nice restaurant
meeting new people your own age	eating a meal with a friend's family
music events geared to your age group	visiting a friend's place of worship
formal concerts where classical music is played	
needing to thank a host family for an overnight visit	
meeting your girlfriend's/boyfriend's parents	

5. Offer the group a chance to practice various skills by role-playing the following:

   ~ shaking someone's hand firmly
   ~ introducing a friend, parents, a teacher
   ~ starting a conversation with someone on the way out of class
   ~ asking someone if it's all right to eat lunch with him or her
   ~ initiating a conversation with a someone on a bus, a plane, the subway, at a bus stop, a party, a recreation center
   ~ making or responding to a comment about the weather
   ~ asking questions as a way of showing interest (beginning with "Do you live around here?" or "Are you new here?" or "What do you think of this class?" or "Do you often come here?" and following that idea with interested comments and further questions).

6. Mention that giving and receiving compliments are important social skills. Ask questions like these:

   ~ How often do you get and give compliments in your family? Among friends?
   ~ On a scale of 1 to 10, with 10 being "very," how easy is it for you to *give* compliments? How good are you at *receiving* compliments gracefully?
   ~ What do you think affects gifted teens' ability to give and receive compliments?
   ~ When is it difficult for you to give or receive compliments? What are you concerned about? (Possibilities: Manipulation; sincerity; being "tested"; being gullible; appearing arrogant.)

7. Ask experienced compliment-givers to demonstrate their skills, with the group giving feedback. Ask them also to demonstrate receiving compliments, with group feedback. (Perhaps you could give a compliment to one or two of them and let them show how to receive it.)

Acknowledge that it is normal to have mixed feelings about compliments. Encourage group members to give compliments when the moment is ripe, for opportunities are quickly lost. Discourage them from automatically rejecting or deflecting compliments.

8. For closure, have the group arrange themselves in pairs and exchange compliments, with the receiver simply saying "Thank you." They can then rearrange themselves into new pairs and repeat the exchange. Then invite them to shake hands firmly (without pumping the arm), and, while holding the other person's hand solidly, to express appreciation for something (for example, "I really appreciate what you say in our group," "I'm glad you're in our group," or "I've really appreciated getting to know you"). Model this interaction by shaking someone's hand. Explain that sometimes a plain, simple, direct, and even clichéd comment is fine. Then have them change partners and wish each other a good day/night/weekend (for example, "I hope you have a good day"), again with a handshake. Collect the sheets and dispose of them.

Being Social

1. How interested are you in other people?

   _____

2. How good are you at listening?

   _____

3. When it comes to being social, what are you most concerned about?

   _____

4. Do you socialize with a group that includes both boys and girls? If not, would you like to?

   _____

5. Do you feel pressure (from family, friends, or yourself) to be in a romantic relationship?

   _____

6. What concerns you most about romantic relationships?

   _____

7. Who do you think has more relationship problems—bright, capable girls or bright, capable boys?

   _____

8. What do you think about two teens with different intellectual abilities dating? being married or in a long-term partnership?

   _____

9. How much do/will your friends' opinions matter when you decide who you go out with? How much do/will your parents' opinions matter?

   _____

10. Have you ever turned down someone's invitation to go out (or not asked someone out)? Why?

    _____

11. If you aren't comfortable socially, what would help you feel more comfortable?

    _____

12. If you socialize easily, including in groups, what advice could you give someone who doesn't?

    _____

Relationships

Authority

Background

Like other adolescents, gifted teens may not deal well with authority. In school, some may give courteous respect and deference to teachers only conditionally, not automatically. Principals, too, may have to *earn* respect. Highly capable and high-achieving students can indeed be quite critical of educators. Some may tangle with police or probation officers. The purpose of this discussion is to offer gifted teens a chance to discuss their relationship with authority.

Complex situations and factors probably contribute to problems with authority, often not readily apparent. Significant conflict with Dad or Mom may carry over into school in the form of resistance to an authority figure of the same gender. Strict parenting and/or harsh discipline, especially without warmth and support, can also lead to acting out in school. Anger about an absent parent can spill over into conflict with the caretaking parent and may affect relationships with adults in school. If there has been no male authority figure in the family, teens may resist directives from male teachers, bosses, administrators, coaches, or police officers and disrespect female teachers or others. When Dad dominates Mom, or vice versa, male and female students may behave accordingly with teachers. In addition, if parental discipline is arbitrary and unpredictable, teens may blame "the system" when it seems inconsistent, when it seems to play favorites, or when teachers and tests seem unfair. All of these responses can affect academic achievement and school relationships.

Children are fundamentally complex and resilient. There are many teens whose difficult family situations do not lead to problems with authority, and a secure home life and lack of obvious problems do not necessarily mean that gifted teens have smooth relationships with authority. They may have decided that they will not allow negative feelings to interfere, or they simply may not be used to expressing feelings. They may also see achievement as an opportunity to control *something*. Sometimes teens with just one parent or an impaired parent find support in a teacher, coach, or boss. Probably more than educators are aware of, students whose parenting has been inadequate or inconsistent look to the school for guidance and support. Educators' poise and consistency can offer access to a less conflicted relationship with an adult.

A gifted teen may resist authority for reasons other than parental absence or abuse. Sometimes one or both parents model resistance to authority, and a teen is simply loyal to a family tradition of troublemaking. Or perhaps parents are highly controlling, have unreasonable expectations, or "overfunction" (that is, do things for a teen that the teen should be doing). It is important to recognize that all of these situations can be found in the lives of highly able youth at any socioeconomic and education level.

Whatever its origin, difficulty with authority can be a lifelong problem, eventually affecting employment, marriages or partnerships, and the next generation of parent-child relationships. However, it is also possible that gifted teens' resistance to, and challenging of, authority reflect their thinking outside of the box. Their creativity and independence may lead to remarkable leadership or success in career and community.

Gifted teens who are "no problem" at school may also have difficulty with authority. Compliant students, including high achievers, may always defer to authority, never question it, and not think for themselves. They may be afraid to question anyone, including an unfair boss, or an abusive boyfriend, girlfriend, or spouse/partner.

A young person's cultural background may also not encourage challenging authority either at home or at school. Such attitudes may cause conflict when teens interact with the dominant culture at school. Group members might challenge students who put family concerns ahead of their own. As a facilitator, model respect for members' cultural values, invite those from nonmainstream cultures to express their views and beliefs, if they are comfortable doing so, and encourage all members to monitor their verbal and nonverbal responses when unfamiliar values are expressed.

Objectives

- Gifted teens consider that complex factors contribute to how individuals respond to authority.
- They learn that unquestioning compliance, like resistance, might be problematic.
- They consider whether changes in their responses would benefit them.

Suggestions

1. Introduce the topic briefly, but do not read the background information aloud. It is simply meant to remind you, as a facilitator, of this topic's complexity—not to encourage analysis or to instruct the group. The value here will be in group members talking with each other about authority, not in your admonitions. Teens rarely have such an opportunity to be heard. Then have the group complete the activity sheet (page 121), which gives them a chance to think about several authority figures in their lives.

2. Encourage the group to share their written responses and/or comments about any patterns they see. Then ask questions like the following to generate discussion. The questions can be directed at the group as a whole. Members can choose to respond or not.

   ~ Does your list of authority figures include all males, all females, or some of each?
   ~ Are there differences between how you respond to females in authority and to males in authority? If so, describe the differences. Is this true only at school? Only at home?

~ Where do you have problems with authority? At school? At home? At work?

~ Are your problems at school mostly with your classroom teachers, with administrators, or with adults who coach and advise extracurricular activities? Can you give an example of a problematic situation?

~ If you have two parents/caregivers at home, are there differences between how you respond to one parent and how you respond to the other? If so, how would you describe their personalities?

~ In general, how much do you have a problem with being told what to do?

~ If you resist authority, what do you gain? What price do you pay?

~ Have your interactions with authority changed? Do you resist authority more now? less? Has this affected your stress level or how you get along with others?

~ If you never question authority figures, even though you would like to, how do you explain your hesitancy?

~ If you have few or no apparent problems with authority, how do you explain that?

~ Are gifted teens more or less likely than others to have problems with authority?

3. For closure, invite summary statements from several students. Did they gain any insights from this session? Thank them for talking about a complex topic. Dispose of the sheets or file them.

Responding to Authority

Name: _____

1. List the adult authorities in your life—people who give you advice, suggestions, or orders. Describe their positions (for example, teacher, principal, coach, father, mother). Then tell how you typically respond to their authority.

NAME	POSITION	YOUR TYPICAL RESPONSE
a.		
b.		
c.		
d.		
e.		

2. If you have problems with the authority of any of the people listed above, what usually sets you off? _____

3. Do you seem to have trouble with only certain types of people in authority? If so, explain.

   _____

4. Do you have any "unfinished business" with people whose authority you have trouble accepting? (For example, are you angry about something they did?) If you do not, go on to #5. If you do, complete this question.

   List the people who fit this category: _____

   What feelings surface when you are confronted by any of them? _____

   What feelings do you have after a confrontation? _____

   What are some other ways you could respond to these people? _____

5. If you have no obvious problems with anyone you listed in #1, when and how did you learn to respond "okay" to their authority? _____

6. In which parts of your life do you believe you have been treated fairly? _____

   _____ Unfairly? _____

7. If you do not deal well with authority in general, how does that affect your life?

   _____

FOCUS Relationships

Who Can We Lean On?

Background

When adults need help, they might call a plumber, mechanic, carpenter, physician, financial advisor, therapist, or spiritual leader. When gifted teens need help—for counseling or for academic assistance, instruction in a skill, or advice—they may not know who to ask, or they may be reluctant to ask at all. They may want to protect an image of competence or believe that high ability means always being able to resolve problems themselves. They may also believe that no one could possibly understand their situation, empathize, or be able to help. Others may avoid seeking help because of barriers between themselves and significant adults in their lives. They may turn to a peer, but, even then, they may feel uncomfortable making themselves vulnerable. Gifted teens may not know that school counselors, if available, are a resource for them. School counselors are usually involved in responding to school or individual crises, and veteran secondary-level counselors have often worked individually and collectively with thousands of students. Like anyone else, they may have biases about giftedness, but nothing shocks them. They are prepared to hear anything, and their complex ethical code guides their actions. This session invites gifted teens to explore the idea of asking for help when help is needed. A caring adult and a supportive group of peers can "give permission" to ask for help.

Objectives

- Gifted teens learn that it is normal to need assistance at times.
- They explore how they feel about asking for help.

Suggestions

1. Introduce the topic by asking students to recall the last time they asked someone for help—at school, at home, with friends, or on the job—and describe these situations. You might share (briefly) an example or two from your own life; however, if group members are forthcoming, let the focus stay completely on them.

2. Ask, "When is it hard to ask for help?" If group members don't mention the following situations, introduce them, perhaps one at a time, and encourage comments. (Suggestions: For academic problems or direction; for advice about life; for problem-solving; for personal dilemmas; for social situations; for family problems.) Explore with the group why it might be difficult to ask for help in each situation. How do they feel when they ask for help?

3. Ask, "Are there certain adults in your life you would never ask for help?" (For example, father, mother, siblings, teachers, a certain teacher, counselors, a certain counselor, faith-based leaders, neighbor, relatives.) Encourage them to explain their answers.

   If several group members voice reluctance to talk to counselors, consider inviting a well-liked counselor (from the school or community) to come in and speak with the group at another session. Let the group ask how counselors view their work, how they approach personal problems of teens, if it is challenging to work with teen clients, whether gifted students discuss personal issues with them, what kinds of training counselors have, and what ethical principles guide them. Even if there are no apparent concerns about counselors, you might invite a counselor to talk about these areas. Eventually, all students probably deal with a school counselor for college or job recommendations or financial aid information, but they may be unaware of the range of other services, including opportunities to talk about personal, academic, peer, or family issues with a nonjudgmental, objective professional. The guest might also talk about what concerns seem typical with clients/students who are gifted.

4. Remind students that the adult world revolves around help sought and received (see the background information). Asking for help is normal. Acknowledge, however, that many gifted adults do not know how to ask for help, especially about emotional issues. If it is an appropriate reflection of the discussion, tell them it is not surprising that asking for help is difficult for them. Say that you hope the discussion will give them "permission" to ask for help when needed.

5. For closure, ask for volunteers to formulate advice about asking for help. Remind the group that people can support each other in many ways. Remind them, too, that everyone needs help of various kinds throughout life, that asking for help is not a sign of weakness, and that asking for help is always a compliment to the person who is asked. Even asking someone to just talk can be important at a critical time.

FOCUS Relationships

Getting What We Need

Background

Many people do not know how to ask for what they need. Gifted teens may be no more able to do this than anyone else. Maybe they are even *less* able, given their ability to (and expectation that they ought to be able to) think things through by themselves. Perhaps their sensitivity stops them from making requests, since they are concerned about the feelings of others. Perhaps they would rather be givers than receivers, thereby avoiding debt. They might not want to give anyone the satisfaction of helping them, may feel unworthy of assistance, or are afraid of appearing weak. Maybe they do for others what they wish others would do for them. Whatever the explanation, their needs may go unmet, and they might feel sad and discouraged—without knowing why.

Some needs may be related to the feeling that something is missing in life. Perhaps they long for time and attention from busy parents. They may yearn for a sign of appreciation or encouragement—or simply less nagging, television, or arguing in the house. They may wish for support or kind words from brothers and sisters. These wishes may be difficult to articulate.

Gifted students' unmet needs may also be related to school. They may be frustrated in regular classrooms because of undifferentiated curriculum or because of teaching style. When students learn how to express their classroom needs to teachers tactfully, their experience in school may improve. A student might say, "It's hard for me to understand things when I can't see them. I need a summary sheet to look at while you explain things" or "I wonder if I could do some independent study in class. I already know most of what we're learning here, and it's uncomfortable for me when the pace is slow. I realize the pace is probably okay for others." Using "I-statements" usually helps to prevent defensiveness.

Relationships are enhanced when people express their needs clearly and directly. In an ideal world, boyfriends and girlfriends, husbands and wives and partners, friends and roommates, and coworkers all can articulate needs. Someone might say (using I-statements), "I would like to be more involved in decisions," or "I need to have you tell me how you feel about this," or "I need to talk with you more often," or "I feel bad when we don't get to places on time." Unfortunately, couples often do not know how to express their wishes and concerns to each other, and children and parents struggle with this as well. Ideally, children express their needs to their parents. For example, "I feel invaded when you go through my papers. I need to feel that my personal space is mine," or "I need to start making more of my own decisions. I feel frustrated when you make decisions for me."

Objectives

- Gifted teens become more aware of the value of expressing needs directly.
- They clarify their own needs.
- They practice asking for what they need.

Suggestions

1. Begin by asking, "On a scale of 1 to 10, with 1 being 'very poorly,' how well do you express your needs to others—for example, to your parents, siblings, teachers, friends, employers, or boyfriend/girlfriend?"

2. Ask students to describe the nicest gift any adult has ever given them—something that meant a lot, but wasn't something that could be touched or seen. If needed, give a few examples: self-confidence, encouragement, the right words at a difficult time, modeling of some behavior or goal, a sense of fun, a shoulder to cry on. You might mention something specific you wish each of your parents would give (or had given) to you. Remember to quickly move the focus back to the group after your sharing.

3. Hand out "Needs" (page 127). Tell the group to circle items that seem true for them and then code the first section, according to the directions. Then invite them to share their lists. Reassure students that they can choose how many items to share, and remind them of the confidentiality guideline.

4. Instruct the group to look back at the items they circled, put a box around anything they think they could actually ask for, and underline anything they think they could do something about—even today. When they seem ready to continue, ask them to choose one boxed item and put it in the form of a request. Explain that they should begin their request with "I." Encourage them to be clear, direct, and genuine and to phrase the request in a way that does not attack or demand. If someone has difficulty composing a request, ask if he or she would like the group to give suggestions, or offer the following as examples.

   ~ "I would like the TV turned down lower so I can concentrate on studying."
   ~ "I need to be alone sometimes. I would like to have the room to myself at a certain time every day."

5. Begin a discussion about the difficulty of addressing needs directly. Ask closed questions like the following, rhetorically, pausing a moment after each. Ask for comments after you finish.

   ~ Do you ever drop hints about your needs or let your moods communicate them, and then feel angry or sad if no one gets your message?
   ~ Do you sometimes use bad behavior to get the attention you need?

~ Does your school performance—bad or good—help to meet your needs?

~ Do you ever do things for other people in the hope that they will do things for you?

~ How do you feel about the idea of asking for what is needed?

6. Ask, "Is there anyone you know who expresses needs well?" After some examples, ask, "What could you learn from these people?" Then, "How might learning how to ask for what you need benefit you as a college student or an adult in work or personal relationships?"

7. For closure, ask how it felt to express needs. Dispose of the sheets or file them.

Needs

Name: _____

Circle what you would most like to have at home. If from a specific person, mark M (mother), F (father), S (sister), B (brother), or O (other person) to the left of the word.

time	less tension	information
attention	more concern	a compliment
understanding	more interest	better behavior
kind words	encouragement	protection
less competition	honesty	listening
less jealousy	smiles	a good meal
less arguing	patience	a hug
less pressure	advice	_____
less criticism	guidance/instruction	

Circle *general* needs from the list below that apply to you. If a need is not listed, add it to the end and circle it, too.

support during a rough time	a conversation that isn't interrupted
space, privacy at home	someone to love
peace and quiet	someone to love me
more contact with people	something to keep me busy
direction	teachers who care about me
a good night's sleep	a different teaching style
a feeling of success	teachers to ease up for a while
less stress	approval
fewer demands on my time	respect from my peers
a feeling of hope that things will improve	role model
someone to listen	more challenging classes

Relationships

Gossip, Cyber-Aggression, and Other Bullying

Background

Schools are obligated to provide a safe environment for learning. They must therefore deal with bullying in all its forms, including cyberbullying and gossip.

There is usually no shortage of gossip among teens—in school and elsewhere. Gossip has power. It can bully, hurt, control, boomerang, become more and more distorted, and cast a negative shadow on both the gossiper and the person who is gossiped about. Gossip has been called the female counterpart to male aggression. It is much more difficult to know who the aggressor is than when the first strike is physical. Some might argue that rumor-spreading is even more cruel than physical bullying. Both boys and girls can be guilty of gossiping.

Technology allows even new kinds of bullying, including cyberbullying—using the Internet or other devices to post cruel messages about or compromising images of others. Cyberbullying is currently rampant. Social-networking Web sites make bullying an increasing threat in both rural and urban settings. Bullies can coerce passwords, impersonate others, claim no responsibility, and feel free to take risks. They can take photos in the locker room and post them. It is difficult to know who the bullies are and who has seen the postings. A particularly frightening aspect of cyberbullying is that, in seconds, messages meant to harm or humiliate can be disseminated globally, with vicious responses coming from near and far. Internet bullying is a school issue, even if it happens outside of school. When students are hurt or traumatized, strong feelings are brought into the school, affecting school climate and learning.

In the United States, research on bullying began only relatively recently, fueled by school shootings linked to bullying. Internationally, bullying has been studied much longer. It appears that the vast majority of students are bullied sometime during the school years and large numbers are bullies. Some are both bullies and targets of bullies. Repeated absences, anxiety, depression, and even suicide have been connected to bullying. In the past few years, bullying among girls (such as social exclusion and rumor-spreading) has received increasing attention, challenging assumptions about gender differences in bullies. Studies have also found that bullying occurs regardless of race and ethnicity, population density, and socioeconomic factors.

A national study of bullying and gifted children and teens, which I co-conducted (*Gifted Child Quarterly*, 50, no. 2, Spring 2006), found that 67 percent of gifted eighth-graders had experienced bullying sometime during their school years. In grade six, the peak year, nearly half (46 percent) of all participants had experienced at least one kind of verbal and nonverbal bullying. Name-calling and teasing about appearance were the most common kinds of bullying, with the latter the most distressful. Even one-time incidents were recalled with clarity. The percent of male victims declined during grades seven and eight, but not the percent of female victims. In grade eight, the peak year for bullying *by* the gifted participants, 16 percent were bullies. These findings are similar to those in some studies of the general population, although studies have varied greatly in definition, age of subjects, and time span of interest, making exact comparisons difficult.

Bullies may continue their aggression in future relationships. Evidence has linked school bullies to later involvement in corrections and to depression. Educators and parents should not assume that bullies have low self-esteem. Instead, they may enjoy high social status, may feel *allowed* to bully, and may enjoy the drama and control of bullying. Bullying appears to peak during school-transition years, when it may be connected to jockeying for social position and countering social anxiety. Although bullying can occur at any grade level, including kindergarten, it typically peaks during early middle school years.

The good news it that bullying is now on the radar screen in schools and elsewhere. Even state legislatures are getting involved, mandating anti-bullying programs. Such programs are geared to all students—those doing the bullying, those who are bullied, and those silently watching. Bystanders actually have the power to stop bullying behaviors, according to research. When administrators and teachers are all on the same page about what bullying is and what their response should be when they see it, when school counselors do prevention-oriented classroom lessons, and when educators take reports of bullying seriously, climate change is possible in schools. Students can relax and feel safe in their environment. Because bullying often occurs out of adults' sight, increased monitoring of hallways, bus lines, lunchrooms, and restrooms can help decrease bullying.

This session gives gifted teens, whether bullies, bullied, or bystanders, a chance to talk about bullying. Victims sharing experiences and feelings, and bullies, encouraged to focus on feelings and the perspectives of others, can contribute to important raised awareness.

Objectives

- Gifted teens consider the impact of various kinds of bullying.
- Those who have been bullied feel heard, with feelings validated.
- Those who have bullied gain insight about their behavior and its effects.
- Gifted teens understand the importance and impact of passive bystanders.
- They consider how gossip affects their lives and the lives of others.

Suggestions

1. Ask the group to define *bullying*. Avoid presenting information from the background paragraphs at this point. After they have offered their perspectives, tell them that it is usually understood to be intimidating behavior by someone with more power. Most researchers and many school policies include *repeated* in their definitions, but even a single incident can traumatize a sensitive, vulnerable individual.

2. Ask students to brainstorm types of bullying. (For example, teasing, name-calling, excluding, gossiping, posting images and messages on Web sites, knocking books to the floor, taking possessions, hitting, threatening, beating up. Encourage them to consider how bullying differs between girls and boys.)

3. Continue with open-ended questions. Be aware that discussion may need to develop for a while before experiences are shared. Begin with general, abstract questions.

   ~ How serious a problem is bullying in your school? Outside of school?
   ~ What kinds of bullying are you aware of in your school? Outside of school?
   ~ How common is cyberbullying?
   ~ What types of students are typically the bullies? (They should not name anyone.)
   ~ What might make someone vulnerable to being bullied? (Possibilities: Height, weight, appearance, low social status, being new, not having a group of friends, being withdrawn, being highly intelligent, having a disability.)
   ~ How might being bullied affect someone during the school years?
   ~ How might being a bully affect someone later in life? (Possibilities: Domestic abuse, trouble with the law, bullying in the workplace, poor parenting.)
   ~ Do you know anyone personally who has been bullied, including by rumor-spreading or being shunned within a group? (No names.)
   ~ What do you know about their experience? (If they believe it was traumatic, say, "It makes sense that it hurt that much.")
   ~ Do you know anyone personally who bullies others? Anyone who cyberbullies? (No names.)
   ~ What do you think contributes to bullying?
   ~ What grade levels in school do you think have the most bullying?
   ~ What about gifted kids? Can they be bullies or bullied—or both? Are they more vulnerable to bullying than other kids are—or less?
   ~ If you've been bullied, would you be willing to share what kind it was? What it felt like? If you told anyone about it? How you survived it? How, or if, the experience affected your feelings about school in general?
   ~ If you've bullied someone in the past or lately, would you be willing to share what that was/is like? What your feelings about it and about the targeted person were/are?
   ~ How does it feel to talk about this topic?

4. Move into a problem-solving mode. Ask the following:

   ~ What do you think administrators and teachers should do about bullying?
   ~ What can students do to combat it? (Mention that passive bystanders contribute to a bullying climate—and can help to stop bullying.)

~ What should parents do if their child is miserable because of being bullied?

~ How could someone who is bullied become less vulnerable?

~ How do you feel when someone says that bullying is "normal," "just part of growing up," or something kids need to handle themselves?

~ What kind of school policies and rules about bullying would help to make it happen less—or not at all?

~ What can be done about cyberbullying?

~ What do you think the consequences should be for someone who bullies?

5. Ask the group to define *gossip*. Invite discussion about experiences with gossip. Ask closed, polling questions like these, and encourage the group to elaborate when appropriate—discreetly:

~ Have you ever been hurt by gossip or known someone who has?

~ Have you ever passed along some gossip and then found out it wasn't true?

~ Have you ever justified passing along some gossip because it *was* true?

~ Do you knowingly add dramatic details to gossip when passing it on?

~ Have you ever told someone that you didn't want to hear his or her gossip?

~ Are you able *not* to pass gossip along when you have heard something interesting?

~ Does your group of friends gossip a lot? Does your family?

~ Do you think you are a gossip? Do your peers think of you as a gossip?

~ Who do you think gossips more—boys or girls?

~ Do you know someone who refuses to gossip, or who seems not to be excited by it?

~ What do gossips get out of gossiping? (Possibilities: A sense of power and control, a feeling of belonging, a chance to hurt someone.)

~ How would you rank these in importance in *your* social world:
— talking about things (possessions, purchases, clothing, houses, etc.)
— talking about people (who likes whom, friends and acquaintances, deaths and divorces, movie and music stars, people in the news, etc.)
— talking about ideas (thoughts about life, politics, meaning, creative ways to do things, insights about self and others, etc.)

~ How would you rank them in terms of conversation quality?

Important
It is important not to pass judgment or to moralize. Let the group express feelings, experiences, and opinions. The most important information will come from them.

6. For closure, thank the group for being open, genuine, thoughtful, respectful, mature (or whatever other descriptors are appropriate). You might offer a summary statement yourself.

Relationships

Relationships with Parents

Background

Teens with high ability may be given extra responsibility in the family. Parents may in fact defer to the teen's opinions readily—even about major family decisions. In other areas, too, gifted teens may have great attention and autonomy. However, they may not feel comfortable with so much power. On the other hand, some parents may "overfunction" for gifted teens, doing things the teens should be doing for themselves, potentially creating dependency and affecting their sense of competence.

Relationships with parents are complex. Families of gifted teens certainly are not immune to stressful, unexpected life events, accompanied by family distress and parental conflict. Parents may even have mixed feelings about giftedness. Some gifted teens might mirror what a parent dislikes about himself or herself, and parents may feel anxiety when their teen moves into a developmental stage that evokes unpleasant memories for them. Some parents have problems adjusting their parenting to fit a new developmental level. These and other aspects of the parent-teen relationship can create tension as gifted teens, like others their age, work on differentiating themselves and moving toward autonomy.

Objectives

- Gifted teens learn that parent-teen struggles are common.
- They examine their relationship with their parents and articulate complexities.
- They explore the idea that parenting styles differ.
- They gain some understanding of both themselves and their parents.

Important

For discussion purposes, *parents* can refer to biological and/or adoptive parents, stepparents, foster parents, guardians, grandparents, or other significant caretaking adults. Be aware that, if a parent is no longer living, even if the relationship was brief, that relationship might still be significant here. The same may be true for a former stepparent or foster parent.

Suggestions

1. If group members have not already described their family situations in your group, invite them to briefly describe the families they live with. Some, of course, are in situations involving blended families, current or past stepparents, grandparents, absent parents, deceased parents, distant parents, single parents, adoptive parents, gay parents, or unknown parents. Remind them that what was once considered a

typical family may no longer be typical. Encourage them to consider all caretaker relationships as important and worth discussing.

2. Hand out "Relationships with Parents" (pages 135–136) and ask the group to fill out the activity sheet with brief responses, anonymously. Use the responses to generate discussion, or simply give each member a copy to refer to during the discussion, going quickly around the group for brief answers to one question at a time. As always, the value is in raised awareness and experience in expressing concerns. Be aware that the activity may be unsettling for group members who have a complicated relationship with their parents or who have lost a parent. Remind them that they always have the option of passing when it is their turn.

3. Introduce the idea of parenting style. Use the following questions to explore this. Beware of overtly passing judgment on responses, even though biases and values are implicit in several of the questions. The questions for this suggestion and suggestion #4 refer to "parents," but not all group members will have two parents or even one. Those with two might have differing relationships with each parent. Invite group members to consider their parents individually when framing their responses to the questions. Depending on your context, time constraints, and preference for other sections of this session, you might want to ask only a few of the following:

   ~ How unified are your parents/guardians? For example, how much do they agree on rules? In other areas of parenting? How does their agreement or disagreement affect you?
   ~ How clear are their guidelines for you?
   ~ How patient are your parents/guardians? How casual? formal? rule-oriented? consistent?
   ~ When you do something you shouldn't do or break a family rule, is punishment appropriate? immediate? harsh? fair? What kinds of punishments are typical?
   ~ How much do your parents/guardians give advice or lecture?
   ~ How much do they allow you to make mistakes and learn from them?
   ~ To what extent are they able to be your "parent," not a peer?
   ~ How much are you allowed to make decisions?
   ~ How protective of you are they? How affectionate toward you?
   ~ How do they divide parenting responsibilities? Who leads? How do they make big decisions?

4. Ask these questions:

   ~ How easy has it been for you to have your parents/guardians as parents/guardians?
   ~ What kinds of feelings do you have when you think about, or talk about, your parents/guardians? (If needed, suggest feeling words like *grateful, angry, frustrated, sad, lucky, secure,* or *guilty.* Remind them that it is good to practice identifying feelings in self and others.)
   ~ What are the major "jobs" of parents, in your opinion?
   ~ Which of these have your parents/guardians done well?

~ What advice would you give about parenting to someone who just adopted a teen?

~ What advice would you give about parenting to someone with a gifted child?

5. For closure, summarize—or have someone else summarize—the most significant ideas of this session. Thank the group for their thoughtful discussion about the complexities of relationships with parents. Dispose of the sheets.

Important	As with all discussions, remember your obligation to model respect for privacy of group members and their families. Adhere to the principle of protecting confidentiality and remind the group that, especially in discussions like these, it is essential that they not talk outside of the group about what was discussed in the group. Tell them that you will honor their and their families' privacy and that you hope they will do the same.

Relationships with Parents

Use your own judgment about how to answer these questions if you don't live with one or both parents; if you live with a stepparent, but have contact with the parent not living with you; if you live with foster parents or adoptive parents; if a parent is no longer living; if you live with grandparents; or if you live with any other nontraditional family. Feel free to omit some questions or, if your parent is absent, to think about how your parent was when with you. Or refer to a current guardian/caretaker.

1. Describe the relationship you have with your mother. _____

    with your father. _____

    _____

2. How are these relationships different from two years ago? _____

    five years ago? _____ ten years ago? _____

    _____

3. What specific problems, if any, interfere with your having a good relationship with your

    parents? _____

    _____

4. Which parent are you closest to?

    _____

5. Which parent do you resemble the most physically? _____

    emotionally? _____ in interests? _____ in abilities?

    _____ in personality? _____

    _____

6. If one or both of your parents is absent, ill, no longer living, or not around much, how have

    you managed to cope with that? _____

    _____

(continued)

Relationships with Parents (continued)

7. How do your parents cope with stress and frustrations? _____
_____

8. How do they handle parenting? _____
_____

9. How are they coping with your getting older? _____
_____

10. How do they respond when you are ill? _____

   When you are in trouble? _____

   When you do well? _____

   When you don't do well? _____

11. How do they feel about your gifts and talents? _____
_____

12. What do you respect most about your parents? _____
_____

13. What are the most important things your parents have taught you?

_____

_____

14. Write five words that come to mind when you think "Dad" or "Father."

_____

_____

15. Write five words that come to mind when you think "Mom" or "Mother."

_____

_____

FOCUS Relationships

Relationships with Siblings

Background

This session focus might not be appropriate if your group has a large number of "only" children. However, those students might enjoy hearing about others' sibling relationships, and they can respond to open-ended questions about how they view not having siblings. A discussion about sharing space is also of interest, since most gifted students are considering further education and will likely have college roommates. While there are many universal issues and themes related to living with siblings, gifted teens may experience some extra layers of concern, especially if their giftedness is an issue in the family, if it is the focus of family attention, if there is considerable sibling competition, and if siblings' abilities are quite different from their own or are not as valued as theirs by parents or others.

Objectives

- Gifted teens gain insight into their relationships with brothers and sisters.
- They gain skills in articulating feelings and concerns about their family.
- They consider how family conflict can help to form personal identity.

Suggestions

1. Introduce the focus, and then ask each group member to do the following:

   ~ Give the names and ages of their siblings and stepsiblings (even if this was done previously). Describe each with two or three adjectives.
   ~ Explain what kind of relationship they have with each.
   ~ If a sibling no longer lives at home, has died, or is at home only part of the time, describe the earlier relationship and, if the sibling is still alive, how it has changed.

2. Move the discussion toward present conflict (for those with siblings):

   ~ Do you have conflicts with siblings? If so, what kind?
   ~ Compared to last year, has there been more, or less, or similar conflict this year?
   ~ How close do you feel to each sibling, on a scale of 1 to 10, with 10 being "very close"?
   ~ How much conflict do you feel (may not be overt) with each sibling, on a scale of 1 to 10, with 10 being "a lot"? (Be aware that closeness does not preclude conflict, and conflict can indeed contribute to closeness, and vice versa.)

Group members might mention conflict areas such as these in answer to the last question. If they don't, offer them as areas to consider:

competition	guilt	jealousy
criticism	favoritism	age differences
personality differences	different interests	gender issues
personal space	bullying	competition for approval
needing a separate identity	privacy	the "gifted" label

3. Give the group a chance to speak positively about their siblings with these questions:

   ~ What do you appreciate about your siblings?
   ~ How much support and encouragement do you feel from your siblings?
   ~ What worries or concerns do you have about a sibling—if any?
   ~ How have your relationships with siblings changed in recent years?
   ~ Do you know of siblings in other families whose relationships have changed?

4. Offer the idea that children often strive for a separate identity in the family, different from their siblings, and they try to get attention from their parents in various ways. Ask some of the following questions, keeping in mind the social/emotional developmental level, language proficiency, and concerns of your group:

   ~ What kinds of giftedness are evident in your family?
   ~ If you have siblings, have they been identified as "gifted"? If not, is that a concern in the family? for you?
   ~ What are you known for in your family? How do family members usually describe you? How accurate is it? Do you enjoy having that as part of your identity in the family? If not, what don't you like about it?
   ~ How easy has it been for you to gain a separate identity?
   ~ What do you think of the idea that conflict with parents and siblings helps someone carve out a separate identity?
   ~ What kind of attention do you and each of your siblings get in your family? Does it differ from person to person?
   ~ Do you feel you get enough attention? too much attention?
   ~ How do you feel around each of your siblings? (Possibilities: Confident, unconfident, superior, inferior, stronger, weaker, comfortable, uncomfortable, irritated, worried.)
   ~ How do you think having (or not having) a sibling might affect future relationships? (Note: Be aware that sibling bullying and competition can affect self-esteem, and research generally has not found negative effects of not having siblings. Therefore, don't assume that this is a leading question with a right answer. Indicate that you are interested in their views.)

5. For closure, ask for a volunteer to summarize the discussion. Or ask for various students' impressions. What kind of relationships do most group members seem to have with siblings? How did they feel during the discussion? Encourage them to use feeling words—like *guilty, pleased, proud, grateful,* or *irritated.*

FOCUS Relationships

Relationships with Teachers

Background

The teacher-student relationship is often a key element in a teen's school experience. Good relationships with teachers can motivate students to achieve and to cooperate with teachers and peers. Many students learn best when they like the teacher. It might be fair to say that teachers also probably respond more positively to students they like. Good teacher-student communication can contribute to advocacy and support, both of which are important for gifted teens, who may not be as self-confident and secure as they appear. Parents and other advocates may forget to emphasize the importance of that relationship to a gifted adolescent.

An uncomfortable relationship can likewise negatively affect learning. Teachers may have biases and attitudes that preclude comfortable relationships with gifted students. In addition, parents' attitude and style of advocacy, student personality, underachievement, perfectionism, and parent or student arrogance may also negatively affect teacher-student relationships. Cultural differences may also play a role, including that some cultural groups give automatic deference and respect to teachers and are therefore reluctant to advocate for their children.

Students may not realize that teachers are quite human. They worry when students are ill or face difficult situations; they are often hesitant to ask personal questions; and they sometimes wonder how to express concern to students. Teachers do see *individuals* in their classes each day, but numbers and time constraints often make it difficult to make one-to-one connections. In addition, some teachers are shy and private, just as some students are. On the other hand, some teachers and students communicate easily in and outside of class.

Part of what makes teaching satisfying and rewarding is having healthy and comfortable teacher-student relationships. Such relationships probably help to sustain coaches and extracurricular advisors during their great time commitment to activities. Nevertheless, it is important that teachers remain *teachers* in student-teacher relationships, no matter how much gifted students are capable of adult-level conversations and have the same interests. Teachers are not peers of students. Teacher-student relationships always have a power imbalance, for example, and there is a fine line between offering support and advice and interfering and manipulating. Teachers who *need* to be close to students—for their own benefit, not the students'—

may cross another line. And there is a great difference between teachers confiding in students and students confiding in teachers. The adult is always responsible for setting appropriate boundaries. Teachers can be of most help to students when they are teachers first. Students, teachers, and group facilitators may need to be reminded of that now and then. Mention professional boundaries if someone complains that a teacher is not willing to be a real friend or provide constant guidance.

Objectives

- Gifted teens learn that a group can vary in attitudes about relationships with teachers.
- They articulate their thoughts and feelings about relationships with teachers.
- They explore the advantages of having a good relationship with a teacher.

Suggestions

1. If you are a teacher or a counselor, introduce the topic by sharing your own thoughts about relationships with students. What are your roles and responsibilities (and what are not)? What helps you maintain clear boundaries between their lives and yours, even as you become an important teacher/counselor to them? Why are boundaries important? The background information provides guidance and vocabulary regarding boundaries.

2. Hand out "Relationships with Teachers" (page 142) and ask the group to fill out the questionnaire with brief responses, anonymously. Or make it an oral exercise only, with the group using the questionnaire as a visual reference during discussion.

3. Ask the group these questions (some of them perhaps only rhetorically):

   ~ Who are the teachers that most kids appreciate? What qualities are appreciated?
   ~ What are some advantages of having a good, comfortable relationship with a teacher?
   ~ Have you ever known a teacher well enough to trust him or her with personal information? (Avoid asking for details.)
   ~ Has a teacher ever advised you about a personal situation? (Again, avoid prying.)
   ~ How important to your learning is liking a teacher? (Expect that the group will vary.)
   ~ How can students build a good teacher-student relationship?
   ~ How could a teacher benefit from having comfortable, individual communication with a student? With students in general? (If teacher voyeurism is suggested or meeting teacher needs is mentioned, use the background information to clarify boundaries.)
   ~ What type of learning needs might a gifted teen discuss with a teacher? (Examples: An independent curriculum, a faster pace, more open-endedness in assignments, less lecture.)
   ~ Have you ever considered a teacher or counselor a friend? (Suggest that a teacher-friend can be an adult to talk with and to seek guidance from. Teacher-friends and parent-friends can be most helpful when they remain primarily teachers or parents. While peer-friends are equal in sharing

confidences, adult-friends of students are *un*equal and able to offer objective adult wisdom and support. In relationships between teacher/counselor and teens, the teens' needs are primary, not the adults.')

~ How was that relationship different from other friendships? How was it similar?

~ Was your high ability a factor in this relationship, in your opinion?

4. Invite the group to problem-solve:

~ What kinds of issues might gifted teens have with teachers?

~ Is there a teacher you aren't getting along with this year?

~ What would the class be like for you if you had a better relationship with the teacher? What would the teacher be doing? What would you be doing? How would you be feeling?

~ How could you make the problem bigger? (This question helps teens figure out what is in their control. Even gifted kids may not be clear about that.) How could you make it smaller? (Possibilities: Ask for help; make eye contact; make small talk; answer questions in class; recognize that teachers appreciate support, like anyone else; arrange to speak with the teacher about the conflict.)

~ Do you think parents or counselors should ever intervene to try to improve a relationship between a student and a teacher? (Suggest that it is probably best for the student to try to take care of the situation with the teacher alone, perhaps after guidance from parents or a counselor. If that attempt is unproductive, however, then someone else might be asked to serve as an objective third party in conflict mediation or to advocate directly. Parents may also be able to intervene effectively, aided by insights from the counselor.)

~ What do you need personally from teachers?

~ What do you definitely *not* want personally from teachers?

5. For closure, ask someone to summarize what has been shared and/or learned during this discussion. Compliment the group on their ability to articulate thoughts and feelings. Dispose of the sheets.

Relationships with Teachers

1. What kinds of relationships do you have with your teachers? _____
    _____

2. In the past five years, have your relationships with teachers generally become closer and
    more comfortable, or more distant and less comfortable? _____
    _____

3. Name one great teacher you have had: _____. What made this
    teacher so great?_____
    _____

4. What teaching style(s) do you like best? Circle one or more:

    is highly organized, structured

    has predictable schedule

    is flexible

    has many rules

    is warm and friendly

    chats with individuals, groups

    uses a lot of worksheets

    has great variety of activities in each class

    gives information mostly by speaking

    assigns projects that involve art or construction

    is loosely organized, not highly structured

    is unpredictable, with surprises every day

    has few rules

    has clear expectations

    uses humor

    doesn't talk much with individual students

    shows information visually

    uses a lot of technology

    teaches by having kids do activities

    Do your choices here fit the great teacher you named in #3? Yes ❑   No ❑

5. Do you like to have teachers know you well personally? Yes ❑   No ❑

    What kind of information do you like teachers to know about you? _____
    _____

    What kind of information do you *not* want teachers to know? _____
    _____

6. If you were having a very difficult time in your personal life, would you want your teachers
    to be aware of that? Yes ❑   No ❑

7. Do most teachers seem to like you? Yes ❑   No ❑ How do you know?
    _____

8. How do you let teachers know that you approve of their teaching?
    _____

FOCUS Relationships
Male and Female

Background

Sexuality involves much more than just "having sex." It is one way we are distinguished—how we behave in response to emotional and physical sensations, how we interact in social relationships, and how we notice the responses of others. Cultures, families, and regions differ in how they define what behaviors are appropriate for each gender—how a male should "be male" and how a female should "be female." Teens, including those who are gifted, have reason to be confused in regard to gender expectations, behavior, and sexual feelings. Some may actually have little opportunity or invitation to talk about these developmental challenges. As with all other sessions, it is important not to feel compelled to inform or moralize. However, give opinions carefully and sensitively if the group asks for them or seems to be looking for guidance.

This session can introduce a brief series of sessions focusing on gender relations. Suggestion #1 usually generates enough interaction to fill a session. Suggestion #2 might be used as a follow-up session, especially if a film is used. Looking at ads can be an effective second half of an introductory session on gender relations.

Important

You will need to do some advance preparation for suggestion #2. Check with a media center if you would like to show a video/DVD concerning media messages. If you plan to analyze advertisements, direct each member, at the previous session, to bring in five ads that feature females (or parts of females), males (or parts of males), or both males and females.

Objectives

- Gifted teens think about cultural attitudes regarding being male and being female.
- They learn that peers also have anxieties and confusion about sexuality.

Suggestions

1. Have group members make lists on a wallboard of "what makes males male" and "what makes females female." Have the boys make lists for both males and females, and have the girls do the same. Then ask a spokesperson for each group to report.

   This activity usually elicits a wide range of behaviors, from silliness to arguing to quiet pondering, but it will also provoke serious thinking. The teens undoubtedly will consider physical attributes first, but very quickly they will probably list emotional, expressive, and other behavioral characteristics. At times they may find it difficult to assign specific qualities or characteristics to specific genders. Reassure the group that most people wonder how they fit society's expectations for males and females. Ask questions like these when they are done:

~ Is being gentle, nurturing, artistic, and emotional only "female"?

~ Is being assertive, strong, athletic, and a leader only "male"?

~ If you were to create a continuum of traits and personal qualities with "female" at one end and "male" at the other, according to beliefs in our society, how would you distribute the qualities? (This might be a group activity, using a large sheet of paper, a wallboard, or technology. If students express strong opinions or feelings about the need for distinctions, invite them to explain how their views were formed. Be careful to remain nonjudgmental, and avoid suggesting that opinions are right or wrong. Religious and other cultural factors may be the basis for beliefs and values.)

~ Some parents seem to support interests and behaviors in the middle range of such a continuum for both boys and girls. What do you think of that? What are some possible advantages of not being at the extremes of "masculine" and "feminine" behavior? (Possibilities: A wider range of interest and talent areas; ease with both genders.)

~ In our society, who and what sends us messages about gender roles and expectations?

~ What do you wish you knew more about in regard to the other gender? (Stay poised and nonevaluative, no matter what emerges here. If someone speaks disrespectfully about the other gender, ask the group how they feel about the statements. If the group is reluctant to comment, offer something like this: "I think that if I were in your shoes, I'd feel offended by what he/she just said. How do you as a group feel right now?" This kind of response to off-color comments lets group members observe boundary-setting and articulating discomfort and also helps to develop sensitivity to others. As always, *everything* can be processed. See page 11 in the introduction.)

2. Discuss a video/DVD (see "Recommended Resources" on page 276) about media messages related to sexuality and self-image. Or show and analyze ads (requested at the preceding meeting), focusing on gender roles, stereotypes, and subtle messages about gender. Ask these questions:

~ What impact do advertising messages have on beliefs about gender and relationships?

~ How much are female and male bodies used to sell products?

~ What do you think about the possibility that the way men and women are portrayed in ads is related to the way they behave on dates, in marriage/partnership, and at work?

~ How do media images like these contribute to what is expected of males and females—and even to sexual harassment, abuse, and domestic and other violence?

3. Introduce the idea of communication differences between males and females. Ask the group if they believe the following statements are true. Individuals in the behavioral sciences have made statements like these; however, remind students that they do not have to agree with them. In fact, encourage them to question anything that summarizes complex, widely varying populations and personalities with a single statement. Obviously, no statement is true for *all* persons of either gender.

   ~ Girls are good listeners. They accept and support each other's comments.
   ~ Boys offer information and opinions, interrupt each other, change topics, and are concerned with power in a conversation.
   ~ Girls finish each other's sentences in conversation and stick with topics.
   ~ Girls are concerned with keeping friendships going. They smile more than boys do.
   ~ Boys' and men's voices are louder. Girls often feel as if they are not heard when they are in classes with boys.

   If yours is a mixed-gender group, ask if the statements above are true of their group. (They may or may not be true.) Suggest that differences in how males and females communicate—whether great or small, consistent or not—can contribute to communication problems in families, at school, at work, and certainly in couple/partner relationships. Ask the group how they might apply the above information in their lives now or in the future. (NOTE: It is helpful to learn how to communicate effectively with the other gender by learning some of their techniques.)

4. For closure, ask the group how comfortable they were when discussing this topic. Assure them that confusing thoughts about sexuality are quite normal, and that sexuality will probably continue to be an interesting topic for them.

FOCUS Relationships

They're Going Out Now

Background

Depending on how social gifted teens are, they may know plenty about romantic relationships. However, this session acknowledges that there is great concern during adolescence about "going out" with someone, regardless of experience. Sensitivities associated with giftedness may exacerbate challenges related to moving into this and other developmental stages: how to behave, how to attract others, how assertive to be, what to say, how to be genuine, how to kiss, and how to maintain friendships while in a dating relationship. There are also serious concerns about sex, pregnancy, sexually transmitted diseases, and date rape. Unfortunately, it is often difficult for adults and teens to discuss sexual matters together, and teens may have to depend on peers or the media for information—or misinformation.

Some gifted kids have less information and experience than others their age because they are absorbed in schoolwork or other pursuits and perhaps because peers stereotype them as being unsocial and don't include them when discussing social issues. In fact, gifted teens range across a continuum of social skills, social awareness, and social ease. Here, they can share thoughts related to this area of development.

NOTE: You might want to ask your group what relationship words they use. "Going out," "hanging out," "dating," "seeing each other"—what do they call it when two people are in a romantic relationship—at various ages and relationship stages? During discussion, use the language the students seem most comfortable with, while also recognizing that terms can change with circumstances.

Important

Even though this session will probably focus on heterosexual relationships, students who are attracted to their own gender should not be ignored. However, it is not just those who have concluded that they are gay, lesbian, or bisexual who wonder about their place in a society that generally finds homosexual relationships unsettling. Words like *gay*, *dyke*, *fag*, *lezzy*, *fairy*, and *queer* are tossed around freely and negatively in schools. Many teens, certainly including gifted teens, are targets as they form close same-gender friendships, pursue activities and careers considered nontraditional for their gender, and/or have mannerisms that leave them vulnerable. Name-calling resonates, because confusion and doubt are often part of the search for identity. Because of fears and teasing, sensitive teens may self-medicate with alcohol or other drugs, run away, stay home from school, or become depressed and suicidal. Lack of support and of open discussion at home and at school may contribute to alienation and desperation.

Keeping in mind the constraints of your setting and the age and trust level within your group, consider conducting a matter-of-fact discussion about same-gender relationships and partnerships, either as part of this session or as a separate session. If you feel uncomfortable or uncertain about how to do this, you might talk first with a school counselor or other professional who works with gay, lesbian, bisexual, or transgender (GLBT) teens. My own research with gifted GLBT youth found that 50 percent of them had seriously wondered about their sexual orientation before the end of elementary school, although it was not a great concern pre-puberty. Depression was experienced by 88 percent, and 76 percent seriously considered suicide. Some experienced humiliating teasing, including by teachers or coaches, even though they had not yet "come out." Only 31 percent told a parent about their thoughts of suicide, and none told teachers. Most did not know any other GLBT teens and wished there had been information, role models, and support available. Being "gay and gifted," as one subject said, meant being "doubly different."

Few GLBT teens are open about their orientation during the school years. You might therefore simply acknowledge that there may be group members who cannot relate to a discussion of heterosexual relationships. If the group appears to want to pursue that direction, encourage them to express their thoughts, feelings, and concerns. Be prepared with information that might refute stereotypes and myths and challenge prejudices. Explain that it isn't unusual for teens to wonder about sexual feelings, some directed toward people of the same gender. Intense friendships with people of the same gender are also common.

If any group members are openly GLBT, you may want to invite them to talk about what that has meant for them socially. However, be sure to ask them ahead of time if this is okay. Just because they are "out" doesn't mean that they want to be singled out to talk about sexual orientation, and they also may be out to only close friends. Encourage the group to think of same-gender relationships in terms of affection, support, conversation, shared interests, and respect—not just in terms of sexual activity. Most of the questions in this session relate to any type of close, caring relationship, not just to heterosexual relationships.

Objectives

- Gifted teens learn about each others' attitudes about romantic relationships.
- They explore their attitudes about relationships in a supportive environment.

Suggestions

1. Ask if gifted kids are any different from others in the age they begin to date, type of relationship, and what they look for in a relationship. Then ask the following:

   ~ What warnings do your parents give about dating?
   ~ If you have had a dating relationship, how old were you when it began? If not, at what age do you think you might begin to go out?
   ~ How much do you think about being in a romantic relationship?

2. To generate discussion about teen relationship basics, ask the following questions, acknowledging that some students have other priorities at this time in their lives and that discussion can be helpful regardless of dating experiences or interests.

   ~ What are some of your family's rules about going out, if any?
   ~ How many of your friends are going out with someone? How much do your friends do things together as a group? Do group activities involve boys and girls?
   ~ When two people are going out, who pays for movies, food, and concert tickets?
   ~ If one person pays for everything on a date, what (if anything) is expected of the other person?
   ~ What are some guidelines about showing affection?
   ~ Should boys open doors for girls? How should girls respond if boys do that?
   ~ Do all girls appreciate gifts and flowers? Do boys?
   ~ Who should decide where to go and what to do when going out regularly?
   ~ Who should make the first move by asking the other person out? What should the person say?
   ~ If the person who is asked doesn't want to accept, how should she or he say that?
   ~ When should a relationship be ended? *How* should relationships be ended?

3. Explain that the next few questions are for those who are going out (or have gone out) with someone regularly. Alternate between present and past tense to include past relationships:

   ~ How have your parents reacted to the person you are going out with?
   ~ How does their attitude—whether positive or negative—affect the relationship?
   ~ What are some relationship issues the two of you have talked about—or should?
   ~ How well do you talk together about how each of you feels about the other's behavior?
   ~ How able are you to assert your wishes?
   ~ How has your assertiveness (or lack of) affected the relationship in the short and/or long term?

4. One researcher found that girls who were average-ability achievers had more equal, healthy, and less toxic relationships with boys than average-ability girls who were underachievers. Ask students whether they think the same is true of gifted achievers and underachievers. In general, are gifted teens' relationships more, or less, mature or serious than those of other students the same age?

5. For closure, ask how it felt to discuss romantic relationships. Wait for responses. Thank the group for teaching you about their social world.

FOCUS | Relationships

Sexual Harassment

Background

Raising awareness about sexual harassment over the past several years has highlighted appropriate versus inappropriate behaviors in school, in the workplace, and in other environments and situations. The media continue to "teach" how to be male and female, significant adults may model gender behaviors that are inappropriate or simply do not fit well in the current world, and the general liberation of both genders causes many to feel unsure about what is proper and expected in institutions, including in schools. Teens must sort out many messages about how to behave.

Important

If this session takes place in a school or organizational setting, it is important for you to familiarize yourself in advance with the school's or organization's policies and procedures regarding sexual harassment. For example, if someone in your group describes a specific incident of sexual harassment, you will want to know about policies and procedures for reporting and follow-up.

Objectives

- Gifted teens learn about gender differences in communication styles.
- They consider the importance of mutual respect between the genders.
- They consider some possible meanings, intentions, and effects of sexual harassment.

Suggestions

1. Introduce the topic with material from the background information and from Internet or other news stories about sexual harassment. Acknowledge that what we hear about behavior and expectations is often confusing.

2. Explore the idea of sexual harassment by asking these questions:

   ~ What does *sexual harassment* mean? (The key is that it is unwelcome and inappropriate, whether it takes the form of sexual advances, requests for sexual favors, teasing, or other behaviors that are sexual in nature. Sexual behavior that is welcome and appropriate is not harassment. Harassment does not have to be physical, dramatic, or threatening. Whether or not it is frequent, and even if it is only semi-uncomfortable, harassment may lead to general, long-term anxiety in contexts like the environment where it occurred. The harasser is often in a power position. Targets can be male or female. Male victims may feel they have less recourse than female victims do. Sexual orientation, perceived or actual, may also be the focus of sexual harassers.)

~ What kinds of comments and behaviors (by either gender) are you uncomfortable with? What are some possible reasons for comments and behaviors like those? (Examples: Power and control, displaced/misplaced anger, modeling, ignorance, insensitivity.)

~ Where do we learn how to behave toward men? toward women? (Parents are probably every person's first role models. Other significant relatives, peers, and the media instruct as well. Emphasize that we can *un*learn those lessons by becoming sensitive to how our behavior affects others and by practicing new behavior.)

~ Have you ever felt sexually harassed? (Point out that sexual harassment does not have to be by someone of the other gender. You might even ask the boys in your group what they would do if a male coworker made inappropriate sexual comments to them or brushed up against them suggestively during breaks.) Describe the experience. What were your feelings? (Respect and reflect feelings and comments related to this question—for example, "That sounds very uncomfortable" or "I can see how that would be embarrassing" or "I'm glad you recognized that those comments were inappropriate" or "I'm glad you trusted us enough to tell us about this.")

Emphasize that feelings can be strong, even if the harassment is subtle. People who are harassed often blame themselves; fear further harassment if they complain; wonder what the behavior means; feel powerless, embarrassed, or trapped; and feel less free to be themselves. Point out that harassing behaviors are practiced when young. Now is the time to be aware of and change them. The key to successful relationships is respect, not power and control. Just as with bullying, repetition isn't essential for significant effects. A single incident can be traumatic to a sensitive, gifted individual—or to anyone else.

3. For closure, ask students to comment on the discussion. How did they feel? What new thoughts and/or insights did they have? You might also summarize the concerns about sexual harassment you have heard in the group.

FOCUS Relationships

Sexual Behavior

Background

Teens think about relationships and sexual behavior a lot. Gifted teens are probably "normal" in this regard. Adults may underestimate this preoccupation—particularly with high-achieving, high-performing teens, who may be viewed mostly one-dimensionally. An entire year of discussion with a broad population of gifted teens probably could be devoted to just relationships and sexuality. Teens in general and gifted teens in particular, even those who are sexually active, aren't necessarily well informed about sexuality and sexual behavior. This session offers gifted teens a chance to begin exploring the topic of sexual behavior in a safe, supportive group setting. Highly able though they are, they may have very few opportunities to discuss this topic.

Important

Even if you are a professional counselor, you may want to invite an outside psychologist or therapist/counselor who relates well to adolescents to attend this session, perhaps responding to questions the students have written anonymously at the end of the last session. If you do not invite a speaker, use the students' written questions as discussion-starters yourself. (Students might also write their questions during this session for use during your next meeting.) Encourage them to pose questions related to sexuality that they have often wondered about and would like to discuss in a supportive environment where there are no "dumb" questions.

If you are facilitating the discussion yourself, whatever the questions are, check out what the group knows *before* adding information or commenting. Assess maturity level carefully when deciding which resources or suggestions to use—and whether to use this session.

Objectives

- Gifted teens ask questions about and discuss sexual behavior in a safe setting.
- They discover that they are not the only teens with questions about sexual behavior.
- They consider alternatives to being sexually active.

Suggestions

1. Introduce the session with reference to the background information. Then ask this general question: "Do you remember something you once heard about sex that you now know isn't correct?"

2. Hand out "Sexual Behavior" (page 154) and ask the students to fill out the questionnaire with brief responses, anonymously. They can respond to whichever items they choose, being as honest as they want to be. Use the questionnaire to generate discussion. If the group seems shy or inhibited, poll them on several of the questions, and then discuss the results.

Question #10 on the handout addresses sexual activity and offers an opportunity for extended discussion. Offer these as possible nonphysical motivators, if they aren't mentioned:

curiosity; to discover more about the self through a new experience
to feel "adult"
to combat loneliness or a sense of not belonging
to rebel, to escape problems
to express low self-esteem, to self-punish
media messages
peer pressure

3. Question #11 might generate discussion. Choose from among these additional questions:

~ How much bragging about sexual activity occurs in your peer group?
~ How much sexual activity do you think is really going on in your peer group?
~ Might those who are *not* sexually active believe most others are? Might those who *are* active want to believe that most others are?
~ Without naming any names, how do you feel about peers who are sexually active?
~ How much is "safe sex" discussed in your peer group and in dating relationships?
~ How much safe or unsafe sex do you think there is in your peer group? (You might offer the information that oral sex carries risk for sexually transmissible infections—STIs.)
~ In your opinion, is there a trend toward abstinence today in young adults? If so, what might be contributing to that trend? If not, why not?
~ What words describe your and your peers' feelings *about* sexual activity. (Examples: *Confused, intrigued, apprehensive.*) How much do you think young partners discuss those feelings with each other? How much should they? (You might suggest that such communication is good preparation for communication in marriage and other relationships. It might also contribute to delaying sexual activity and to considering other options.) Why is it important for couples to discuss sexual feelings and behavior? (Possibilities: Because of risks; to be sensitive to each other; to communicate needs; to set boundaries.)
~ What sexually transmissible infections (STIs) are you aware of? (Be prepared with information about these and other concerns among teens. Your group may be aware of only one or two.)

4. Question #12 deserves emphasis. Ask for responses, summarize collective responses, and perhaps ask for comments about high-risk socializing in high school and college, alcohol as an excuse for sexual behavior, and personal responsibility for sexual behavior. Note that gifted individuals might use intelligence and persuasion to manipulate someone into having sex. Compliant, sensitive gifted teens might also be unable to set a boundary when being manipulated.

5. Ask, "When you think of a creative dating experience—as one couple or with several couples in a group, with activities that are both fun and helpful for getting better acquainted—what comes to mind?" (Encourage the group to think beyond alcohol/drugs and sex.)

6. Bring up the topic of mixed messages—verbal and nonverbal:

   ~ Do girls sometimes send boys mixed messages about their sexual interests—so that boys are confused about what behavior is wanted or appropriate? Give an example.
   ~ Do boys also send mixed messages—so that girls feel confused? Give an example.

7. For closure, summarize what you have heard in the discussion. Emphasize that sexual behavior involves choices. Even if they have been sexually active, they can choose to change. Then ask the group how they felt during the discussion—comfortable/uncomfortable, amazed at the openness, relieved, fascinated, embarrassed? Collect and dispose of the questionnaires.

Sexual Behavior

1. Do you feel well-informed about sex? Yes ❑ No ❑ Where have you gotten most of your information? _____ If you had a question about sex, whom would you ask? _____
_____

2. What are some ways to express love, affection, and caring with a partner—besides having sex? _____
_____

3. What would you do if your date was insisting on oral sex and/or sexual intercourse, and you did not feel ready for it (in general or in that relationship)?
_____

4. Do you worry a lot about sexual issues? Yes ❑ No ❑

5. Do you worry about HIV/AIDS and other sexually transmissible infections? Yes ❑ No ❑

6. What do you think about *not* having sexual intercourse or oral sex before marriage?
_____

7. Why might someone want to wait—even if in a serious relationship?
_____

8. What is the potential harm (to either gender) in having sexual intercourse at an early age?
_____

   Outside of a committed and mature relationship? _____
_____

9. When is a person psychologically ready for sexual intercourse? _____
_____

10. What are some of the reasons someone your age might be sexually active—besides sexual drive? _____
_____

11. What percentage of boys in your class do you believe are sexually active? _____
What percentage of girls? _____

12. Why should people be concerned about alcohol or other drug use in regard to sexual behavior? _____
_____

FOCUS Relationships

Sexual Aggression

Background

Date and acquaintance rape is a serious social problem. Media attention to this kind of sexual aggression (as opposed to rape by stereotypical strangers) is increasing, and many health centers now display brochures about it. No one knows how prevalent it is, but surveys and clinical histories indicate that it is not uncommon.

All girls and women are vulnerable to sexual aggression. Intelligent, compliant females may be especially vulnerable. The "good girl" self-concept may prevent a young woman from leaving, asserting herself, struggling, screaming, and seeking help after the fact. Most sexual attacks during middle school, high school, and college are made by someone the victim knows. Even though most victims blame themselves for being naive and too trusting, drinking, or not being able to control the situation, a lapse of discretion or safety precautions never justifies a rape. (Keep in mind that boys and men can be victims of sexual aggression as well. Whether the aggressor is female or male, the experience can be traumatic, with long-lasting effects.)

Social upbringing often does not prepare teens for sexual aggression (perhaps especially among those who fit the gifted-student stereotypes), and it often does not provide survival skills. Not just school-age teens, but also new college students and young adults in the working world, eager to make friends, need to be alert and wise. Assess the maturity level of your group carefully when considering whether to use this session, but beware of underestimating the vulnerability of even middle school students to sexual aggression. Expect a wide range of interest and readiness if your group is composed of young teens.

Important

If you are not a counselor, check with (depending on venue) your program director or school counselor about how to report a rape or assault, since someone might reveal an experience during the discussion (see pages 13–14 in the introduction) or tell you afterward (more likely) about a date/acquaintance rape or attempted rape. Whether or not you are a counselor, be clear at the outset of the session what you are mandated to report (for example, sexual abuse, statutory rape, neglect, and suicidal or homicidal thoughts). Then be prepared to listen attentively and compassionately. It is probably difficult for the individual to talk about the experience, and it is appropriate to commend the teen's courage in speaking of it. Remind the group, if they have been trusted with important, sensitive personal information, that you expect them to respect the privacy of the teller. However, it is unlikely that anyone will reveal a rape in the group.

Objectives

- Both boys and girls consider the phenomenon of date/acquaintance rape.
- Through discussing realistic situations, gifted teens become less vulnerable to date/acquaintance rape, and potential aggressors become more informed, self-aware, and empathic.

Suggestions

1. Introduce the topic with reference to the background information. Some group members may feel uncomfortable speaking about it, but most will discuss expectations, vulnerabilities, responsibilities, pressures, and socialization about gender behavior. Note that probably all parents worry that their children will find themselves in situations they can't handle—involving sexual aggression, for example. Encourage the group to be discreet in answering these questions.

   ~ Does anyone have the right to insist on intercourse or oral sex under any circumstances?
   ~ How prevalent is date or acquaintance rape in your age group, in your opinion?
   ~ Have you ever been in a situation where sexual aggression caught you off guard?
   ~ What do you know about the effects of date rape?
   ~ What are some strategies for dealing with sexual aggression?
   ~ What can contribute to date/acquaintance rape? (Possibilities: Alcohol, dress, being alone, intimidation, flirting, attitudes in both boys and girls.)
   ~ We usually think of girls and women as the victims here. What might contribute to boys and men being victims of sexual aggression—and in what situations?

2. Brainstorm and list differences among consensual, manipulated, coerced, and forced sex on a wallboard, or provide a handout with the four terms on it. Group members might suggest the following:

   ~ Consensual sex probably involves smiles, closeness, affection, mutuality, comfort, and verbal and nonverbal communication.
   ~ Manipulated sex might involve music, alcohol or other drugs, planning and expectations, playing to vulnerabilities, concern for the other person and self, and "consensual" aspects.
   ~ Coerced sex probably involves power and strength, guilt, threats, debt, and discomfort, and might involve alcohol and other drugs and lies.
   ~ Forced sex probably involves fear, fighting, physical touching unlike with consensual sex, aggression, threats, submission to survive (not consensual), and possibly momentary paralysis of movement. (Psychologically coerced or physically forced sex is illegal.)

3. Emphasize that individuals can minimize their vulnerability. Have the group make a list of recommendations. Suggest the following if they are not mentioned:

   ~ Think through the limits you want to set on sexual behavior prior to going out.
   ~ Express feelings honestly and communicate assertively and with certainty.

~ Pay attention to what you wear (even though dress should never excuse a rapist) and make sure that your verbal and nonverbal messages agree—and that they agree with your intent.

~ Don't leave a friend alone in a situation where he or she is vulnerable.

~ Don't give in to pressure to have sexual intercourse or oral sex or give it to return a favor.

4. Create some scenarios for the group to discuss and problem-solve, or hand out "Problem Scenarios" (pages 158–159). Discuss what makes the person vulnerable in each situation. The last three involve males, two as a potential victim and one as the aggressor. Your group might want to discuss more situations where males feel uncomfortable about sexual activity or are in situations where they perceive that intercourse or oral sex is expected.

For Scenario A, encourage the group to address the issue of the young woman's wish to talk at the point when she learns that the young man's parents are gone for the weekend. For Scenario B, pay attention to the vulnerability of the girls. Scenario D was written with a female in mind, but if someone mentions that the victim could be male, explore that possibility. The scenarios that describe situations on college campuses are included here because it is likely that gifted teens will attend college, and also because of the particular vulnerability of students who enter college unaccustomed to sexual aggression and, possibly, to drinking. The scenarios may be appropriate even for a group with young teens, depending on who is in the group, since your group members will soon be older and vulnerable.

5. For closure, tell the group what you have heard them say, or have one or two of them summarize the discussion. Compliment them for handling the discussion well or for articulating difficult matters, if appropriate. Emphasize that if they are ever raped or are otherwise sexually assaulted, they should seek help immediately, make a report, be examined, and be counseled. Counseling will be important, since feelings related to self-worth, sexuality, and relationships undoubtedly will be affected. Many who are raped do not report the attack because they blame themselves. Remind the group that loss of control *never* justifies one person forcing sex on another. In addition, warn them about making false accusations.

Problem Scenarios

A. You are a female high school junior and have been going out with someone from another school casually for a few weeks. You do not feel committed to the relationship and have strong reservations about having sex with him. You enjoy talking with him. In fact, he is the first person you have dated who is intelligent and talented and interesting to talk with. You look forward to the conversations. After a movie and pizza, which he paid for, he asks if you would like to see where he lives with his parents. You arrive at his home, he asks if you would like some wine, you say yes, and then he tells you that his parents are gone for the weekend.

B. You are an eighth-grade girl and attend a dance in a nearby town with your older sister, who drove. A cute guy, apparently in his early twenties, dances with you, and you enjoy flirting and dancing with him for most of the night. You would like to go out with him again. He asks if he can take you home. You see that your sister is also quite occupied with someone. You get her attention, wave good-bye, and leave with him.

C. You are at a party with your friends. There is alcohol, and everyone is drinking. Some are dancing, some are disappearing, and you are beginning to feel a bit drunk. You are dancing with someone you've been casually involved with for a week or two.

D. You were raped by an acquaintance three nights ago after a party. You are uneasy about telling even your best friend, since you feel that you shouldn't have let yourself be vulnerable, and you know that the acquaintance has a great amount of credibility. You are very upset, feel violated and depressed, are shaky, and haven't slept much since then.

E. You are an attractive, high-achieving college freshman woman and are attending a dance sponsored by your sorority and a fraternity. It is your first college dance. You are not naive about sexual behavior (in fact, you and your former boyfriend were sexually active during your senior year), but you are uneasy about what you have heard are the sexual expectations of this particular fraternity. You are getting a lot of attention from one of the fraternity men.

F. You have never considered yourself to be a physically attractive woman. In fact, you are quite self-conscious. Your strengths are, you feel, your intellect and your ability to read others well, to be nice to everyone, and not to be confrontational and demanding. You were surprised when you were invited to join a university sorority of the "beautiful ones." One night, your sorority has a party. A good-looking, fairly smooth guy asks you to dance. You are flattered when he dances with you for the next four dances, even though you wonder if someone has dared him to, and he seems overly complimentary. He radiates confidence and sexuality. The dance is nearly over, and he's asking to take you to his friend's apartment, where some of his friends "probably are."

(continued)

Problem Scenarios (continued)

G. You are a female commuter college student and need to make a phone call, but your cell phone battery is dead. You know several people in a coed dormitory and decide to stop to call there. In the lobby, you see a guy you've met in a class, and you tell him about your need to call. He invites you to use the phone in his room.

H. You have not dated much. You're a conscientious, fairly quiet guy who doesn't feel comfortable at parties and is shy around girls. An aggressive, sexually experienced girl asks you to dance at the first party you have attended all year. She seems to have taken on the responsibility of instructing you in sexual behavior. You and she are now in the back of her friend's pickup truck. You feel quite uncomfortable about the way things are going, but you are aroused and feel unable to leave the situation. You are very concerned about what she might think of you—no matter what you might say right now.

I. You are a sexually experienced young man. A beautiful woman your age has accepted an invitation to come to your apartment for a drink after a party. You know that she is not inexperienced sexually, because you know others who have dated her. She has been flirting with you quite obviously. The two of you have been kissing on the sofa, but she has said she wants to go home now, and when you persist with more physical aggression, she begins to cry.

J. You are a respected college sophomore male, known for your athletic achievements. You have been in a relationship with a female classmate. You are quite sure you have never behaved improperly with her. She was very upset when you quietly told her last night that you wanted to break up. Today you heard she is claiming that you raped her. She might even press charges.

FOCUS Relationships

Violence in Relationships

Background

The topic of abusive relationships can be approached with statistical information (available on the Internet), in the context of a changing society, as a response to media violence, as connected to adult modeling of violence, or as a power and control issue, among many possibilities. Abusive relationships occur at all levels of society, in all age groups, and at all ability and education levels and are perpetuated from one generation to the next. Both genders learn how to treat a partner and what to expect from a partner through the media and by observing adults. People may stay in abusive situations because they learned young to accept abuse. Unfortunately, many in such relationships, including teens, do not feel they can do anything to help themselves. They fear what the abuser might do if they leave; they worry about the abuser's well-being if they leave; or they are afraid of being without a relationship. They believe they have no choice but to stay. The abuser's behavior likely has damaged their self-esteem.

Actually, changes in the response to abuse and in beliefs about the self can sometimes, in fact, provoke positive changes in the abuser, depending on the kind of abuse and the depth of the pattern. Abusers, too, can take steps to change patterns of response to stressful situations and beliefs about themselves and others. Raised awareness through discussion may encourage a young abuser or abused individual to seek help. Individual or couple counseling can help a couple take stock of a relationship, examine abusive sequences, empower the abused, and dissolve a relationship when appropriate. Teens need to be made aware that marriage does not cure an abusive dating relationship. Unless changes are made, the abuse will continue.

Important

This session encourages a realistic look at abusive relationships that may help to prevent them or give teens courage to leave them. Although you should be prepared that group members may share experiences with past or current abuse, eliciting that kind of information is not the intent here. There can be great value in this session without self-revelation by anyone. However, some individuals may seek you out individually. Be aware of laws regarding reporting by someone in your position before addressing this issue, inform the group at the outset about limits of confidentiality in that regard, and be clear about the purpose of your group. If sensitive information is shared, discreetly or indiscreetly, immediately remind the group about confidentiality and trust.

You might bring in a speaker from a domestic-violence shelter or a mental health agency. If you will be providing information as a school counselor, find out what your community offers in counseling resources related to relationship abuse and protective services. You should have an up-to-date list available for anyone who asks about resources for self, mother, father, other relative, or friend. If you are in a school and are not a counselor, channel requests and concerns to the school counselor. If your groups are in a summer or other program, know program protocols related to reporting abuse and assault.

Objectives

- Gifted teens learn that abuse can occur in relationships at all levels of society, in all age groups, and at all ability and educational levels.
- They learn that patterns of abuse can become firmly established, that stopping them requires courage and effort, and that leaving the relationship may be the best option.
- They consider that abusive teen relationships are related to abusive adult relationships.

Suggestions

1. If you have arranged for a speaker, open the session by inviting him or her to present information about abusive relationships and helpful suggestions for avoiding or stopping them. The focus might be on patterns that develop in teen relationships or on factors that contribute to violent and abusive behavior and to vulnerability to abuse. Other possibilities are the cycle of violence, options for support, therapeutic approaches, and pertinent laws.

2. In addition to, or in place of, a speaker's presentation or your information, the group can respond to the following statements. You might put the statements on separate pieces of paper and have group members read them in turn. Ask them whether the statements are believable.

   ~ Abuse is about dominance, power, and control.
   ~ Abuse can happen at all levels of society, even among people with advanced degrees, wealth, and status, and at all ages, including among young children.
   ~ Relationships during middle school and high school can be abusive.
   ~ Abuse can be physical, verbal, emotional, and/or sexual. The abused person can be either male or female. Females are more likely to abuse verbally than physically, but are capable of physical abuse. Verbal and emotional abuse may be harder to stop than physical abuse.
   ~ People who are abused may believe that they are responsible for the abuser's behavior and that *they* are the ones who need to be better. Abusers sense that and take advantage of it.
   ~ People who are abused may believe they don't deserve respect.
   ~ People who are abused fear "rocking the boat."
   ~ People who are abused often do not believe they have options.

- Both abusers and abused may be afraid of their emotions and deny, "stuff," or numb them. Strong emotions may be perceived as too scary to feel and deal with.
- People who are abused may fear their abusers so much that they are reluctant to request or force changes.
- Abusers and abused both may fear rejection. That fear may increase the danger of abuse if the abused leaves or threatens to leave the relationship.
- People who are abused might keep picking abusive partners because they confuse love with abuse—perhaps because that was the "love" that was modeled at home.
- Men and women are often attracted to the pattern of experiences they grew up with. If their experiences contributed to solid self-esteem, and if they experienced and witnessed healthy relationships, they will probably be attracted in a healthy way to others. The pattern they grew up with is *familiar*.
- People who were abused in the past have the potential to become abused *or* abusive. Suffering abuse early in life can be seen by a victim as proof of his or her low worth as a person. Abuse can lead to abusing in order to play out or undo what was experienced as a child.
- Teens may be in toxic relationships that, although they look more mature than their peers' relationships, are really unequal and unhealthy.
- The pain and emptiness of abusive relationships leaves people vulnerable to addictions (often referred to as self-medication), because the emptiness wants to be filled by something. Self-injury (such as cutting, burning, or rubbing) may be connected to present or past abuse, but not necessarily.
- Victim and abuser behaviors are learned behaviors, not innate, and can be changed with effort and assistance.
- Counselors can help victims and abusers heal and make positive changes.

3. Ask the group how they would know if they were in an abusive relationship. (Possibilities: Being hit, shoved, or slapped; being constantly or frequently criticized; feeling controlled; being physically or psychologically coerced to have sex or to behave in other ways that are contrary to personal values.)

   Brainstorm options for avoiding and stopping abuse. Emphasize that everyone is worthy of respect and kindness in relationships, and no one "makes" an abuser abusive. Inform them that there are effective groups to help abusive partners change.

4. For closure, summarize the discussion (and thank any invited speaker) and commend the group for their attentiveness and comments. Emphasize again that they do not deserve abuse in *any* situation and that abusive behavior is *never* appropriate or justified.

FOCUS Relationships

Marriage and Partnership

Background

Some gifted teens may have a happily-ever-after view of marriage, expecting to find a perfect partner, who will fulfill all dreams. Others have doubts about marriage and/or committed relationships. Perhaps they have seen sadness and distress in their parents'/caretakers' relationship, the impact of divorce or spousal abuse, or the tensions of employment brought home. They are probably aware of the challenges of raising children. They might even wonder if they will, can, or should marry. Gifted teens are usually quite concerned about the future. Because they observe a lot and think a lot, they feel a lot. They give future relationships and responsibilities a great deal of anxious thought because they are able to consider and anticipate the complexities of the future, including marriage.

This session offers gifted teens, perhaps representing a variety of cultures and religious beliefs, a chance to sort out the real, the ideal, and the feared. Open exchange can contribute not only to affirmation of diversity, but also to an appreciation of cultural support for marriage and family.

Objectives

- Gifted teens articulate their attitudes and thoughts about long-term relationships and marriage.
- They consider the impact of the media on their expectations about marriage.
- They consider the impact of their own experiences on their attitudes and concerns about marriage and partnership.

Suggestions

1. Invite the group to define *marriage* and then *partnership*. Expect that some might mention lesbian and gay relationships, and some might feel that commitment without official sanction constitutes a marriage. The focus should be on their expression of thoughts, not on your presenting information. If only a few are expressing opinions, invite those who are quiet to share their thoughts (for example, "I'm guessing that more of you have thoughts on this and may even not agree with what has been said. What are you thinking?"). Then expand the discussion:

   ~ What makes a marriage?
   ~ Is there a difference between "marriage" and "just living together"? (Expect that this question might provoke disagreement. Consider the theme of #4.)

~ What might be gained by living *alone* before marriage? (Possibilities: Developing a sense of self, management skills, competence, and independence—to help to avoid an unhealthy level of dependence in marriage/partnership later.)

2. Steer the discussion toward the students' feelings about marriage and other committed relationships.

~ What qualities will you expect in a spouse/partner?
~ What anxieties do you have about marriage?
~ Are you optimistic or pessimistic about being able to sustain a long-term relationship?
~ What experiences have affected your views of such a relationship?

3. Ask the group what makes it difficult to sustain long-term relationships in the current world. They might mention some of the following factors in society. If not, add them.

~ dual-career couples, with more daily contact with other adults for both spouses than in the past
~ economic self-sufficiency for some women and the option of leaving an unhappy marriage
~ less stigma associated with divorce than previously
~ unrealistic expectations of marriage/partnerships
~ lack of commitment to relationships
~ poor skills in conflict resolution (and no role modeling of it)
~ geographic mobility, with no extended family or long-term friends for support
~ high stress and poor coping skills
~ money problems; inability to manage finances
~ partners growing and changing in different ways and at different speeds
~ longer life spans, with marriages tested over a longer period
~ overcommitment to work and community, with resulting physical and emotional exhaustion, making couple's contact minimal and/or strained
~ men and women being socialized in ways that don't encourage expression of feelings
~ women and men expecting their needs to be met without verbalizing them
~ the distractions and commitment involved in raising children
~ the fact that both partners bring psychological "baggage" into the relationship
~ couples not seeking counseling from an objective professional early enough in the relationship

4. Discuss commitment. As always, the emphasis is on discussion of development, with listening and responding skills the primary goals—in addition to becoming informed and making connections. Use some of the following questions to extend the discussion:

~ What does *commitment* mean?
~ What are your thoughts about commitment in regard to marriage versus living together without marrying?

~ How much is commitment role modeled today? Is there a couple you know or can think of who seem like a good model of commitment?

~ What are your thoughts about how commitment is related to working through problems?

~ Have you seen successful relationships with a lot of give-and-take, ups and downs?

~ What are your thoughts about the notion that society does a better job of training people to compete than to cooperate? (NOTE: Some nonmainstream cultures have a cooperative, collaborative value-orientation, different from the mainstream culture's competitive, individualistic orientation.)

~ How much do you agree or disagree with this general statement: People are trained by families and society to blame others when they have problems.

5. Focus on what kinds of images the various media present about marriage. Ask these questions:

~ What are some images of marriage in daytime TV? Disney movies? Fairy tales? TV sitcoms? Romance novels? Popular movies? Magazines? Among celebrities?

~ How do these images affect a young person's expectations of marriage?

~ How do they affect attitudes about commitment and ability to sustain a relationship?

~ How can a couple contemplating marriage prepare for the everyday, the inconvenient, the realities of making a living, and the need to compromise?

~ What should a person expect from the marriage relationship or partnership? From the spouse/partner?

~ Where can couples find balance and support that does not threaten the relationship, yet lightens the burden of needing to "be everything" to each other? (Examples: Friends, family, activities, work.)

6. Focus on expectations by asking for comments on the following statements:

~ Some teens believe that all of their needs will be taken care of in marriage.

~ Such expectations can put unreasonable pressure on a spouse to "be everything."

~ Friends, extended family, and colleagues can all "be something" for a person who is married.

7. For closure, thank the group for sharing their feelings and insights. Ask how it felt to discuss marriage/partnership. Ask someone to assess group consensus about this topic.

Relationships

Tolerance, Compassion, and Altruism

Background

Because many gifted individuals are sensitive to social justice, they may be distressed by what they see and hear related to negative cultural stereotyping and harassment. Even at young ages, gifted children may lie awake at night, sad and concerned about how classmates are treated and about news reports of intercultural conflicts. Gifted teens may be hateful and bigoted themselves, of course. Depending on parental and other models and information received, they might even be negative leaders, passionately fueling racial and cultural conflict in school or community.

In a pluralistic nation, tolerance and compassion are critical for smooth and mutually satisfying relationships among diverse groups. How can we encourage these qualities in young people so that they will not participate in gay-bashing, racial bigotry, hate groups, immigrant harassment, and rigidity about who deserves fair and respectful treatment? Discussion groups can raise awareness about the importance of promoting interpersonal and intercultural sensitivity.

Within the context of a caring, concerned group, questions can provoke examination of important feelings related to living in a complex, constantly changing world. Scholars have associated giftedness with altruism, particularly as related to translating sensitivity to injustices into selfless action. Altruistic gifted teens have the potential for leadership in working toward interracial and intercultural harmony and respect for the rights of all citizens. Talking with intellectual peers about pertinent issues may serve as inspiration toward this end.

Objectives

- Gifted teens consider the importance of tolerance and compassion in human relations.
- They consider ways to develop these qualities in themselves and others.
- They consider the concept of altruism.

Important

Part of this session involves a discussion of hate groups. Be prepared to present basic information about such groups—what they believe, what motivates them, who belongs to them, and so on. If possible, bring in some current or recent articles about domestic or foreign hate groups or racial/ethnic bigotry or conflict from newspapers and magazines. Group facilitators must always beware of taking advantage of a vulnerable captive audience by imposing political beliefs. Therefore, choose articles and other materials carefully, and be confident that raising awareness of cultural, religious, and political conflict in the United States and abroad is important. However, since the focus of this session is on group members' feelings and attitudes, it is important not to get sidetracked into loud political or religious debate. It is important that "gentle comments" also be heard.

Suggestions

1. Ask the group to define the terms *tolerance* and *compassion*. If necessary, offer brief definitions. (Examples for *tolerance*: "live and let live," "respecting individual differences," "not trying to change or hurt someone whose ideas and lifestyle are not the same as mine, even if I don't approve"; examples for *compassion*: "empathy," "understanding," "trying to understand someone without judging.") I use the term *tolerance* in this discussion because of its widespread use in our society. However, I prefer the term *affirmation* rather than *tolerance*, and you might choose to discuss the difference between these terms with your group. For instance, the word *tolerance* might suggest a begrudging acceptance, as in "barely tolerable." The word *affirmation* suggests a more positive, proactive attitude.

2. Invite students to give examples of tolerance and compassion from the "real world"—what they have seen or experienced at school, in their families, at work, or in the community.

3. Generate discussion about tolerance by asking questions such as the following:

   ~ On a scale of 1 to 10, with 10 being "great," what is the level of tolerance for "difference" in your school? in your community?
   ~ How much do you hear people, including other students and family members, speaking negatively about those who are different from the majority? What are some of the reasons they give for their views?
   ~ Do you see our society as becoming more tolerant or less tolerant? Give examples.
   ~ Do you have any fears or anxieties about how various cultures in our country, or in the world, are getting along lately? If so, what kinds of concerns?

4. Turn the discussion to the topic of hate groups. Begin by presenting some of the information you prepared ahead of time. You might mention economic factors, fears, hate, anger, abuse, demagoguery, vulnerable minority populations, power differences (socioeconomic), misinformation, and religious and political trends. Then ask questions like the following:

   ~ Have you ever seen or read anything about hate groups?
   ~ Why do you think teens might be attracted to hate groups? Gifted teens in particular? (Possibilities: A wish for clarity in a confusing, complex world or because they are uncomfortable with the gray areas between right and wrong.)
   ~ What is the message of hate groups?
   ~ What ethnic or cultural groups are targeted by hate groups today?
   ~ What makes young people especially vulnerable to hate groups' messages?

(Possibilities: Lack of information, media selection, parents' extreme attitudes, feeling powerless.)

~ Why might an ethnic or cultural group be vulnerable to violence in a society?

~ What are some common stereotypes of targeted groups?

5. Invite group members to explore and describe their own feelings regarding tolerance and compassion. Ask questions such as the following:

~ How tolerant and compassionate are you? your family?

~ Are gifted kids different from others in how they view race and ethnicity?

~ How much contact have you had during your life with people of racial and cultural groups other than your own? What kind of contact? How has that contact affected you? How comfortably do you interact with people who are different from you?

~ If a couple of a racial or cultural group different from yours moved next door to you, how would you feel? (If they do live near you, how do you feel about them?) (Some examples of U.S. racial and cultural groups: White, African American, Asian American, Mexican American, Native American, Russian, Guatemalan, Palestinian, Middle Eastern, Kenyan, Iraqi.)

~ If a family who practiced a different religion than yours moved next door, how would you feel? (Some examples of religious groups: Jewish, Mormon, Jehovah's Witness, Pentecostal, Catholic, Presbyterian, Southern Baptist, Lutheran, Hindu, Muslim.)

~ If a gay or lesbian couple moved next door to you, how would you feel?

~ If you or a sibling fell in love with someone from a racial, cultural, or religious group different from yours, how would you or your family react?

~ If you would/do feel uncomfortable with a neighbor whose ethnic or religious background or sexual orientation is different from yours, how would you explain that feeling? If you made your feelings clear, how do you think your neighbor might feel or respond?

~ Have you ever been in a situation where you were in the racial or cultural minority? Are you now? If so, how did/do you feel?

~ Do you think it would be possible for your religion or culture to become the target of a hate group? Why or why not?

~ If a hate group targeted your religion or culture, what would you do? How would you feel?

~ How easily are you drawn into prejudiced conversations and attitudes?

~ What would you say to a member of a hate group who told you that "all immigrants should leave this country because they are taking jobs away from 'real Americans,' ruining the welfare system, and corrupting American values"? Or that "the only people who deserve to live in the United States are whites." (Give these statements careful thought prior to the group meeting. You might ask how many in the group had family who came as immigrants to this country.)

~ What are the potential strengths of a nation made up of many cultures? (Possibilities: Homogeneous populations might have no counterbalance to majority attitudes. Each culture's good values, such as work ethic, volunteerism, and helping the poor, can have a positive influence.)

~ How are tolerance and compassion important to our lives—to your life—today?

6. Ask the group to think about how they can develop tolerance and compassion in themselves and in younger children. Suggest the following if they aren't mentioned: Education, modeling tolerant behaviors, a conscious effort to learn about and get to know people whose backgrounds and beliefs are different. Ask, "What can schools do to help students and teachers develop tolerance and compassion?"

7. For closure, ask if any in the group would like to express feelings about tolerance and compassion. Encourage them to continue educating themselves about pertinent issues.

FOCUS Feelings

FOCUS Feelings

General Background

Giftedness has been associated with high levels of sensitivity and intensity, and gifted teens may therefore have particularly strong feelings and reactions to major and minor life events and developmental transitions. The social climate at school may be competitive and volatile, with relationships continually changing. Rough language may be aimed at gifted teens' behaviors, personality, or talent. They probably feel disappointed and upset when things don't work out as hoped. They experience losses and transitions at home, and they grieve. They say and do things they know they should not, or they feel guilty about their giftedness. They may "replay" uncomfortable conversations and situations endlessly. They experience the rush of romantic love, and they suffer when relationships end. They suffer if their parents' relationship ends, and they experience anxiety as parents remarry and families blend. They perceive that holiday celebrations are not what they used to be. They are no longer children, and their families may have changed. They may long for the past.

Then there are the perplexing mood swings. Minor events may feel like major traumas. Teens do not have the wisdom from experience to know that nothing stays the same—situations change, time heals, and feelings pass. Gifted teens, especially, may believe that no one feels as they do, or could understand, and they are lonely in their distress. If they lose heart, they may flirt with dangerous behaviors and may become seriously involved with alcohol and other drugs. Sometimes they show their feelings, sometimes not.

It's good to talk about feelings. Building expressive vocabulary and the skills of articulating concerns will probably help future relationships—with friends, coworkers, spouses, partners, and children. Learning to identify and accept feelings can help to stay balanced in a complex world. Because gifted teens may not be encouraged to talk about feelings elsewhere, instead focusing largely on academics and talent areas, they might especially appreciate discussions here.

General Objectives

- Gifted teens feel emotions in the present, affirm them, and talk about them.
- They look at past emotions and gain perspective.

FOCUS Feelings

Mood Swings and Mood Range

Background

The sensitivities and intensities of gifted teens may contribute to extra layers of moods, but how teens have been socialized influences whether and how moods are expressed. Other factors may also be at work—protection of a positive image, a need for control, hard-wired temperament, and perhaps even a collective family mode of expressing emotion. This session sets the stage for those that follow in this section. It is helpful to look at mood range. On a scale of 1 to 10, some individuals experience the full range, some a narrow range, some a moderate range, some a range that stays buoyantly above 5, and some a range that never rises above 5. It is interesting for teens to consider their own and each others' fluctuations in morale, especially when mood swings seem to be the norm. Do all people have intense emotions, but only some express them intensely? Do we protect ourselves from "1" feelings by narrowing our mood ranges, thereby precluding "10" feelings as well? These are interesting questions for teens to ponder.

Well-functioning, compassionate parents often want to (and try to) protect their children from feeling bad. But such protection takes away opportunities to develop resilience. Adults' preoccupation with keeping children happy may lead to the children's fearing the "bad." Children need to learn that it is all right to feel bad, that bad feelings are survivable, and that thinking affects feelings. One way to move past them is to feel them and go *through* them. That can include talking about them. Much emotional energy is spent keeping the lid shut tight on uncomfortable emotions. Gifted teens can benefit from hearing about others' mood ranges and expressing concerns about moods, including sadness and depression.

Objectives

- Gifted teens learn that mood swings are common, and vary, in their age group.
- They feel less strange after listening to shared experiences and thoughts about moods.
- They practice positive self-talk as a way to cope with downswings in mood.
- They consider the effect of thoughts on feelings.
- They consider how mood range may affect life and vice versa.

Suggestions

1. Ask the group what they have heard or know about mood swings during adolescence. Depending on what is offered, you might mention aspects of development that may contribute to mood swings:

~ rapid physical growth, other physiological changes, increasing awareness of sexuality
~ concern about romantic relationships
~ changes and conflicts in their social world
~ greater awareness of, and frustration about, family stresses
~ the tug-and-pull of beginning to separate from parents and explore the world
~ the bumpy process of forging identity
~ family style of coping with stress

2. Ask the group for suggestions for coping with mood swings:

~ What do you do that helps you cope with your mood swings—if you have them?
~ How are your parents and/or guardians coping with your mood swings—if you have them?
~ What strategies for dealing with them have they offered (if any)—for them or you?

3. Pass out sheets of paper and ask group members to draw a line representing their moods during the past week, perhaps with moderate ripples, sharp peaks and dips, or consistently high or low lines. Invite the group to display their lines and describe any changes in their moods.

4. Psychologists and counselors keep in mind that thinking (how a person interprets situations) can affect feelings. They may focus on helping clients alter thinking in order to alter or cope with negative and unsettling feelings. Introduce the idea of self-talk as a way to affect thinking and feeling. Invite group members to close their eyes and repeat silently one or two of the following statements. You may want to go around the group first and ask which statement(s) might be most helpful for them—today or on a daily basis. Practicing positive self-talk can help them prepare for future situations.

~ "I have a right to be imperfect."
~ "I have a right to make mistakes."
~ "(She/he/they) (has/have) a right to be imperfect."
~ "I will feel better soon."
~ "I'm really stronger than I feel I am right now. I'll get through this."
~ "I've gotten through times like this before."
~ "I'm still learning."
~ "They said growing up was tough. I'm surviving it."
~ "I need to be (patient, gentle with) (kind to) (understanding, tolerant of) myself."
~ "I'm not alone. Others my age are riding this same roller coaster."
~ "I'm okay."

5. If time is short, go to #8 and delay going further with this focus until a later session.

6. Ask for their present moods on a scale of 1 to 10 (with 10 being "fantastic"). Invite them to comment on what might have contributed to their moods. You might want to spend time discussing some of their situations, but be sure to allow time for each person to report. Even if only five or ten minutes remain when this discussion seems to be winding down, ask questions like these:

~ What is your usual range of moods, perhaps over one week's time? 1–10? 3–7? 5–9?

~ When are you likely to go up or down?

~ How often do you swing up? down?

~ How often do you feel sad or depressed for no apparent reason?

~ How has your mood *range* changed over the past three years, if at all?

7. Invite the group to think about others' mood ranges:

~ How similar are you to other family members in mood range?

~ How similar are you to your friends in mood range?

~ Whose mood range is like yours? Whose is quite different?

~ How do you feel about those people?

~ How much control do you feel you have over your mood range?

8. For closure, ask, "What in the discussion was helpful? surprising?" Dispose of the sheets or file them.

FOCUS Feelings

Sensitivity to Fairness

Background

It is not unusual for teens to indict people and systems as unfair. That makes sense, since they are carefully looking at the adult world as they prepare to enter it—and at adult behaviors, practices, and policies. Gifted teens are likely to have a few extra layers of idealism, sensitivity to social justice, and discernment.

Objectives

- Gifted teens gain skills in articulating feelings about situations that seem unfair.
- They practice seeing fairness issues from more than one perspective.

Suggestions

1. Begin by asking the group to brainstorm things in life that seem grossly unfair. Tell them you want to hear about situations, institutions, or people that provoke intense emotions about unfairness. (Be prepared for anything from school evaluation and corporate and political systems to gender issues, wages for teens, and parental rules. The group might also mention specific actions by adults in their lives, including teachers and school principals.) Then ask these rhetorical questions about their list to provoke thought or generate discussion.

   ~ Are any of these the result of poor *adult* judgment or behavior?
   ~ Are any of these problems somewhat universal across society?
   ~ Are some associated with strict limits or rules?
   ~ Are some unavoidable—that is, "necessary evils"?

2. Change direction with some of these questions. As always, keep the focus on group members and avoid evaluation, moralizing, or "fixing."

   ~ How do you react when things seem unfair? What do you feel?
   ~ What feelings about unfairness cause problems for you? What kinds of problems?
   ~ How and where do you release your frustrations?
   ~ Do you tell anyone how you feel? If so, whom do you tell?
   ~ In general, how long do the feelings about unfairness last?

3. Put unfairness into a somewhat different light with these questions:

   ~ How do you think "unfair" actions by adults might help you move into adulthood? (Possibilities: They give teens something to react against and help them clarify their own values. They give teens a chance to assert themselves and gain confidence.)

~ What is a smart way to deal with perceived unfairness? (Possibilities: Figure out how to get "the system" to work for you. Decide to let it go instead of dwelling on it. Talk with someone about it. Become a political activist. Talk directly to whoever is being unfair.)

4. Most people would probably agree that it is the job of parents to set wise limits for their children and encourage impulse control. Protecting and nurturing means firm and consistent guidance and discipline. Children are owed that. With this in mind, pose some of the following:

~ Can you think of something "unfair" your parents said or did that turned out to be wise?

~ Was there a time when they did something you didn't like that was important to your safety or growth?

~ Can you recall a time when a parent, relative, teacher, or coach made a demand of you that was unfair (and might have been an abuse of power)? How did you respond?

~ Have you ever been given great responsibility as a child—for taking care of the family, making family decisions, being a "parent" to others in the family (including being a parent to a parent), or doing most household chores? If so, how have you handled it? What are your feelings about it? What have you learned through it? (These situations represent an inappropriate family hierarchy, but a teen may perceive accurately that there is little or no choice in having adult responsibilities. Teens may also feel quite mature as a result. Gifted youth, because of their abilities, sometimes have such responsibilities, called "parentification" by scholars.)

~ Would you like *more* rules and limits in your life? (Preface this by saying that some teens do, in fact, wish for more guidance and limits, even those whose bravado or rebellion suggests that guidance and support are not wanted or needed. Invite the group to consider why a gifted teen might want more support and guidance.)

~ What are you owed as adolescents—by teachers, parents, employers? (This is not meant to convince them that they are owed nothing. The adults who are responsible for them *do* owe them care, nurturing, protection, and guidance.)

~ How does it feel to talk about fairness and unfairness? (Possibilities: There is benefit in learning how to put strong feelings into words. Sometimes that is how we find out what we think and feel. Maybe we don't know we feel something is unfair until we apply that word to it—and find that it fits. There are indeed personal and societal injustices that need to be rectified.)

5. For closure, ask someone to summarize the session, or tell the group what you have heard. You might also ask what they thought about during the discussion. Thank them for their helpful sharing, if that is appropriate.

FOCUS Feelings

Disappointed

Background

This session provides another chance for gifted teens to practice articulating thoughts and feelings and to peel off the protective façade that they, like others their age, wear in order to present an image of ease and confidence and hide insecurities. All teens experience disappointment, but sensitivities and intensities related to giftedness may intensify these experiences. In the inherently competitive school environment, some disappointments may be especially deflating. Your group will probably welcome the chance to hear others' stories of coping. Perhaps they will recognize the value of learning to deal with disappointment—and of not having others protect them from it.

Objectives

- Gifted teens articulate experiences of personal disappointment and express their feelings about those experiences.
- They recognize that disappointment is part of life, is instructive, and can build resilience.

Suggestions

1. Begin by asking the group to define *disappointment*. Then ask if they feel they have experienced it a lot, an average amount, not much, or hardly ever.

2. Encourage them to share moments of disappointment in their lives. First, ask them about disappointments in school—at any age, including the present. Then ask if they have had disappointments in friendships or relationships or at home. (An option here is to provide paper and a pencil/marker, direct them to draw a disappointed face, and list at least three disappointments underneath it. You might also construct a questionnaire, based on the questions that follow, or simply use them to guide discussion around the shared experiences.)

   ~ How did you handle the disappointment?
   ~ How did you react? What did you feel?
   ~ How long did it take to move past the disappointment, if indeed you are past it?
   ~ What did you learn about yourself or about coping with negative experiences?
   ~ What advice about disappointment can you offer to others?
   ~ Should someone have protected you from disappointment? (If examples are related to material desires or to academic, social, or not-being-selected situations,

the answer is probably no. However, adult negligence or irresponsibility probably warrants a yes.)

3. If #2 did not already move in this direction, ask the group to think about possible effects of experiencing disappointment. Some might mention negative effects on motivation, self-confidence, faith in people, and trust in relationships, besides feelings of powerlessness and pessimism. However, others might speak of maturity, increased confidence from building resilience, increased drive to succeed, or compassion for others. Ask questions like these:

   ~ When and how have you moved beyond a disappointment? (Perhaps they talked to a good listener/counselor, used positive self-talk, immersed themselves in an activity, or tried again.)
   ~ How much disappointment is normal? Can there be too much? too little?
   ~ What disappointments have you experienced in competitive school situations? What are possible effects of always winning? of always losing?
   ~ What can be gained through overcoming disappointment? (Ask the group to define *resilience*. In psychological terms, it is the ability to recover from and adjust to unfortunate experiences. Ask for examples of resilience that they have observed.)

4. For closure, ask the group what has been thought-provoking during this session. Thank them for sharing, commend them for expressing their feelings well, and wish them a life with just enough disappointments to help them build resilience and develop compassion for others.

FOCUS Feelings

A Sense of Humor

Background

A sense of humor can mean having an eye for the ridiculous, the ability to respond with delight to comical situations, or the ability to laugh at ourselves. Humor can also be a way to cope. From the grimmest childhoods can come nationally known comedians, joke-tellers in the break room at work, and nimble conversational wit. Laughter is helpful and healthful. "Sense of humor" is often listed among characteristics of giftedness, but can probably be found at any ability level.

Use this session simply as a break from heavy topics, or use it to gain a serious perspective on the function of humor. Be guided by your group's needs and abilities. If your group normally has difficulty sustaining dialogue because one or more gifted comedians use humor to avoid serious conversation, you might prod group growth by addressing that humor as a serious topic. It also can be productive to discuss how humor can hurt. Sometimes other people's humor is uncomfortable, and we don't know why. Gifted teens might register uncomfortable moments more intensely than others because of the amount of environmental information they are taking in and responding to. They may also appreciate looking at humor analytically.

Objectives

- Gifted teens appreciate the value and functions of humor in daily life.
- They consider their own sense of humor.
- They consider how humor can be helpful and hurtful.

Suggestions

1. Ask questions like these to begin:

   ~ Who do you know who has a sense of humor you appreciate?
   ~ What do you appreciate about that person's sense of humor?
   ~ How would you rate your sense of humor on a scale of 1 to 10 (with 1 being "nonexistent" and 10 being "terrific")?
   ~ Does your sense of humor show, or is it mostly inside—shown only in chuckles or smiles?
   ~ To what extent are you usually around people who have a good sense of humor?
   ~ What kind of sense of humor are you most attracted to?

2. Back up a bit. Move in these directions:

   ~ What is a sense of humor? (Does it mean joke-telling; making terrible, gross, uncomfortable things seem funny; warmth and sensitivity; repartee; dry wit; practical jokes; satire; irony?)
   ~ Describe your sense of humor.
   ~ Do people develop a sense of humor, or is it natural?

3. Invite the group to consider the function of humor:

   ~ What can humor do for us? How can it help us? (Possibilities: It can help us relieve tension and not take ourselves and others too seriously, and be a balance to seriousness.)
   ~ Can you think of examples where humor (yours or someone else's) has been helpful for you?
   ~ Can you think of examples where humor (yours or someone else's) has been hurtful? offensive? a put-down? critical? a practical joke that caused great discomfort?
   ~ What about the possibility that humor can interfere with, or shut down, conversation? Some people use humor in tense, uncomfortable situations. Can you think of examples of this? Have you ever been frustrated by someone who continued to joke when you needed to be serious? (NOTE: There are times when uncomfortable emotions need to be expressed.)
   ~ What is sarcasm? (Possibilities: Mocking; ironic; meant to unsettle; sending a negative message about something or someone.) Can you think of examples of it, including when you have used it yourself? Can you think of examples when someone has been sarcastic to you?
   ~ What might be some guidelines for telling jokes? (Possibilities: Never use humor to hurt, harm, or create discomfort. Avoid jokes that callously demean any group. Use good taste and be discreet regarding language and content. Be aware that there might be people in the audience with understandable sensitivities related to gender, sexual orientation, culture, age, religion, political affiliation, physical characteristics, disability, ability, socioeconomic status, and occupation.)

4. Ask if anyone has a joke to share. You might also ask the following:

   ~ Is there a particular kind of joke that is popular with your friends lately?
   ~ Do you enjoy hearing jokes? What kinds?
   ~ Do you know any families who banter a lot among themselves, even criticizing with teasing?

5. For closure, ask for a volunteer to summarize the session, or ask what was enjoyable, interesting, thought-provoking, or feelings-provoking. As your closing statement, affirm humor as complex and interesting, and affirm laughter as good for health.

FOCUS Feelings

Angry!

Background

Anger is a powerful emotion. It is full of energy and demands release. It can be expressed in violence, aggression, cruelty, vindictiveness, or sullenness—but also with quiet words or silence. It can be expressed both effectively and ineffectively. It can provide short-term control, but have long-term repercussions. Anger can hurt, and it can be perpetuated. It can also be bottled up and turned into sadness and even physical and emotional problems over time. Angry individuals may be defensive and aggressive. The target of anger may not be the person or situation actually provoking it. Anger can also be directed toward, and find a voice in, political and social action.

Anger can tip people off balance. People can also be discounted when they are angry too often and too intensely. Sometimes anger is not allowed in a family. Many girls and women, and, of course, some boys and men, do not feel permission to express anger. Gifted teens may hide anger, like other strong emotions, afraid to express something so potentially out of control and shameful, in their view. Other sensitive gifted teens may suddenly "explode" with anger, to the surprise of peers, teachers, and parents. Sometimes they do not even recognize anger. It may be expressed in another form—like depression.

Anger can tell us a lot. If we pay attention to it, we can discover what we feel—and even what is contributing to the anger. Some feelings may not be comfortable for us. Perhaps our needs are ignored (by self or others), we feel taken advantage of or taken for granted, we are not assertive enough, we feel "stuck," or we feel that someone is crashing through personal boundaries. When we can identify the parts of anger, we can do something to help ourselves. We can change something—if not the situation itself, then maybe our responses to it. We can ask for help from an objective person outside of the situation. By understanding our behavior, learning to assess feelings accurately, and learning how to express anger in productive ways, we can enhance our relationships with others and feel empowered.

Objectives

- Gifted teens learn to recognize, acknowledge, and articulate feelings of anger.
- They learn that anger simply *is*—not something one chooses or should/shouldn't feel.
- They have a chance to speak about anger-producing situations.
- They learn what they have in common with other gifted teens regarding anger.
- They learn that all feelings are okay, but not all behaviors are.

1. Introduce the topic and ask the group to fill out the "Being Angry" questionnaire (pages 184–185) with brief responses, anonymously. Assure them that they will not be asked to share all of their answers. Invite them to share whatever they are willing to.

   Encourage the group to respond, ask questions, and offer suggestions. You may want them to concentrate on only one of their situations—that is, just *a* or just *b*. If some members prefer not to share either one, they may pass (always an option). The group should not press anyone to share. Some may prefer to name the situation, answer yes or no to the other questions, and not elaborate. Gifted teens in your group should be able to read down all their answers for *a*, for example, transforming them into statements ("It lasted a day," "Yes, it happens often," and so on). Keep the focus on their responses, and avoid responding with, "Yes, but . . ." That kind of response usually invalidates feelings, suggesting that the feelings are "wrong" (for example, "Yes, but wouldn't it be better if you . . . ?"). Since it is a useful skill for anyone, you might even call attention to your avoiding such invalidation (for example, "It would be easy for us to say, 'Yes, but you shouldn't feel hate.' But that would imply that feelings are wrong. Behaviors may be hurtful, but feelings are simply feelings. They just *are*. Our job is to figure out how to express them and respond to them effectively.").

2. Instead of, or in addition to, #1, have them fill in an outline of a human form with colors (perhaps from yellow to red to even black) representing various levels of anger according to where angry feelings are felt in the body (for example, in the head, in the clenched jaw, in the stomach, in the heart, in tense shoulders). Group members can then take turns describing how anger feels and where their bodies reflect anger. Perhaps each can also use a metaphor to describe the feelings (for example, flooded, white-hot, cold). Gifted artists in the group may especially enjoy this activity, but others, too, may find it interesting to consider visceral emotional responses.

3. Another option is to bring children's books that focus on anger, and invite the group to read and critique them regarding whether they can relate to them, whether the books accurately portray anger, and whether it would have been helpful to them to read this book at a younger age.

4. Go around the group and invite each person to finish this sentence: "The time I was most angry in my life was when . . ." Assure them that they have a right to pass, as always.

5. Share some of the background information. Encourage reading about and talking about anger in the future. Make a handout from the following, perhaps with members reading statements in turn, or simply offer the thoughts to generate discussion.

   ~ Anger is energy. As a feeling, it is not bad or immoral. We should pay attention to it. It can tell us what needs to be changed.

   ~ We can channel anger energy constructively into competitiveness in sales and athletics.

~ We can channel anger energy constructively into political action, protests, and social causes.

~ Anger energy can be channeled destructively and hurt people and things.

~ We express anger in many ways—silent withdrawal, moodiness, foul language, insults, criticism, manipulation, tantrums, violence, or heartfelt, rational words.

~ It is possible to be angry with someone we love. It is also easy to transfer anger to those who simply happen to be around—especially at home.

~ It is important to understand why something "pushes our anger button."

~ We can be frightened by our own anger. It threatens our sense of control.

~ Learning how to deal with anger while we're young is important.

~ Women and girls may feel less permission than men and boys in our society to be angry. They may feel sad when anger is more appropriate. Males may feel more permission to be angry than to be sad, and therefore express anger when they feel sad. Like anyone else, gifted teens of both genders may express anger as sadness or sadness as anger.

~ Talking about strong feelings with a good listener is helpful. When we feel heard, we begin to move beyond the feelings. Talking with the target of the feelings is good. An objective third person, such as a counselor, can listen and respond in helpful ways.

6. Ask, "Is there someone you are often angry with? Do you argue a lot or exchange angry words? Do you find yourself saying the same things over and over?" Encourage trying something different next time. For example, instead of defending or attacking, they might respond with, "I hear you. I know you're angry." Point out that changing a pattern (in this case, a communication sequence) is a personally powerful thing to do. When the other person feels heard, he or she might listen in return. Eventually *both* may feel heard, which can help resolve conflict and diminish anger.

7. If time remains, ask, "How did you learn to 'do anger'? Did someone show you how?" (Some in the group may propose that ways to express anger are inherited. Ask them to consider instead that we learn how to "do emotions" by observation and permission. We can also, then, unlearn behaviors and learn and practice more effective ways to express anger.)

8. For closure, invite the group to summarize the discussion, offer thoughts, or share feelings that surfaced. Encourage them to be alert to angry feelings during the coming week and to share observations at a later meeting. Dispose of the sheets.

Being Angry

1. Briefly describe the last two times you were angry.

   a.   b.

For questions 2–12, your "a" answers should relate to situation "a" described in question #1, and your "b" answers should relate to situation "b."

2. What led to, or contributed to, each situation?

   a.   b.

3. How did you act? (Did you say anything? Were you aggressive? assertive? Did you do something physical? hurt anything or anyone? cry? yell? leave? withdraw? show your temper?)

   a.   b.

4. How long did your angry feeling last?

   a.   b.

5. Did you feel that something or someone was being unfair?

   a.   b.

6. Did you feel that you were being attacked or invaded or harmed somehow?

   a.   b.

7. Does this angry situation happen often for you?

   a.   b.

8. Did you or someone else bring up "old garbage" that had nothing to do with the situation? If so, what?

   a.   b.

(continued)

Being Angry (continued)

9. Is your anger about the situation done, or is it likely to come up again?

a.   b.

10. Did you "talk out" your anger later with someone who was not involved in the situation?

a.   b.

11. Have you discussed your anger with the person or persons involved in the situation?

a.   b.

12. If not, what would you like to say to that person or those persons?

a.   b.

FOCUS Feelings

Anxious and Afraid

Background

Some gifted teens may experience little anxiety. For others, worry and fear are constant companions. They may worry about giving a speech, performing in a recital or concert, or having no one to eat lunch with. They may worry about the safety and health of their parents or of themselves. Gang violence, random shootings, natural disaster, and terrorism may lurk in their thoughts. They may wonder about sexually transmissible infections or simply about germs and health risks. They may fear bullies at school, Internet bullies and predators, and abuse at home, even being afraid to go home after school because home is dangerously unpredictable. There may also be anxiety about romantic relationships, parents' marriage, or parental unemployment. They may also feel anxiety about the future—because it seems bleak, carries heavy responsibilities, or is simply an unknown—and be unable to relax in the present. They may have vague social and sexual anxiety—and may wonder and worry about their sexual orientation. For some, anxiety might be a constant, vague dread. College-bound students may "catastrophize" that the ripple effect of today's fatigue will ultimately affect college acceptance in three years. It might be difficult to imagine getting over all the hurdles between present and future—a formidable whole, not a series of manageable steps.

It is normal to feel anxiety when facing new or challenging situations. Anxiety can be a catalyst for personal growth. When a person is able to embrace it and not avoid challenging situations, life can be an adventure. In contrast, when anxiety constrains life, some freedom is lost. Life satisfaction is probably related to the ability to deal with anxiety and adapt to change.

Even though worries are not bringing their lives to a halt, gifted teens need encouragement to pause and appreciate the present—and even laugh a little about themselves and their anxieties. In this anxious era, they need to name their dread—in a place where it is safe to talk.

Objectives

- Gifted teens openly communicate about their worries and fears.
- They learn that anxiety is part of being human.
- They learn that their peers also have worries and fears.
- They practice identifying and distinguishing between rational and irrational fears, and productive and unproductive anxiety.

- They consider ways to diminish irrational fears.
- They practice articulating concerns about the future.

Suggestions

(NOTE: There are too many suggestions here for just one session. Choose directions according to what you think your group would benefit from most. It is also possible to split this into two sessions: a fear focus and an anxiety focus, perhaps.)

1. Hand out "Being Afraid" (page 190). Have the group fill out the activity sheet, anonymously, as a way of tuning in to past and present fears. Depending on trust level, invite members to share some responses—perhaps just #1, #2, and #3. For #1, they might mention bad dreams, fire and water, spiders and snakes, or being lost, for example. Then move away from the sheet and ask the following questions. Responses on the sheet may help them articulate responses here and later.

   ~ Have some of your early fears continued until today? Which ones? (Don't pry. *Pass* is okay.)
   ~ Were some of your early fears provoked by specific things that happened to you? (Let yes or no suffice. Again, don't ask for specifics.)
   ~ What did you do when you were afraid?
   ~ Who comforted you? (If no one) How did you cope?

2. Move the discussion into the present. Choose questions from the following:

   ~ What kinds of fears do kids your age have? (This general question lets the group put the question at arm's length for a moment. It may nevertheless elicit personal examples.)
   ~ What do these fears feel like? (Encourage similes and metaphors. If needed, give one or more of these examples: "heavy weights," "lurking monsters," "a hand around the heart," "a knot in the stomach.")
   ~ What are some times when you get "butterflies" in your stomach?
   ~ Which fears and anxieties are vague—not about a specific person, thing, or situation? (Possibilities: About the future, social relationships, or being criticized or evaluated.)
   ~ Which fears are real and specific? (Perhaps a parent's unemployment, a family member's poor health, a bully.)
   ~ How much do you worry about violence at home? on the street? at school? Do you ever feel unsafe?

   Let the discussion move freely in any direction. Complex situations might come up, and sharing might be spontaneous and interactive. Encourage the group to communicate feelings. If they tell a story about something fearsome, reflect feelings (for example, "That does sound scary"). Invite them to put words on the feelings (for example, "What did 'scary' feel like?"). Focusing on feelings helps to prevent long narratives, which limit broad participation within the group.

3. Ask the group to list orally a few *rational* fears, which make sense because there is real danger. Then ask for fears that are *irrational*, not likely to happen. Then ask these questions:

~ When do you worry most about things that are *un*likely to happen?

~ Have these fears ever stopped you from doing important things? What things? What other feelings do you have when you worry or are afraid?

~ What could you do to make these fears bigger? (Example: Worry even more— even every waking hour) smaller? (Examples: Self-talk in an encouraging way; look at the fears and figure out why they are so powerful; label them as irrational.) (These questions intentionally suggest "agency"—that is, the ability to control feelings.)

~ What would be different in your life if you didn't have irrational fears?

4. Ask the group to define *anxiety* (vague worry and concern). Then ask, "What vague worries occupy your thoughts?" Perhaps each group member can share three things. Going around the group, ask each student to rate his or her *general* anxiety/worry level on a scale of 1 to 10. Then ask how much their anxiety affects their lives:

~ How much does your anxiety keep you from doing something?

~ How much of your free time is spent thinking anxious thoughts?

~ What are the catastrophes you worry about—terrible things that might happen if you do or don't do certain things? (You might ask for an example of a "small worry"—like a bad grade—and then "catastrophize" as a group: "What's the worst thing that could happen if you got a bad grade?" "Then what might happen?" "And then?")

~ How much does your personal well-being depend on whatever you are concerned about?

~ (Ask those with low levels of anxiety) How do you view some of the worry-filled situations the others have shared here? What advice would you give them? (Comment that anxiety levels vary greatly from person to person. Some have very little anxiety.)

5. Introduce the idea of "productive anxiety"—worry that helps people get a job done or take care of personal care and safety. Ask the following:

~ What are some worries that help you get things done? (Possibilities: Assignments, test or talent performance, locking the door at night, not losing a wallet or house key.)

~ What are some examples of excessive, unproductive worry? (Possibilities: Social situations in general, criticism, imperfection, mistakes, "what ifs"—like moving, parents divorcing, fire, natural disasters, death, not measuring up in the future, not finding someone to marry, getting sick.)

6. Ask them to think of several things they felt quite anxious about a year ago. They might even write them down so that they can study them for a moment. Then ask these questions:

~ How many of those situations turned out all right?

~ Which ones were not worth worrying about? (Similar situations in the future will probably also work out all right.) In retrospect, which ones did warrant worry?

7. Ask the group, "Who is the biggest worrier you've ever known? What did/do you notice about that person? What did/do they worry about?"

8. Explore self-talk as a tool for coping with anxiety. Ask what they tell themselves when afraid or anxious. Encourage the group to change the following anxious self-talk to more rational statements (choose statements according to age level):

   ~ "I've got to get an A on this test."
   ~ "I'm not going to be able to remember what to say."
   ~ "I'll be crushed if she says no."
   ~ "I'll be devastated if she doesn't want to be friends anymore."
   ~ "I know I'm not going to do well in the game."
   ~ "If I don't get a job, I'll have a miserable summer."
   ~ "If we move, I'll never see my friends again. And I'll never make new friends."
   ~ "If I don't have a date for prom, I'll never be able to show my face in school again."
   ~ "If we break up, I'm going to die."

9. For closure, ask someone to summarize the session. What was helpful? Wish them a relaxing, only-productively-anxious time until the next meeting. Dispose of the sheets.

Being Afraid

1. As a young child, I often had these fears:

   a. _____

   b. _____

2. Later on, I had these fears:

   a. _____

   b. _____

3. Of the fears I listed in #1 and #2, these were *rational* (they could really happen):

   a. _____

   b. _____

   c. _____

4. Of the fears I listed in #1 and #2, these were *irrational* (they were highly unlikely to happen):

   a. _____

   b. _____

   c. _____

5. My *rational* fears at the present time (real fears of real possibilities) are:

   a. _____

   b. _____

   c. _____

6. My *irrational* fears at this time in my life (fears of things that probably could never happen) are:

   a. _____

   b. _____

   c. _____

7. Of the fears I listed in #5 and #6, these are the most intense:

   a. _____

   b. _____

   c. _____

FOCUS Feelings

The Dark Side of Competition

Background

Viewed through an anthropology or social psychology lens, the U.S. dominant culture appears to be steeped in individual, conspicuous, competitive achievement (see pages 31–34, "What Does *Gifted* Mean?"). Since most U.S. schools reflect dominant-culture values, it makes sense that they are inherently competitive and that individual achievement in academic, athletic, and other talent areas gets considerable attention. Gifted teens are probably quite conscious of the competition, not only those who are highly invested in the pursuit of prizes, awards, and victories, but also those who are cynical about that aspect of school culture, question the competitiveness in society, or become dispirited and enervated in the competitive school culture. Those who do embrace it may find themselves highly stressed, jealous of and negative toward the competition, and envious of those who make winning look easy.

Objectives

- Gifted teens put competition into perspective.
- They recognize that jealousy, envy, and other negative feelings are often found in competitive situations.

Suggestions

1. Introduce the topic by inviting the group to explore the element of competition in the typical U.S. school culture—in the present.

   ~ How much are you aware of competition in school?
   ~ How much do you think about it?
   ~ What kinds of situations are competitive in school?
   ~ What fuels competition in school?
   ~ To what extent are gifted teens involved in it? Who (of gifted kids) might not be?
   ~ How much are you involved in competition(s)?
   ~ What is the upside of competition in schools? the downside?
   ~ What feelings are involved in competition in academics? athletics? music? art?
   ~ What feelings might be directed at the competition?
   ~ What feelings might be directed at peers who are successful in competitions, even if the peers are competing in different areas?
   ~ If you have feelings about the competition, what are they?
   ~ What might be a positive effect of those feelings? a negative effect?

~ What would schools be like without competitive activities? (You might mention that, although there certainly are countries with intense competition for academic success, there are indeed countries and cultures that do not value being "outstanding." Instead, they value collaboration, humility, teamwork, and mutual help—even lending a hand to others in a class so that the class can stay together over the school years. Schools in many countries have no extracurricular activities at school, with those available only in the community. The U.S. cultural phenomenon of interschool competitions and rivalries seems strange to many foreign visitors.)

~ What would *you* be like if schools did not promote individual, competitive, conspicuous achievement? Would anything change socially or in achievement, health, or well-being?

~ In general, what are your feelings about competition? Do you thrive in it? Retreat from it?

~ How big a role do you think competition will play in your future?

2. Move more specifically into a discussion of past jealousy, envy, and competitiveness.

~ Do you recall being jealous or envious of someone at school? If so, what was that like? How long did it last? What effect did the feelings have on you or others?

~ What contributed to those feelings? What do you understand now about yourself then?

~ How much are those feelings a part of your life now?

~ What advice or guidance might you give to someone younger about such feelings?

3. For closure, ask for a volunteer or two to summarize the session or to make some statements about competition, jealousy, and/or envy. If appropriate, thank them for their serious discussion of a cultural (and school-culture) phenomenon.

FOCUS Feelings

When We Were at Our Best

Background

This might be a light, upbeat session for most, but it may be distressing for gifted teens who have low self-esteem or are in particularly difficult situations. In either case, it has the potential for affirming personal strengths, especially when a group has established a good level of trust.

Objectives

- Gifted teens affirm their own and each other's "best selves."
- They recall a time when they were at their best or affirm their present "best."
- They explore ways to recapture their best selves.

Suggestions

1. Pass out paper and invite group members to write something positive, personal, and appreciated about each of the others. (Especially if some have not been showing a positive side, others may have difficulty affirming them. Give some suggestions: courage, personality, warmth, kindness, acceptance, ability to listen, faithful attendance, independence, energy, creativity, insights, deep thinking, eye contact, unusualness, quietness, assertiveness, respect for others, sensitivity, or smile, for example.)

   Holding the focus on one person at a time, invite the rest of the group to offer affirming statements, with the recipient saying "Thank you" in response.

2. Invite them to remember a time when they were at their best. If they like to write down ideas before sharing them, ask them to list on paper a few of the characteristics of this "best self." Then ask each group member in turn to share the context of this positive period in his or her life. Following are directions that may be followed if they don't appear spontaneously:

   ~ How old were you?
   ~ What helped you feel so good?
   ~ What kinds of comments were others making about you?
   ~ How was the rest of your life affected by your being at your best?
   ~ What were you doing for yourself at that best point in your life?
   ~ If these best parts of yourself haven't been showing lately, where are they?

~ What could *you* do (or what would help you) to bring your best parts to light again? (Encourage them to think about what they can do for themselves, rather than focusing on what others can do for them—perhaps especially in neglectful situations.)

Suggest that the group problem-solve together for the last question, if appropriate. Be careful, however, to validate situations or feelings that are perceived to be keeping the best self down. Do not minimize their difficulties. To validate their feelings and difficulties, you might say, "Yes, it sounds as if you're in a challenging situation right now"; "That sounds like a lot of pressure"; "It's hard to remember the best of ourselves when our world seems out of joint." Then affirm the best parts from the past, without "cheerleading" (for example: "You were a good friend to him" or "I'm sure your grandma saw what a good person you are"). Their best parts were real—and are still part of them. Express confidence that they will be able to have them again, especially since they have gained strength from managing difficult situations since then.

3. For closure, tell the group that it was good to hear about their best selves. Ask for summary comments about feelings and thoughts. How was it to talk about this topic as a group? Dispose of the sheets or file them.

FOCUS Feelings

Proud or Arrogant?

Background

It is probably fair to say that gifted teens, programs for gifted students, and the field of gifted education all have an image problem. Why should there be concern for kids who are bright and capable, for programs that are able to work with the well-endowed, and for a field that gets to work with and plan for those with high potential? After all, they are talented, smart, and filled with promise. But common stereotypes of "the gifted" belie their vulnerabilities and needs, and many sub-populations within the gifted ranks are unfortunately not part of public perceptions about gifted kids. Then, too, educators are advised to raise the performance of bottom quartiles, not the top. Differentiating curriculum, career guidance, and counseling services for the top are not usually a priority. The public often reacts negatively to any suggestion that there are critical needs for gifted kids that need to be addressed—academically, socially, and emotionally.

So what happens when stereotypical gifted kids are proud of, and feel value in, their achievements? When they express pride, no matter how legitimately, there is social risk. Others' perception might be that pride is too much of a good thing—for those who are already so "unfairly gifted." If they go one step further, and are overbearing or haughty with self-importance, they are perceived, probably fairly, as arrogant. What is the difference between pride and arrogance? Is it okay to be proud? Is it okay to be arrogant? What harm does arrogance do to the arrogant individuals themselves, to programs, and to the field? What fuels arrogance? There is a lot to discuss here. In my experience, when groups focusing on social and emotional development are part of programs for gifted students, arrogance is diminished, as a result of raised awareness of shared concerns.

Objectives

- Gifted teens consider the difference between pride and arrogance.
- They consider political, social, and emotional aspects of pride and arrogance.

Suggestions

1. Ask the group to define or describe *pride*. What does it feel like? look like? When is a person likely to feel it? Invite them to mention (or list on paper) times when they have felt pride—deep satisfaction, dignity, and value. Celebrate these moments with them with responses such as "Congratulations" or "That sounds wonderful"

or "That's certainly something to feel proud about." Your group context might offer a rare and safe opportunity for expressing pride. You might even comment, "It's nice to have a place to say that, huh? Thanks for sharing these experiences with the group." Ask the group for times when it's quite natural for someone to feel pride—and also if or when they think it's ever *not* appropriate to feel pride.

2. Check out whether any in the group have ever had negative thoughts about feeling pride in what they have accomplished. Has anyone told them that pride is not a good thing? Can they feel pride at home for what they do there or in school or elsewhere? Do they feel proud in school without worrying about feeling proud? Do they think any gifted kids feel uncomfortable, vulnerable, or guilty when feeling proud? The group might want to explore this last possibility at length.

3. Ask the group to define *arrogance* or think of synonyms. (Examples: Haughtiness, self-importance, being overbearing.) Then ask, "Have you ever witnessed it? felt it? demonstrated it yourself? worried about being perceived as arrogant? assumed that all gifted kids are arrogant? never seen arrogance as a problem? seen arrogance in media stars? thought of all pride as arrogance?

4. Explore whether there is a cost for arrogance. If so, who pays? What might arrogance reflect? (Possibilities: Insecurity, insensitivity, not feeling part of the humanity, being excessively competitive.) Ask the group what they feel when they see or hear a peer being arrogant? What would they like to say? Is arrogance a problem in their school among students in general? Among gifted kids in particular?

5. Ask them to consider arrogance in regard to being politically effective. What effect might arrogance have on whether gifted students are able to have a special program that is supported by teachers, administrators, and community? on getting funding for teachers, materials, and activities for gifted education programs? on passing legislation that supports programs?

6. For closure, ask for volunteers to summarize the discussion or express feelings and thoughts about the discussion.

FOCUS Feelings

Happy

Background

Happy is a word teens use often, whether describing the feeling of a moment or telling how they wish they could feel. Gifted teens are probably just as likely to talk about "happy" as anyone else. This session can move in many directions.

Objectives

- Gifted teens learn that there are many ways to view happiness.
- They consider whether happiness is something to be achieved, is a choice, can be pursued, is relative, or might sometimes simply be unrecognized.

Suggestions

1. Begin by asking, "What does *happy* mean to you?" Encourage them to describe happy feelings, speak metaphorically about happiness, or give examples of times they have felt happy. (If your group likes to draw, invite them to draw a small picture representing "happy." You should probably begin the discussion before everyone has completed the picture. Invite them to make a statement or two about their picture.) Then ask these questions, rhetorically:

   ~ Do things like success, love, security, quietness, contentment, rest, competence, weather, faith, friends, favorite activities, or gifts "make" us happy? (Remind them that *interpretations* of experiences contribute to feelings. Thus, we have some cognitive control.)
   ~ Is happiness related to anything particular? Or does it simply happen?

Important

Be alert for group members who might actually be saddened by this discussion. Some might be cynical and pessimistic about happiness. Encourage them to express their feelings. Validate their feelings—that is, don't express doubt about their feelings (for example, "I can't imagine why you would feel that way"), but rather affirm their feelings (for example, "That does sound sad" or "I can hear your frustration"). It is important that they feel heard and not squelched. If their thoughts affect the mood of the group, comment about that (for example, "I'm sensing that hearing her say that just changed the climate in here") and discuss it, but without judgment. Those who are not happy probably are aware of the power of their feelings and might be hesitant to speak. The group can practice listening attentively and affirming (for example, "It makes sense you're still upset"). Feelings always make sense, of course. It's what to do with them or with the absence of them that is the challenge.

2. Ask questions like the following after group members have expressed their thoughts:

~ How much do you think about happiness?

~ Does anyone *not* think about happiness much?

~ How often do you feel happy?

~ (To those who say they aren't happy) Can you remember times when you were happy? (If so) What was different then? What were you doing then? How were you being? How did you accomplish "happiness"?

~ What do you associate with "happy thoughts"?

~ Considering everyone's responses so far, what would you say about yourselves as a group?

Important

Be prepared for the mention of altered states—through alcohol, inhalants, or other drugs, for example. If so, explore that kind of happy—perhaps short-term effects, escapism, danger, addiction, or poor coping habits that are counterproductive. Sexual activity might also be seen as a route to happiness. Affirm that the sexual drive is certainly powerful and that it is fueled by feelings and desire for feelings. Your group might consider that sexual activity can also be a potentially dangerous or manipulative way of coping with stress and pursuing happiness, especially if it is seen as a means to that end. It is important, if either of these areas comes up, to hear students' thoughts and opinions first before offering adult views. Be aware that they will be watching your responses. Responding without teaching, preaching, advising, or evaluating will provide them with an opportunity to express feelings and be young and vulnerable. Moving quickly to advice can stifle important discussion.

3. Continue the discussion by asking questions like these:

~ What do you think about the idea that happiness is like a butterfly that gently lands on our shoulders unexpectedly, instead of something that can be pursued and captured?

~ Can a person choose to be happy, even in bad circumstances? Are some people in reasonably good situations *not* happy? If so, have you seen examples?

~ Is mood beyond a person's control? What are you basing your opinion on?

4. If someone brings up depression, the group might pursue that spontaneously. You probably will want to prepare yourself by reading through the "Dark Thoughts, Dark Times" session (pages 208–213) in advance of this session. If depression is not mentioned, delay that topic.

5. For closure, ask someone to summarize the discussion, or ask for feelings experienced during the discussion and opinions about the topic *as* a topic. Compliment them, if appropriate, on expressing thoughts and feelings well.

FOCUS Feelings

Loss and Transition

Background

Many situations and events involve loss: the death of a loved one; the death of a pet; the loss of a friend who moves away; the loss of childhood; the loss of innocence; the loss of security and trust; the loss of family "the way it used to be"; an accident, illness, or other situation that changes the ability to do favorite things; a relationship that does not work out; the shattering of an image (one's own or someone else's). Gifted teens experience these losses, even in the best of family and school circumstances. Life happens. Not all members of a group will have experienced dramatic events and transitions. However, those who have will probably feel support through this discussion, and those who have not will gain compassion for those who have.

Grieving is certainly not just for losses through death. Every change, even positive change, leaves something behind. For every loss there is grief, which may or may not find a way to be expressed. And with every loss comes a transition: to life without the person, pet, place, friend, family the way it was, trust, or relationship. The transition period may feel uneven, as new resources and new rhythms are found. It may last a long time. When there is a major loss, perhaps one never gets over it, but simply becomes accustomed to the pain of loss and copes increasingly better.

Objectives

- Gifted teens learn that many life experiences involve loss.
- They learn that it can be helpful to share such experiences discreetly with others.
- They gain hope through hearing how others have successfully navigated transitions.

Suggestions

1. Introduce the topic with material from the background information, or ask the group to brainstorm life experiences that involve change and loss.

2. Hand out "Experiencing Loss" (pages 201–202) and ask the group to complete the questionnaire with very brief responses, anonymously. Use it to generate discussion. You might take one question at a time from #1 and ask for volunteers to share what they have written. Be sensitive to the fact that some members might not feel comfortable sharing all of their responses. Simply state that they can decide what to share. You might also ask each member to list *all* parts of #1 that were answered with yes.

As each member reports responses, ask some of the following questions. (If someone's loss is in the present, adjust the wording accordingly and omit the last two questions.)

~ What are some feelings that you recall from that time?
~ What was the hardest part of going through that experience?
~ Did anyone give you support? Who?
~ What did you do to help yourself through it?
~ How long did it take you to move past the intense feelings of loss?
~ What advice would you give to someone just beginning the same transition?

You might offer the following suggestions, if the group does not mention them:

~ Go ahead and feel.
~ Understand that feelings help us to start going *through* a difficult experience. We can survive them. Feelings can be painful, but they move us forward. They are important to the process.
~ Talk to a friend or an adult—someone you trust. Or talk to a counselor.
~ Find ways to keep going. Return to routines. Distract yourself when necessary and know that distractions have a function. Keep busy. Make plans for your altered life. Reach out to others.
~ Remember that time does heal scars, and though the painful loss will remain in memory, it will gradually lose its intensity.
~ If the loss was of a beloved person, find ways to cherish the memory of that person.

3. For closure, ask a few group members to summarize what they thought or felt during the discussion. Dispose of the sheets.

Experiencing Loss

1. Have you ever experienced loss through . . .

   . . . the death of someone you were close to?   Yes ❑   No ❑

   Who? _____

   . . . the death of a pet?   Yes ❑   No ❑

   What was the pet's name? _____

   . . . moving away from friends?   Yes ❑   No ❑

   Who? _____

   . . . having friends move away?   Yes ❑   No ❑

   Who? _____

   . . . losing trust in someone?   Yes ❑   No ❑

   Who? _____

   . . . losing trust in something?   Yes ❑   No ❑

   What? _____

   . . . an illness or accident?   Yes ❑   No ❑

   What happened? _____

   . . . a change in family life that made it
   different from before?   Yes ❑   No ❑

   What was the change? _____

   . . . the loss of a special friendship?   Yes ❑   No ❑

   Who with? _____

   . . . being disappointed in a special person?   Yes ❑   No ❑

   Who? _____

(continued)

Experiencing Loss (continued)

... loss of innocence, or childhood, or the past? Yes ❑ No ❑

Which one? _____

... the loss of feeling secure? Yes ❑ No ❑

When? _____

... a major change in your life? Yes ❑ No ❑

When? _____

... another kind of loss, not mentioned above? Yes ❑ No ❑

When?_____

2. Pick two of the circumstances described above. What feelings do you recall from each time?

   a. _____

   b. _____

   How long did it take before you felt better?

   a. _____

   b. _____

FOCUS Feelings

Divorce

Background

Some in your group have probably had experiences related to divorce. Some may currently be in the middle of custody battles or decisions about where to live, with loss of concentration, acting out, anger, and/or depression. The process may also be undramatic, with no acrimony and obvious effects. Normal confusion about sexuality may be exaggerated by divorce.

Divorce often involves considerable upheaval. But it is unfair and inaccurate to characterize all divorced families as unstable and "broken" or to assume that single parents are inadequate in child rearing and that "intact" families parent adequately. In many cases, divorce stops abuse and mutual destruction that even counseling cannot alter. Those who divorce and can address important personal needs may then be healthier and more attentive parents than they were before.

What contributes to a high divorce rate? Media messages foster unrealistic expectations of marriage. Mobility deprives couples of the support of extended family and long-term friends. Couples are often unable to communicate personal needs to each other. Couples grow and change uniquely and at different speeds. Too few go for counseling *early*, when adjustments can be made more easily than later, when acrimony reigns.

Young people—even gifted individuals—may marry without first forming separate identities and clear ego boundaries. When something goes wrong, they are unable to deal with imperfections in themselves or their partners. They cannot look at their relationship in parts and address what needs fixing. People who are not healthily separate individuals tend to form and leave relationships quickly. They continue familiar, unhealthy patterns that reflect their poorly defined sense of self, because they lack the skills to change them.

Divorce is not easy for those involved, particularly the children, who likely do not receive the same "benefit" as the adults. How children cope and thrive afterward depends on what parents do to finish the *emotional* divorce. Sometimes divorce escalates conflict instead of stopping it, with rancor and court battles keeping the focus on what is wrong. Mediation or working with legal and other professionals can help to lessen the fallout. When parents can separate spousal issues from parental issues, they may be able to keep the children in mind during the divorce process.

There are many similarities between death and divorce in how people react. Divorce means change, change means loss, and loss means grief. Grief needs mourning, a process that may take years. The sensitivity and intensity that scholars have associated with giftedness may make transitions surrounding divorce especially distressing to gifted children and teens.

Children of any age need to understand that they are not responsible for parents divorcing, that it is difficult to be the messenger, that it is easy to idealize the absent parent and have conflict with the custodial parent, that even late teens and young adults can feel devastated when parents divorce, and that the need for co-parenting after a divorce does not end when children are grown. Under most circumstances, children deserve some sort of consistent contact with both parents.

Important

Some group members might welcome a discussion of divorce; others may not. With this topic, give permission at the outset for students to remain silent, if they prefer. The comfort/trust level of the group, how recently group members have been touched by divorce, and the number who have been affected will likely determine if and how much they share and interact. During the previous session, you might invite everyone to tell you on paper if their parents are divorced and, if so, when the divorce occurred; if they are in a new family; and if they are willing to talk about their experiences in the group. Explain that you will be addressing the topic soon, but they will be in charge of whether they share anything about their experiences, and you will not ask them about divorce unless they indicate willingness to be asked. Mention that those who have not been affected by divorce might learn more about it and become more sensitive to those who have, and that everyone can benefit by hearing what others have to say.

This topic, like some others in this book, may not be appropriate for discussion in a large group. A counselor might do an informative presentation on divorce instead.

Objectives

- Gifted teens learn about how children and teens respond to divorce.
- They learn how children of divorce adjust to altered families.
- They learn that it can be helpful to share feelings about divorce.

Suggestions

1. Familiarize yourself with the background information and organize an appropriate introduction to the topic. You might affirm that good people sometimes have difficulty living together and acknowledge how common divorce is in your school or institution, in case some feel that no one can understand their situations. In a small group, support from those who have "been there" can be valuable for those currently experiencing divorce.

2. If you followed the suggestion in "Important," and if some group members have indicated that they are willing to share, ask the following questions:

   ~ How much of a surprise was the divorce for you?
   ~ How did various members of your family react to the divorce?

~ How did you react? (Here, you might have group members draw quick outlines of each member of their family and fill in each with a color that represents a reaction.)

~ What roles did family members have before and after the divorce? (For example, leader, helper, bill-payer, house-cleaner, dishwasher, car-fixer, family organizer.) How have roles changed?

~ How has your life changed since the divorce?

~ What feelings and attitudes have you gone through since the divorce?

~ What contact do you have with the parent who doesn't live in your "main" home?

~ What strengths have you discovered in yourself during this experience?

~ What advice would you give someone whose parents are divorcing now?

Ask the group members who are willing to share if others may also ask them questions. It will be your responsibility to encourage discretion (for example, "Think carefully about your questions, and be sensitive to feelings and the need for family privacy") and, if necessary, intervene (for example, "Is that question too personal?"). Some answers might generate helpful discussion.

3. For closure, if appropriate, thank the group for sharing and offering support. Remind them that talking helps healing and also is practice for future relationships.

FOCUS Feelings

Family Gatherings

Background

This session, like others in this book, is included because it resonated powerfully with the middle school and high school groups of gifted teens I facilitated over several years. Even when no unexpected personal and family transitions require adjustments during major holidays, normal development makes each year's gathering something new. This discussion is best scheduled *after* the holiday. Holiday gatherings can bring out the best or the worst in extended families and bring into sharp focus the adjustments required when families break up, are reconfigured, or are joined by new in-laws.

The traditional holiday event may simply not have the wonder that it used to. In addition, older teens often work many hours at jobs over the holidays. Some may have to travel to one parent's distant home and meet the family of a new stepparent. Holiday get-togethers may be painful reminders of loss and how things used to be. The week after the holiday break might not be full of happy memories. Expect a variety of experiences and feelings —from "best ever" to "worst possible" to no family gathering at all.

Objectives

- Gifted teens learn that frustrations and sadness are often part of holiday experiences.
- They put feelings into a developmental perspective.
- They learn to articulate complex and varied feelings associated with the holidays.

Suggestions

1. To direct attention to feelings, the focus here, have group members report how they are feeling at the present moment on a scale of 1 to 10, with 10 being "terrific," and some reasons for their state.

2. Ask the group to tell about their holidays—what was fun, stressful, new, and where they were. Or have them list on paper some times of good feelings and some of stress, and share some of these.

3. Then move the focus to interactions with family members. If some members gather with extended family at times other than this season, encourage them to think back to their last large get-together. If someone indicates no extended-family contact

(because of vacation travel, economic constraints, family accident/illness, family conflict, extended family in another country), be poised and make a calm, validating comment (for example, "So your holiday situation didn't fit the stereotype" or "So something interfered" or "It was just your immediate family"). For other students, ask the following:

~ Which relatives attended your family gatherings?
~ What kinds of relationships do you have with them?
~ What were some changes in your relationships or your feelings since the last time you were together?
~ How would you describe your extended family when/if they get together in a large group? (If positive) Who is particularly enjoyable for you? What kinds of things do you do together? If we were your extended family at a gathering, what would we all be doing right now?

4. Focus on feelings generated by holiday experiences. In fact, if the discussion seems to be focused solely on activities, foods, and descriptions of people, you might want to steer it purposefully toward feelings. Ask these questions:

~ How did you feel at these gatherings? (Expressive vocabulary might include *happy, sad, bored, disappointed, nostalgic, loving, affectionate, grateful, excited, inspired.*) (Encourage group members to give situations for each feeling they identify, but respect reluctance to share. Affirm that the holiday world usually is not tidy, just as families are not.)
~ Were any feelings connected to your life in the past? (Possibility: Losses—of childhood, the family's "good old days," familiarity, a sense of place, comfort, a relative, a sibling to marriage.)
~ How were the holidays different for you this year compared to last year (if at all)?
~ How were *you* different (if at all)?
~ Sometimes teens feel stress from too much family, too many work hours, or adjustments to new family situations. Did any of these apply this year?

5. Ask, "How would you describe the perfect holiday? Which family members would it include? exclude? What would you want to do? What would you *not* want to do?

6. For closure, ask someone to give a one-sentence summary about school breaks and family gatherings for teens, based on what has been shared during this session. Were there any discoveries or insights about adolescence? Were there common feelings and experiences?

FOCUS Feelings

Dark Thoughts, Dark Times

Background

Only in the last few decades has the topic of depression been freely discussed. What used to be largely closeted has been much researched in recent years, with significant breakthroughs in treatment. Advances in the understanding of brain chemistry and the chemistry of stress have led to an ever-increasing number of effective drug therapies. Cognitive therapy that works to change the way people think about themselves and situations has also been effective, and generally it is understood that counseling and medication together are more effective than medication alone. People still experience depression, and much of it goes untreated, but more are being helped now.

Sometimes teens use the term *depression* loosely—for being in a bad mood or for a situational sadness that will soon diminish. If, however, they mean a moderate level of clinical depression, they may be experiencing fatigue, changes in sleep patterns and weight, physical pain, difficulty with memory, lessened interest in former activities, withdrawal from friends, and a general feeling of hopelessness. At this level, they might also act out. To improve their mood, they may turn to alcohol (itself a depressant) and other drugs. With severe depression, they may consider suicide.

Because teen mood swings are common, it is difficult for adults to know when to be concerned about a teen's dark mood. There is also a tendency for others to withdraw from someone who is depressed, just when focused attention is crucial. Because pained teens are so concerned with remaining socially acceptable, they often keep smiling. In addition, they are often reluctant to ask for help, especially those who are gifted, since they may believe they should be able to figure it out themselves. Others may not want to burden parents who appear to be already overburdened. If they do ask for help, they may hear, "All you need to do is get up and get moving" or "It doesn't make sense for you to be depressed when you have so much going for you." But for the clinically depressed, there is little or no energy to move ahead.

Several varieties of depression exist, according to current thought. They include a mild, chronic category; minor and major depression; depression associated with an event or situation; cyclically recurring depression; low periods that alternate with highs; and even a depression involving a perpetually gloomy and negatively critical outlook. Clinical assessment of depression looks at frequency, duration, and severity. Treatment varies, depending on kind and level. In fact, depression may be related to physical illness, and whatever is involved, it is important to treat it early. It is important that anyone feeling depressed be seen by a professional if his or her feelings are interfering with normal life.

Suicide is near the top of the list as a cause of death among teens and young adults. However, many adults are fearful of bringing up the subject. They may have a vague awe of the depth of feelings involved, or they may be wary of being engaged in a dialogue on this heavy topic. Teachers, parents, and even counselors often fear that they will "plant the idea" in those who may be "just depressed," and they also worry about the possibility of cluster suicides when there has already been one. Though understandable, those concerns should not preclude discussion. No research has shown that talking about suicide increases the likelihood of it.

In addition to brain chemistry, contributing to thoughts of suicide in teens in general are family problems, loss, abusive relationships, relationships breaking up, sexual and other physical abuse, alcohol and other drug abuse, concerns about homosexuality, and earlier abuse that rears its head with increased sexual awareness. When these factors converge in a teen's life, hopelessness can set in. No matter what the situation, those who contemplate suicide may not want to die, but they feel that nothing will change and that life is too painful as it is. Children and teens do not have an adult perspective. They may not believe that change is inevitable.

Gifted teens are no more or no less vulnerable to depression and suicide than others, according to scholars. However, anonymous, informal written surveys of my discussion groups of gifted achievers and underachievers from grades seven to twelve consistently found that more than one-fourth had seriously considered suicide for more than one day at some time. Sensitivity to stress and feedback from others, especially about expectations, may be a factor in the suicide risk of highly able teens. In addition, their emotional maturity might not match their intellectual or talent level. They may struggle with existential questions and social justice issues even at young ages. They may be highly self-critical, and others may treat their feelings lightly. However, their defenses may be so intact, their emotions so controlled, and their achievement so impressive that, when social and emotional difficulties arise, no one recognizes their vulnerability, and they may not ask for help.

Discussion groups are an ideal forum for discussing the troubling phenomenon of suicide if there is a good level of trust. Those who struggle with depression may find comfort in knowing that they are not alone and perhaps will ask for help outside of the group. Those who have not experienced it can learn about it and feel compassion for those who have. Peer support can be an important line of defense.

Some group members may know peers or family members who are depressed and suicidal or have known someone who died from suicide. Treat the subject sensitively—and yet in a matter-of-fact manner. Model that such topics can indeed be discussed.

Assess the maturity and trust levels of your group when deciding if and how this topic should be addressed. It is most appropriate for older teens, although depression can occur even at very young ages. The format is more appropriate for small groups than large. If you do not use this session with your group, use the information in it to raise your own awareness. This session can easily be divided into one on depression and one on suicide.

Objectives

- Gifted teens become more knowledgeable about depression.
- They learn that ups and downs are part of life and growth, but feelings of depression should not be treated lightly when they interfere with normal activity.
- They learn how to articulate feelings and thoughts associated with sadness.
- They are exposed to information about suicide.
- They learn that even sad and scary topics like this one can be discussed.
- They learn that it is important to ask for help when feeling depressed.
- They learn that they should seek help for people who are suicidal.

Suggestions

1. Introduce the topic by connecting it to stress, which is related to depression. (The first few sessions in the Stress section might be helpful to you in preparing for this session.) Ask the group, "How stressed do you normally feel? About what?"

2. Use parts of the background information to provide information about depression (but do not read that section aloud), or invite a mental health professional to speak. When dealing with topics like this one, do not claim to be an authority unless, in fact, you are. Resist the impulse to share personal examples, since you should not be the focus here. Simply say that the topic relates to teen development. As always, there is potential value in the group simply talking about this, with no adult "teaching," "fixing," or giving first-person accounts.

3. Ask the group to fill out the "Feeling Bad" (page 213) questionnaire as a sorting exercise. Explain that they will not share the whole questionnaire with the group. Make a general comment, when they finish, that if they have been feeling deeply sad for a while, they may see you individually for suggestions about getting assistance (if in a school, and if you are not a counselor, it is appropriate then to offer to accompany the student to the school counselor, who can evaluate and make a referral, if warranted). Give them specific times when you are available. Tell them that if they do not feel comfortable coming to see you, they should see someone else—a school counselor, parent, grandparent, mentor, youth leader, or clergyperson.

Important

You are probably a mandatory reporter, and you need to follow protocol for notifying appropriate resources if someone seems to be suicidal. (See "Handling the Unexpected," pages 13–14.) If someone responds to your invitation in #3, it is appropriate for you to ask about thoughts of self-harm and if he or she has a plan—and the means—for self-harm. If you are working in a school setting, and if you are not a particular student's counselor, see the student's counselor *immediately* if there is cause for concern. You might first say to the teen, with direct eye contact, "Are you okay? Let's talk a few minutes about the mood you were describing today. I'm concerned." (Later) "Should I worry about you? Have you ever thought of harming yourself?" If you have followed the informed-consent directive in the introduction (page 12), the student knows you will have to follow through if the answers are yes.

4. Use the handout questions in a poll-taking manner. The discussion is less invasive if you do not insist on an answer from everyone—so that no one needs, self-consciously, to pass. Questions #4 and #5 ask about symptoms of depression (see background, paragraph 2).

5. Ask the group these questions:

~ What do you think adults don't understand about teenage stress?
~ It has been said that teens often assume that everyone *else* is "fine," but not they themselves. Do you ever feel that way?
~ We are more aware today that teens can suffer from depression. Aside from biochemical factors, what might depression reflect about society at this time? (Possibilities: Life is complex and confusing. People are not patient with problems. Media messages, rapid and dramatic changes in society, national disasters, wars, and the incidence of divorce contribute to feelings of insecurity. Society is mobile, and families often have no extended family nearby for support. Teens may not have relatives available for emotional support. Parents' jobs may seem insecure. The future is unknowable, but rapid change is likely.)
~ How much do you think young children understand (or feel, but do not understand) during times of grief and family stress?

6. Depending on the social/emotional developmental level of the group, you might share a few or all of the following items in a handout or simply by reading them.

~ Isolation and alienation contribute to suicide, but the key factor is depression.
~ Teen suicide may be the result of easy access to drugs, glamorizing of death by the media, an unrealistic view of death (not fully realizing that it is permanent), pressure to succeed, and lack of family cohesion, among many possible contributing factors.
~ Warning signs of severe depression, with thoughts of suicide, include changes in behavior, appetite, sleeping patterns, school performance, concentration, energy level, interest in friends, attitude toward self, risk-taking, and a preoccupation with death.
~ Most people who attempt suicide send signals first—comments about hopelessness or worthlessness, increased isolation, making arrangements for pets or possessions, or changing from agitation to peace and calm (because the decision has been made).

~ Anyone who suspects that someone is suicidal should ask direct questions about whether the person has thought of suicide or whether he or she has a plan in mind.

~ Anyone who believes that someone is in danger should immediately notify someone who can evaluate the situation and help to set up a support system and/or referral for professional help (in a school, a school counselor is an appropriate person), including medication. This holds true for gifted teens who are concerned about a friend. Teens, no matter how intelligent they are, cannot solve this problem for someone else. And promises of confidentiality cannot be kept when someone is a danger to self. If the person is talking about desperate feelings, he or she is asking for help and hoping for change.

~ Because antidepressants usually do not have an immediate effect, support is crucial until they do.

~ Suicide is a permanent solution to a temporary problem. Eventually despair is likely to fade away.

~ Suicide can devastate the lives of the surviving family and friends.

7. For closure, ask the group for summary statements. What was learned? felt? If time remains, ask, "What was this discussion like for you?" This topic often leaves groups quiet and pensive. Invite the group to write their name on the activity sheet, if they would like to. In this case, glance at the sheets before filing or shredding them to learn if anyone needs attention.

Feeling Bad

1. Have you felt significantly sad . . .

   . . . in the last year?   Yes ❏   No ❏   . . . in the last month?   Yes ❏   No ❏
   . . . in the last week?   Yes ❏   No ❏

2. What seems to get you down?

   _____

   _____

3. Do you sometimes feel bad for no apparent reason?   Yes ❏   No ❏

4. Do those feelings affect your sleeping?   Yes ❏   No ❏

   If so, do you sleep *more* than usual?   Yes ❏   No ❏   *Less* than usual?   Yes ❏   No ❏

5. Describe "feeling bad." How does this feeling affect you?

   _____

   _____

6. How long does the feeling last? _____

   _____

7. Does there seem to be a pattern to that feeling (for example, every two weeks, once a month, every spring, every January, every holiday)? If so, explain.

   _____

   _____

8. Does this feeling interfere with school?   Yes ❏   No ❏

   With your job?   Yes ❏   No ❏   With relationships?   Yes ❏   No ❏

   If so, explain how it interferes:

   _____

9. What do you do to deal with feelings of sadness?

   _____

10. Have you ever talked to someone about feeling sad?   Yes ❏   No ❏
    If so, who?_____

11. Have you ever written about feeling sad—just for yourself?   Yes ❏   No ❏

    Have you ever written about it for someone else to read?   Yes ❏   No ❏

FOCUS Feelings

Eating and Not Eating

Background

In the United States, the mainstream culture seems to be obsessed with physical appearance, particularly with thinness. Ads equate it with sex appeal, mannequins feature "perfectly thin" bodies, runway models lack figures, celebrities are underweight, new diets compete in the media, and food products are marketed for the weight-conscious. Possible positive aspects of this are an awareness of fitness and nutrition. Among many negatives is the reality that a sizable number of young women—and an increasing number of young men—may develop eating disorders and be nutritionally deficient. However, this trend stands in contrast to the current prevalence of obesity, a phenomenon that often affects both self-concept and health.

Added to media messages are comments and actions closer to home. If a family overemphasizes appearance and thinness at a time when a girl's normal growth conflicts with that value, the foundation for an eating disorder may be established. In addition, coaches and directors may turn a blind eye to routine purging in the interest of having competitive teams and troupes.

What results too often is an eating disorder, especially for girls and young women and especially for those who are culturally, biologically, or psychologically vulnerable. Eating disorders may reflect power and control issues; difficulty expressing uncomfortable feelings; anxiety; fear of maturity; dependency; difficulty with problem-solving; childhood trauma; or difficulty with trust and intimacy. High-achieving, perfectionistic, nice, compliant gifted females are among those at risk, a reality which has received only rare attention in scholarly writing. Low self-esteem and feelings of powerlessness may contribute. Chronically dieting, addicted, chaotic, neglectful, violent, overprotective, or perfectionistic families; early dieting; and personality or impulse disorders—any of these can also contribute to vulnerability. Eating disorders usually begin during adolescence and can go on indefinitely. Teens may learn about eating disorders through the media; some even turn to the Internet and chat rooms for instruction. Discussion groups can raise awareness and sound the alarm.

Because they also can be afflicted, males need to become aware of eating disorders. Probably no less than for females, media images of athletes, actors, musicians, and other celebrities send the message to young boys and men that perfect thinness or perfect abs are ideal. Dancers and athletes in certain sports (such as wrestling) are likely to suppress anger, have high expectations, and have high tolerance for physical discomfort. It is good to raise awareness about compulsive exercising or excessive dieting for school athletics, since negative lifelong habits may become established. In addition, because their comments have impact, and because they may have vulnerable girlfriends, sisters, mothers, or friends, young men need to understand how dangerous eating disorders are.

Eating disorders are complex, and individual and family therapy is usually basic to recovery, the time required varying with the factors involved. Such disorders can become life-threatening, progressing until heart failure, decreased kidney function, elevated blood pressure, stroke, cardiac arrhythmia, rectal bleeding, loss of normal intestinal function, electrolyte imbalance, enlarged salivary glands, dental enamel erosion, seizures, or depression and suicide result.

Before discussing this topic, make a list of Internet or library resources about eating disorders or obtain brochures from a medical or mental health facility to distribute to the group. Offer these definitions:[1]

> *anorexia nervosa:* "refuses to maintain a minimally normal body weight for age and height"; distorted perception of actual body shape or size; intense fear of gaining weight

> *bulimia:* "binge eating and inappropriate compensatory methods to prevent weight gain" such as self-induced vomiting; misuse of laxatives, diuretics, or other medications; fasting; or excessive exercise

As mentioned earlier, obesity also is a major health concern. However, in stark contrast to eating disorders, simple obesity is not automatically a psychiatric diagnosis, since psychological or behavioral factors are not consistently associated with it. Instead, unless psychological factors are involved, it is viewed as a medical condition. It is not clinically discussed as an addiction, per se.

Like many conditions that are connected to behaviors, obesity is complex. Certainly, in terms of the general culture, lack of physical activity and the availability of unhealthful snacks and fast-food meals are easy to blame. However, genetics, body type, metabolism, occupation, a sedentary lifestyle, fitness, family environment, and culture have all been discussed, depending on context. Obesity is not easy to explain, even though it might be easy to see. Even with a media culture preoccupied with thinness and buff bodies, and with talk and reality shows carving up "the willing guilty," it is important not to pathologize obesity and make simplistic assumptions about the behaviors or psychological health of individuals struggling with it. It also is important not to assume that self-knowledge and knowledge of associated risks are enough to provoke someone struggling with obesity to make dramatic changes. Change probably means a long-term, lifelong commitment, which is not easy for anyone with firmly established behaviors in any area of life.

---

1.   American Psychiatric Association, *Diagnostic and Statistical Manual of Mental Disorders, Fourth Edition, Text Revision (DSM-IV-TR)* (Washington, DC: American Psychiatric Association, 2000), 583–584, 589.

With these cautions in mind, it is encouraging that insurance companies, businesses, and other institutions are promoting lifestyle changes related to eating habits and weight in the interest of a healthy workforce. They would cheer your including obesity in this session with teens. However, be aware that obesity is no more comfortable for teens to discuss than are anorexia nervosa and bulimia—certainly for those who are struggling with it. Obesity also is highly visible, in contrast with these two disorders. Given the sensitivity of teens about appearance, discussion of obesity needs to be carefully facilitated. It will be important that you not single out any group member to illuminate how obesity feels or affects life. It also will be important that tactless comments, if they occur, be processed immediately. The groups promoted in this book are not meant to encourage confrontation or intervention, since the emphasis is on prevention and development. As always, it will be valuable to stay focused on inviting group members' views (for example, of fitness, eating habits of teens). If someone who is overweight offers insights, that will be a welcome bonus, but that should not be expected.

Important	One option is to invite a local expert on eating disorders to make a presentation to the group. (School counselors and nurses do not have the time, staff, or collective expertise to address eating disorders adequately; such disorders often require intensive in-patient treatment.) Remember, however, that the purpose of this session is to generate discussion, not to offer therapy. It is highly unlikely that anyone will reveal serious concerns. However, if they do, encourage them to seek medical and psychological help immediately, and to seek help for anyone who might have an eating disorder. Encourage individuals to see you privately for referral possibilities, and have resources available.

Objectives

- Gifted teens become better informed about eating disorders.
- They explore possible contributing factors to eating disorders.
- They consider that media and social pressures are associated with eating disorders.

Suggestions

1. If an expert makes a presentation to your group, follow it with discussion. If this meeting will be entirely discussion, introduce the topic by asking what the group knows about eating disorders. Caution them against mentioning anyone by name, even though a personal experience or the experience of an acquaintance may have provided general knowledge that can be shared. Supplement what they report with material from the background information. Remember that discussion among peers, in your presence, is in itself potentially valuable. You may be surprised by their understanding of eating disorders, but be prepared to hear a great deal of misinformation. If the latter, wait until it is appropriate to gently ask if they would like some current information. Present information calmly. Listen to their concerns. If you can accomplish this, a group member or a group member's friend might approach you outside of the group. They will know that you can talk about this troubling subject objectively.

2. Invite the group to comment about the following in regard to eating disorders:

   ~ societal pressures and media messages regarding appearance
   ~ expectations and comments from families and boyfriends/girlfriends
   ~ feeling little control in life—and wanting control
   ~ the incidence of eating disorders among highly capable, high-achieving students
   ~ the incidence of eating disorders among dancers, models, cheerleaders, actors, and athletes in certain sports—both male and female
   ~ aspects of personality and environment that can contribute to vulnerability

3. You may want to offer additional information during the discussion:

   ~ The publicly perceived ideal weight, by American standards, has become lower and lower over the years.
   ~ Women need a fat level of approximately 22 percent of body weight to menstruate normally.
   ~ Bingeing is the body's response to excessive dieting. The more one diets, the more one feels the need to eat. The best defense against binge eating is to eat healthfully and regularly.

4. If you wish to broaden the discussion to include obesity, ask these questions (you might decide to address this suggestion before moving into the discussion of #2):

   ~ In general, how does our society feel about food and weight? How "big a deal" are they to most people? How do teens feel about food and weight?
   ~ What have you noticed lately on TV about food and weight? (Possibilities: Attention to healthful cooking, fitness, health risks associated with being overweight.)
   ~ (If the consensus is that teens have poor eating habits or lifestyle) What do you think would help teens eat more healthfully or have a more healthful lifestyle? (Possibilities: More physical movement, less time with video games and at computers, less fast food, fewer soft drinks, more family dinners together, and more attention to cooking healthfully.)

5. For closure, offer an appropriate summary of the session, or ask group members to summarize the discussion.

FOCUS Feelings

Cutting and Other Self-Harm

Background

Deliberate physical self-harm, not connected to suicidal intent, is the focus of this session. Self-injury/self-mutilation can take many forms—for instance, cutting; intense scratching or rubbing of the skin; burning the skin on one or more body parts, such as arms, torso, or legs; biting oneself; or head-banging. This behavior may occur only a limited number of times or may be repetitive and compulsive.

Anyone, at any age, can be involved in this kind of self-harming behavior. Many gifted teens are familiar with the phenomenon, and therefore it deserves attention in this book. Although the behavior is usually secretive, self-injury can become competitive, with students trying to out-do one another with dramatic revelations and suggestions of "bravery." Internet chat rooms may add to that spiraling effect.

Some "cutters" and other self-injurers may seem rebellious or highly stressed, and others, including gifted teens, may appear to be functioning well socially and academically in school and elsewhere. However, the behavior of self-injury often reflects anxiety and depression, isolation and alienation, rage and powerlessness, and failure to cope with highly stressful situations. Those who self-injure may feel unable to stop the behavior. When life seems out of control, and emotional pain feels overwhelming, self-injury can bring a feeling of relief; emotions take physical form—visible and controllable.

The purpose of this session is not to teach group facilitators how to intervene and stop the behaviors just described. (There are indeed effective strategies that mental health professionals can employ to address this behavior, often working toward improved problem-solving and coping, and replacing self-injury with other forms of expression of emotional pain and other alternatives for stimulating the senses. However, school and other proactive, prevention-oriented groups are not appropriate environments for intervention.) Rather, the discussion is intended to give gifted teens a chance to talk with peers, in the presence of a nonjudgmental adult, about this behavior—a behavior which likely seems strange and frightening to parents and teachers. It often provokes a simplistic response in adults and peers, such as "That's horrible. Stop it!" Sometimes adults even become punitive. However, the behavior may be difficult to unravel, since complex emotions are involved.

It is important for adults, including group discussion facilitators, to control the impulse to moralize. The emphasis of this session is on raised awareness. Talking and listening can help troubled teens to normalize emotions, make genuine connections, develop expressive language, and gain skills in expression of emotion. Those who are not self-injuring and who are not inclined to do that can become more informed about the phenomenon, gain compassion for troubled peers, offer support, and also gain skills in healthy forms of self-expression. This session should be longer than a brief meeting. A class-period length is probably sufficient, however.

Objectives

- Gifted teens learn about the phenomenon of self-injury.
- They gain some perspective about emotional pain.
- They learn skills related to healthy expression of emotion.

Suggestions

1. Invite individual group members to make a list on paper of ways they express extreme emotions. (Possibilities: Crying, screaming, withdrawing, sulking, sleeping, eating.) Ask the students to share their lists, if they are willing. This activity might spark discussion, which leads easily to the focus of this session.

2. Ask group members what they know about "cutting" and other forms of self-injury. Let them share their various understandings before offering any background information. Remind them not to name names if they share information about peers or family. This suggestion may provoke enough discussion to last the entire meeting. It is appropriate for you to ask, after something is shared, "How do you feel about that?" If someone says something shocking, process that (for example, "What was it like to hear that statement?").

3. If the group seems to need more information than they already have, share some details from the background information.

Important

You might want to prepare for this session by learning more about self-injury, particularly related to contributing factors. (See "Recommended Resources" on page 276.) However, do not present yourself as a clinically trained expert, unless you are one. Self-injury is a complex phenomenon, and offering "truth" about it (that is, strong statements suggesting "*the* cause" or "*the* effect" or "*the* way to solve it") may not only be insensitive to, and judgmental of, group members who may be struggling with the behavior, but also may convey an inappropriately narrow view of something that can be troubling, persistent, and addictive. Professional assistance is often required to stop the behavior. Above all, even if you believe a first-person account might be helpful to the group, do not ask if anyone in the group has self-injured, since shame is likely involved, and it is important not to appear to be prying for details if someone reveals involvement in self-injurious behavior (which is always a possibility). Rather, thank and commend them for their courage in sharing that personal information.

4. For closure, thank group members for their serious consideration of this complex phenomenon. Ask what they felt or thought during the discussion. Invite one or two students to summarize the discussion.

FOCUS Family

FOCUS Family

General Background

Some families are great nurturers, and some are not. Some have overt conflict, and others rarely raise voices or tension levels. Some adapt well when new situations arise, and some do not. Some families are emotionally close, some distant. Some families talk easily and well, and some have difficulty sustaining conversations—or are simply not inclined to talk. Some have experienced great trauma, some none. Some must worry about providing basic needs, and some have no such concerns. Some fit comfortably into mainstream culture, some not.

Regardless of what the family of a gifted child or teen is like, it strongly influences whether the student trusts, expresses anger (and expresses it without hurting others), lives optimistically or pessimistically, has empathy, is concerned about others, and is successful at school. Even when gifted students have severe disabilities or chronic illness, whether they are emotionally healthy depends to a large extent on how well the family nurtures them.

Teens typically are in the process of figuring out how they can become autonomous—to an extent appropriate within the family culture. That process affects family interaction. Sometimes relationships are strained even before a child enters adolescence. Sometimes there is little tension even during adolescence. It can be assumed, however, that the expected gradual separation process, as the child grows into adulthood, will involve some stress and strain for those involved. Identity development and the process of differentiation from family may be particularly intense for highly able youth.

The sessions in this section look specifically at the family as an entity—as a system. The sessions are meant to be informative and thought-provoking, but not invasive. Gifted teens are usually interested in peer comments here and amazed at how varied families can be. The activities do not suggest "better" or "worse" values or behaviors or styles. Avoid passing judgment—even with nonverbal behavior.

Important

Family, for purposes of discussion, includes anyone who lives (or lived) together and may include grandparents, aunts and uncles, cousins, married older siblings, and even pets. It may also include people in more than one household, especially when a child's time is regularly divided among them. *Extended family* usually refers to whatever generations of the family are still living, whether near or far away. *Nuclear family* usually refers to parent(s) and children, although the adults may be same-sex partners, foster parents, guardians, or grandparents.

Depending on their cultural heritage, family traditions, and family situation, group members may vary in their beliefs about what constitutes a family. It is important to be sensitive to, and accepting of, *all* group members' situations and perceptions. Emphasize that the various perceptions are simply different, not greater or lesser. Some may even speak of close friends as family and may not want to speak at all of blood relatives. A discussion group is a good place to increase appreciation for diversity of families.

General Objectives

- Gifted teens take a closer look at their families.
- They think about their place in the family context.

FOCUS Family

Family Communication Style

Background

Though this session looks at family communication in general, the idea of emotional boundaries also deserves mention here. Each of us is most healthy when we are clear about where our responsibilities begin and end. When we are clear about who we are, we are not as likely to feel sucked into others' problems and emotions and to feel responsible for their behavior. We are also more likely to be able to say no when we should, to set limits, and to protect ourselves from being used or used up by people and situations. Compassionate, sensitive, altruistic, and conscientious gifted teens may especially struggle with emotional boundary-setting. Looking carefully at communication patterns may illuminate patterns that reflect both effective and problematic boundaries.

Objectives

- Gifted teens learn that families differ in the ways they communicate.
- They recognize that adults model how to make requests, offer help, show affection, encourage or discourage, express anger, vent frustration, and share the day's events.
- They consider how their own families communicate.
- They practice effective communication by role-playing problem situations.
- They consider the idea of emotional boundaries.

Suggestions

1. Ask the group what forms family communication can take. (Possibilities: Oral and written words; gestures; affection; gift-giving; phone calls; electronic communication; and smiles, frowns, and pouting.)

2. Hand out "Family Communication" (page 226) and ask the group to briefly complete the sheet anonymously. You might choose only a few of the questions for discussion, rewrite the questionnaire with fewer items, or poll for each question (for example, "Who said 9 or 10?" "Who said 3 or 4?"), inviting a few students to explain their response or give an example.

   Validate feelings that are expressed (for example, "I can feel your emotion when you say that," "I can hear that it's important to you," "That came from the heart, didn't it?"). Avoid judgment (for example, "I can't understand why you would feel that way" or "Your reaction doesn't make sense").

If a high-stress situation is mentioned, encourage the individual to express feelings about it. The student might also be testing the group for response—to see whether the situation is too awful for discussion and whether the group will pass judgment. Thank the student for sharing and offer a compliment for being able to put words on a difficult situation. Simple statements can validate feelings and the experience (for example, "That must have been hard for your family" or "That must cause a lot of stress and frustration"). The group may even be willing to brainstorm problem-solving, if the student asks for help. However, be aware that this moves the group into the "fixing" mode, which may leave the sharer feeling unheard. As always, allow anyone to pass on any item.

Emphasize that what works for some families might not for others. There is no "right" way. Rather, what is most helpful is to consider how *effective* a particular communication style is for getting needs met. Expression of affection, for example, differs among cultures and even among culturally mainstream families. Ideas for enhancing communication may come out of the discussion.

3. As an alternative, use the questionnaire as a continuum activity (see #4 in "Developing—Similarly and Uniquely" on page 29 for guidance). Not only do some groups like to move around, but bold answers through physical movement may have more impact than spoken numbers. Keep in mind, however, that any format can lose its appeal.

4. A big communication issue among families is fighting and arguing. Ask students if they frequently hear family members say, "You never…," "You always…," "Remember when you…," or "Doesn't anyone else care about…." Ask about the effect of *never* and *always*.

5. Especially if your group is made up of older teens, introduce emotional boundaries. The sensitivities of gifted teens may contribute to difficulties in setting emotional boundaries—or any kind of boundaries. Ask the following questions as scaling questions (on a 1 to 10 scale) or to elicit narrative responses. Or, if time is a concern, change the open-ended questions here to closed questions, beginning with *Do* and *Are*, and ask them in a yes/no poll-taking manner.

   ~ How able are you *not* to be drawn into other family members' moods?
   ~ How much do you get drawn into arguments with an unhappy parent or sibling?
   ~ How much do you feel responsible for other family members' feelings and behavior?
   ~ How much are you uncomfortably affected by a family member?
   ~ How much do you draw others into your unhappiness?
   ~ How much do you blame others when things go wrong in your life?
   ~ How much do you think emotional boundaries are a problem for you?

6. Rehearse some boundary-setting statements in the group. Call the group's attention to the use of "I" in the following.

   ~ "I can see that you're upset, but I'm not going to get into an argument with you."
   ~ "No, I didn't *make* you do that."

~ "I realize that no one *makes* me do or feel anything. I have a choice about how I react."

~ "I'm responsible for my own emotions, not theirs."

~ "I feel that you want me to take sides, but I'm not going to do that."

~ "I'm going to try to take better care of myself. It's easy to be drawn into other people's emotional situations, and that exhausts me sometimes."

7. Hand out "Family Communication Role Plays" (page 227). Explain that the group will be acting out some or all of these situations. Divide the group into pairs or small groups and assign the roles. Discuss each role play after it has been presented, inviting others in the group to offer suggestions for more effective communication. If time allows, have the students role-play both negative and positive interactions for some situations.

8. For closure, emphasize that communication within the group is good practice for later relationships—with roommates, coworkers, spouses, partners, or children. If they can learn to talk about what matters to them, what they feel, and what worries them, they will be better able to ask for what they need, express support and concern, and work out problems in relationships. Collect and dispose of the questionnaires.

Family Communication

On a scale of 1 to 10, with 10 being "very" or "a lot" and 1 being "not at all," rate your family on each of the following questions:

____ How well do family members communicate with each other?

____ How often does your family eat a meal together?

____ How much conversation is there at mealtime (when most members are there)?

____ How much is arguing a part of your family's way of communicating?

____ How well (positively, undramatically) do family members deal with their own mistakes?

____ How well (positively, supportively) do family members deal with each other's mistakes?

____ In general, how critical are family members of each other?

____ How good are family members at listening to each other?

____ How much do family members express anger (in any form—"good" or "bad")?

____ How free do members of your family feel to express emotions?

____ How clear-headed is your family, in general, when there is a crisis?

____ How easily do family members compliment each other?

____ How much do family members use words to express personal feelings and wishes?

____ How well can your family talk comfortably about difficult topics, including feelings?

____ How openly affectionate are family members with each other?

____ How well do you think you know what each family member thinks and feels?

____ How much communication is there with extended family (such as aunts, uncles, cousins, grandparents)?

Who are the *most* talkative members of your family?

_____

Who are the *least* talkative members of your family? In what ways do they communicate their needs?

_____

Who in your family expresses his or her needs most effectively?

_____

Family Communication Role Plays

1. You have been losing sleep because someone in your family is making too much noise when coming home late at night. Talk to that person, using I-statements ("I've been feeling . . . ," "I need . . . ," "I feel . . . ," "I'm concerned . . ."). Try to avoid putting the other person on the defensive.

2. You have a need for more privacy at home (for sleeping, studying, or just being alone), and you've come up with an idea you'd like to try that would give you more privacy. Talk to the family at mealtime about your suggestion and your need for a change. Use I-statements ("I've been feeling . . . ," "I need . . . ," "I have an idea for how I could . . . ," "I'm worried . . .").

3. You want to tell a parent or sibling that you are proud of something he or she did recently. Talk to the person, expressing your feelings and asking for further details of the situation.

4. You just spilled a bottle of syrup on the floor. Your entire family is there. Interact with your parent(s) about the incident. (Perhaps role-play a negative, escalating reaction, as well as an acceptance-of-error reaction.)

5. You are terribly angry about something your brother (or father, mother, sister) has done. Interact with that person. (Perhaps role-play a negative, escalating reaction, as well as one involving positive I-statements about feelings and clear statements about anger. For a positive result, try to speak about the deed and its effect on you, not about the person. Avoid statements that begin, "You always . . ." or "You never. . . .")

6. Come up with your own real-life situation to role-play involving family communication.

FOCUS Family

Family Values

Background

This session looks at family values as reflected in how a family interacts socially and how it feels about various issues that reflect values. The gifted teens in your group will consider their family values and see how family priorities expressed in the group differ.

Objectives

- Gifted teens consider what is important to their families.
- They consider how similar or different their personal values are to other family members' values.
- They learn that attitudes and values vary within their group.

Suggestions

1. Ask the group what they think of when they hear someone use the word *values*.

2. Ask the group to complete the "Family Values" activity sheet (page 229), anonymously. Use the statements to generate discussion, noting that they are not meant to be moral truths. Perhaps go around the group for one statement before moving on.

3. As an alternative, if you haven't overused the format already, make "Family Values" a continuum activity (no writing and no photocopying involved). (See #4 in "Developing—Similarly and Uniquely," page 29, for guidance.)

4. For closure, ask a volunteer to name common values in the group. Or ask what thoughts and feelings the discussion or continuum activity evoked. Remind them that talking about values is one of many ways people learn about themselves and others. Dispose of the sheets.

Family Values

Read each of the following statements. For each, ask yourself, "Would my family agree or disagree with this?" Rate the statements from 1 to 10, with 1 being "They wouldn't agree at all" and 10 being "They would agree strongly."

_____ Being social is important.

_____ Work is good—it feels good, and it offers more benefits than just money.

_____ It is important to know what is going on in the news.

_____ Parents, not others, are responsible for giving their children moral guidance.

_____ Parents should communicate moral values to their children clearly and often.

_____ Everyone needs a balance of work and play.

_____ It matters what the neighbors and other people think of us.

_____ Family traditions are important (such as food for special events, family reunions, camping, hunting together on opening day, dinner together, reading before bed).

_____ High achievement is very important—in school, at work, or in the community.

_____ Giftedness should be celebrated.

_____ Getting a good education is important.

_____ It's good to be creative. Unusual creations deserve respect and support.

_____ The arts are important—music, dance, painting, drawing, theater, etc.

_____ Risk-taking is good—socially, personally, on the job, financially, and in play.

_____ Being physically fit is important.

_____ Family privacy is important. What is said and done in the family should stay in the family.

_____ A family should solve its own problems and not ask others for help.

_____ It's a family leader's responsibility to decide how to solve family problems.

_____ Eating healthfully is important.

_____ Athletic ability is important.

_____ Being associated with a faith community is important (church, temple, mosque, for example).

_____ It's best to put the past behind you.

_____ Change is good—and desirable.

_____ The more experiences a person has in life, the better.

_____ Being respectful of others' lifestyles and beliefs is important.

FOCUS | Family

Family Roles

Objectives

- Gifted teens become aware that family members play various roles in the family.
- They think about how personal needs are met and not met in the family.
- They recognize that roles might be altered—with effort.

Suggestions

1. Ask the group to consider that members of any family play various roles in the family—and that they themselves have roles in their families that have advantages and disadvantages.

2. Hand out "Family Roles" (page 232) and ask the group to fill out the questionnaire anonymously. Tell them that there is no correct or incorrect way to interpret the words and phrases. However, encourage them *not* to list an animal, cat, or bird under "pet," but rather to consider that a person might have that role. The terms in quotation marks are roles any family member can take on and should not be interpreted literally (for example, "adult" might in fact be a child and "child" might be an adult). This activity is usually very popular with gifted teens. It provides a safe, individualized way to be known to others.

   In a typical school group setting, with limited time, I recommend that group members *not* note all family members' roles, but rather only their own, since those will be of greatest interest. Have members list all roles that are *theirs*. For example, "I'm the responsible one, peacemaker. . . ." Then, ask students if they heard anything surprising. People often are not the same at home as they are in school, of course.

   You might choose to tally the number of times each role is mentioned. Afterward the group can guess which roles were mentioned most often. Perhaps they can make a statement about the group, based on the family roles the majority have. Then ask if these roles seem typical of most gifted teens—and unlike the roles of others their age.

3. Ask the group if they have ever wondered, even though they might *despise* how a family member behaves, if they might *let* that person take care of a particular emotion or behavior for the family. For example, one person might "do" all of the anger in the family, or all of the sadness, responsibility, seriousness, emotionalism,

rebellion, or risk-taking. Gifted teens, especially those who have well-defined roles, may be interested in exploring the following:

~ How might being respected as "the emotionally strong person" in the family affect someone? (Possibilities: A unique kind of loneliness; not feeling allowed to be weak, sad, frustrated, angry; not feeling able to ask anyone for support; not receiving as much sympathy or support as other family members during difficult times.)

~ How might being seen as "*not* strong emotionally" affect someone? (Possibilities: Not being asked for help; receiving too much assistance; having family members "hovering" protectively; not being depended on during crises; not feeling respected.)

~ Who in the family seems most sensitive to the needs of other family members? What might be the upside of that sensitivity? the downside?

~ Who in the family seems least sensitive to the needs of other family members? What might be the upside of that lack of sensitivity? the downside?

~ What would happen if all members of your family were *equally* serious—if each *shared* that characteristic at a low or moderate level? What if all members of your family were equally angry, equally sad, equally responsible—at a non-extreme level?

~ How might it affect various individuals in the family if emotions were *expressed* equally by all family members? Whose identity might change within the family?

~ Can only one person in a family be gifted (or *very* gifted)? hot-tempered? happy? sensitive? worried? depressed? What do you wish your family recognized in you? (Mention that the "gifted" label can be a point of conflict in a family. Ask the group if their families recognize different *kinds* of giftedness. See "What Does *Gifted* Mean?" pages 31–34.)

~ What do you think happens when we mentally label our family members according to their roles? (Possibilities: Siblings or parents are not seen as complex individuals. They live up to their images and believe they do not have what someone else is noted for—including giftedness.)

4. Ask if anyone in the group would like to change a role they play in their family—and what they'd have to do to change it, who would be affected, what other changes might result, and what a first step would be.

5. For closure, ask for volunteers to tell what they learned, thought about in a new way, or felt. Thank them for their thoughtful contributions. Dispose of the sheets. You might also invite group members to take a blank activity sheet home to work through with their families.

Family Roles

Which family member(s) do you associate with the following roles? Your group leader might ask you to mark only your own roles. If you are asked to show all family members' roles, use initials rather than full names.

leader	teacher of skills	"adult"
planner	"child"	sensitive
responsible	easily upset	gets the most respect
gets the most attention	calm	gets the least respect
gets the least attention	social	hot-tempered
playful	peacemaker	joker
happy	sentimental	sad
emotional	instruction-giver	disciplinarian
business manager	worrier	map-reader
caretaker	angry	full of ideas
rule-maker	not taken seriously	"pet"
"wise one"	"smart one"	perfectionist

Use these spaces to write in other roles that apply to your family:

_____   _____   _____

_____   _____   _____

Now go back and circle any roles that bother you. You may circle more than one.

FOCUS Family

Becoming Separate—But Staying Connected

Background

Having emotional comfort with family members helps a person handle stressful situations. Resolving conflict among family members is desirable as teens move into adulthood, yet that process is a long and bumpy journey for some. According to family-systems theory, those who are most entangled in family emotional conflict have the most difficulty separating from the family even if they can't wait to leave, move far away, and cease contact. Intense needs, fears, and anxiety can continue for decades. Those who are not so involved in family conflict have less trouble becoming autonomous and carry less anxiety into adult life.

Success in marriage is often related to healthy separation from families, having identity, and having clear boundaries, a sense of competence, and autonomy. Then, adults are not as likely to feel responsible for others' emotions, to be overly involved in them, to rush to fix others' problems, or to be hypervigilant. If important needs were met prior to adulthood, or if they have figured out ways to meet their needs themselves, they are not as likely to be overwhelmed by their own or others' needs— or to overwhelm friends or a spouse or partner with theirs.

For many individuals in the United States, movement into adulthood has no clear rite of passage. No special cultural ritual celebrates it, and therefore, for some, general risk-taking, substance use, and experimenting with lifestyles (including some related to talent and interest areas) that contrast with those of parents/guardians become a means to separation. That transition is further complicated by prolonged financial dependency on parents/guardians for higher education, which is probably a reality for most gifted teens. In well-functioning families with not much to fight against, the process of differentiation may be especially challenging. What the U.S. dominant culture sees as healthy "interdependent autonomy" (in which an individual plays a responsible role in relation to the group) may be long delayed.

Objectives

- Gifted teens gain insight into the often difficult process of forging a separate identity and achieving healthy differentiation from parents/guardians.
- They learn that conflict can play a part in the differentiation process.

Suggestions

1. Introduce the topic with some comments about how conflict is often part of the transition into adulthood, which can begin early and last a long time. Conflict may involve clothes, friends, decisions, curfew, car, homework, or any other area in a teen's life—and it may be major or minor. Suggest that what students see as their parents'/guardians' mistakes and stupidity might even be doing them a favor by giving them something to fight against and encouraging them to become separate, competent individuals, who will create their own lives rather than living with parents as adults. On the other hand, conflict that is not resolved as a person moves through adolescence can continue to bind, entangle, and interfere with progress toward healthy adult autonomy and interdependence.

   Ask the following questions:

   ~ In what areas of your life are you becoming more and more self-sufficient?
   ~ In what ways are you letting your family know you are a unique person?
   ~ In what ways are you still dependent on your parent(s)/guardian(s)?

2. Address conflict with questions like these for those experiencing it:

   ~ What are some areas of conflict (overt or silent) between you and your parent(s)/guardian(s)?
   ~ Which ones might still be issues five to ten years from now?
   ~ What will it take to resolve those conflicts?
   ~ What effect is the conflict with your parent(s)/guardian(s) having on your life and their lives? What does the conflict feel like?
   ~ How much do you worry about your current level of conflict?
   ~ How soon do you think your situation will change? How will you know when it has changed? What will your relationship be like then? What will you be doing differently then?

   Assure the group that nothing stays the same, including conflict. It can diminish or escalate as circumstances change. My own studies of gifted teens and young adults have found that conflict seems to lessen as developmental tasks are accomplished (for example, finding direction, establishing autonomy, forging an identity, developing a mature relationship).

3. Address the separation/differentiation process more directly with these questions:

   ~ What do you think your parent(s)/guardian(s) are worrying about as you become more and more independent?
   ~ What are your own fears and worries as you move toward autonomy?
   ~ Is "separation process" a good way to describe what you are going through? Or does that description seem inappropriate?
   ~ What does the process feel like to you?
   ~ How far away from your parent(s)/guardian(s) do you think you will want to live as an adult?
   ~ What might your mother/father/guardian have a difficult time with when you leave?
   ~ What would be an ideal relationship with your parent(s)/guardian(s) when you are twenty? thirty-five?

4. Invite the group to give examples of what they consider healthy and unhealthy separation from parents/guardians. You might mention that the *amount* of contact with parents/guardians is not the main determinant. A person can have frequent contact with parents and still be an independent adult. A person can be completely cut off from parents and still be connected to them in an emotionally unhealthy way—with intense, ongoing inner conflict. The ideal is a comfortable adult relationship with one's parents/guardians. Some keys to achieving such a relationship are the following:

~ feeling competent about making personal decisions independently
~ taking responsibility for one's own life
~ being able to resist involvement in "old" family conflict

5. For closure, ask one or two students to summarize what they have heard the group say or what they have thought about or felt during the discussion.

FOCUS Family

Making Predictions

Background

Some brief or extended life events mean significant change for a family. For example, births, deaths, illnesses, accidents, moves, job changes, unemployment, separation, divorce, marriage, remarriage, and eldercare all can create major ripples. Someone starting kindergarten, adolescence, high school, or college (or finishing high school or college) is also a developmental event for a family. Some events are anticipated for months and are followed by extended periods of adjustment. Yet families are often unaware that present tension may reflect preparation for, or entry into, a new stage of family development. Developmental shifts happen gradually, outside of awareness, and are easily overlooked. Normalizing developmental changes can help teens feel less out of control as they occur. Gifted teens may be hyperaware of their changing environment during family transitions. Yet they may not perceive the tensions as reflecting individual and family development.

Objectives

- Gifted teens look to the future and imagine altered relationships with their families.
- They recognize current, ongoing changes in their families and anticipate other changes.
- They discover that others in the group are also experiencing family transitions.

Suggestions

1. Introduce the topic by drawing, or having the students imagine, a timeline of their family development during their lifetime. Mark off events—for example, births, first child to kindergarten, last child to kindergarten, first child into adolescence, first child to college, last child to college (anticipated), first child launched into adulthood, grandparent unable to care for self, death of grandparent, death of immediate-family member, divorce, remarriage. Then invite comments about what happens as a family moves through each stage.

   ~ What changes in the home are likely to happen when the first child is born?
   ~ How might sending the first child off to kindergarten affect the parent(s)?
   ~ What ripples are caused when a child enters adolescence? (Possibilities: Parents may begin to relive their own anxieties from that stage of their development; the family has to deal with the teen's mood swings or lack of communication;

parents may feel less and less control as the teen's activities and peers become increasingly more important.) How has your family handled your adolescence?

~ Has your being gifted had any effect on your family's development? on the family's expectations of you? If so, when did you first feel those expectations?

~ What effect does launching the last child into adulthood have on the parent(s)? (Possibilities: Children are no longer the focus; parents must relearn how to focus on themselves and each other.)

~ What happens when a parent must take care of his or her own parent? (Possibilities: Additional physical and emotional strain, more financial responsibility, resistance in the elderly parent, marital disagreement.) Has your family experienced this?

2. Hand out "Family Predictions" (page 238), and ask the group to provide brief responses, anonymously. You might invite all members to respond to one question orally, moving quickly around the circle or class and then doing the same with the next question. Encourage the group to be alert to common themes. As always, allow anyone to pass.

3. For closure, ask one or more students to summarize the discussion. Was it a new experience for them to consider families as developing? Was it interesting? (Let nods to these closed questions suffice.) Collect and dispose of the sheets.

Family Predictions

1. What changes are likely to happen soon in your family?

    a. _____

    b. _____

    c. _____

    d. _____

    Of the above, which changes are related to children growing up?

    _____

    Which changes do *not* seem to be related to children's growth and development?

    _____

    Who in your family will be most affected by these changes?

    _____

    How will you be affected?

    _____

    How do you think your parent(s) will be affected when you eventually leave home?

    _____

Finish the following sentences:

2. My biggest problem in the family, which is _____ , will

    eventually (improve, get worse, go away, etc.) _____.

3. When I'm an adult, I plan to live in (location) _____.

    I probably will have a (comfortable, close, distant, friendly, etc.) _____

    relationship with my (mother, father, sister, brother, other relative) _____

    and a (what kind of) _____ relationship with my (relative) _____

    and a (what kind of) _____ relationship with my (relative) _____.

4. I think my family will eventually become more _____.

FOCUS The Future

FOCUS The Future

General Background

During the school years, gifted teens probably hear that doing well ensures success at the next level, which, they hear, is more important. So elementary school is preparation for middle school, which is preparation for high school, which is preparation for college, which is preparation for another next step, which is . . . ? Parents might also speak in terms of "when we get this done, we can relax and really *live*." However, looking at each successive stage as preparation for something yet to come means that no stage is seen as real life, the life that is longed for. Each stage, in fact, *is* life—lived *in the present*. "Now" can be missed by many gifted teens.

In contrast, some seem to live only in the present. They may be impulsive and spontaneous, unpracticed in delayed gratification, procrastinating with important preparation for the future, closing doors with unwise choices, resisting advice, and seeing little value in school and other responsibilities. Stereotypical gifted teens may not fit the second description, but it is indeed accurate for those who don't fit the high-achiever stereotypes. However, underneath, the latter may have great anxiety about the future—when thoughts of it intrude.

How can gifted teens find middle ground? How can they focus on the future without becoming anxiety-ridden and joyless? How can they enjoy the present without letting it blot out concern for what is coming? This final section helps them look ahead.

General Objectives

- Gifted teens look realistically into the future, while understanding the importance of living in the present.
- They look at themselves as moving along a continuum of development.
- They contemplate direction, meaning, and change.

FOCUS | The Future

What Is Maturity?

Background

Because of uneven, asynchronous development, some gifted teens may hear that they are immature. Their cognitive development may be far beyond their age peers', but socially and emotionally they may be less developed. Even if they are socially, emotionally, and physically on target, teachers may consider them immature because of intellectual or talent precocity. This topic should generate discussion easily, regardless of group members' developmental level.

Objectives

- Gifted teens learn that *maturity* is defined according to the lens of the viewer.
- They apply the term to both teen and adult behavior.
- They realize they are *in the ongoing process* of maturing.
- They enjoy discussing a term that is often used to point out what they are *not*.

Suggestions

1. Ask the group to define *maturity*, orally or in writing. Then ask them to explain what they think various groups (teens, parents, employers, teachers, elderly adults) mean when using the term.

    Then pursue the following ideas. (The discussion is intended to provoke self-reflection and expression of feelings and thoughts. There are no right or wrong responses.)

    ~ When do you feel mature now?
    ~ When do you not feel mature now?
    ~ How will you know when you are mature?

2. Ask the group if others often comment about their being or not being mature.

    ~ (For those who often hear that they are mature) How has that affected you? What do others see as maturity in you?
    ~ (For those who often hear that they are immature) How has that affected you? What do others see as immature in you?

3. Invite them to consider the following:

    ~ What is immature behavior?
    ~ Can adults be immature? If so, give some examples of immature adult behavior.

~ What is the upside of being mature in behavior? Of being immature?

~ What is the downside of being mature in behavior? Of being immature?

4. Move the discussion to the topic of early and late maturers. Ask the following:

~ What are meant by the descriptors *late maturing* and *early maturing*?

~ If a girl matures early physically, how might that affect her socially? emotionally? academically? during adolescence? as an adult?

~ If a boy matures early physically, how might that affect him socially? emotionally? academically? during adolescence? as an adult?

~ If a girl matures late physically, how might that affect her socially? emotionally? academically? during adolescence? as an adult?

~ If a boy matures late physically, how might that affect him socially? emotionally? academically? during adolescence? as an adult?

~ Do you think you are ahead, behind, or right on schedule in the process of maturing physically?

~ If you have matured early, or seem to be maturing relatively late, how has that been for you? (Convey that there is a normal range of development within every life stage.)

~ On a 1 to 10 scale, with 10 being "on target," where are you in mental development? social? emotional? (If their numbers are inconsistent, explain that gifted kids often have uneven development, with intellectual or talent development being relatively advanced.)

5. For closure, thank and compliment the group for their insights and comments, and either summarize the session yourself or ask someone to do so.

FOCUS The Future

Satisfaction in Life

Background

During middle school and high school, especially for teens who are not satisfied with themselves or their situations, their relationships with peers and adults, their success in the classroom or in activities, or their prospects for the future, it can be helpful to step back, take the focus off themselves, and consider the future in broad terms. Gifted teens whose performance or nonperformance preoccupies adults may especially appreciate this.

In an era when material wealth, personal amenities, travel, and even access to surgically enhanced beauty seem to be symbols of success, it is important for teens to consider what contributes to satisfaction in adulthood. Sober, serious thought about this often elusive state might even help them with current developmental tasks related to identity, direction, relationships, and the differentiation process. In fact, eventually having a good sense of self, a comfortable career, a mature relationship, and a separate-but-connected relationship with parents and siblings may help them feel satisfied with their lifelong developmental journey. Accomplishing developmental tasks is as much of a challenge for gifted teens as for anyone else. It might even be argued that "normal development" might be *more* difficult for sensitive, intense, performance-driven (or performance-aversive) gifted teens.

Objectives

- Gifted teens ponder what helps adults feel satisfied with their lives.
- They look to the future while contemplating the present.
- They consider their tendency to be optimistic or pessimistic about the future.
- They contemplate how circumstances might affect a person's view of life.

Suggestions

1. Introduce the topic by asking the following questions:

   ~ What do you think helps adults feel satisfied with their lives?
   ~ What might help a retired person feel satisfied?
   ~ What might help a thirty-year-old feel a sense of satisfaction?
   ~ Which adults do you know who seem satisfied with their lives? What do you think helps them feel satisfied? What do you think their sense of satisfaction was when they were your age?

~ What seems to be most important in life, based on the adults you know:

a satisfying job	health
a satisfying relationship	social status
children	faith/religion
money	family

(You might ask the group to rank the above eight items from most to least important in helping people feel satisfied as adults.)

2. Invite group members to evaluate their current satisfaction in life and to consider their level of optimism regarding the future.

~ How satisfied are you with your life right now?
~ What do you think could help you feel more satisfied? (Receive all responses without judgment. Respond with reflective statements like "Sounds like things aren't feeling good right now" or "So getting along better at home would help.")
~ Are you optimistic or pessimistic about finding satisfaction in adulthood? Explain.

3. Provoke thought about how various life circumstances might affect one's view of life. Assure the group that you are interested in their individual views and that you expect their responses to differ.

~ How might pain and struggle affect a person's view of life?
~ In your opinion, do struggles in life have any value? Give reasons for your answer.
~ Is it possible to have no struggles during an entire lifespan? not enough? too many?
~ Do you know any adults who struggled as kids (for example, with family difficulties, poverty, individual or family health problems, parental death, divorce, frequent moves, loneliness, parental neglect and/or addiction) but seem to feel satisfied with their lives now?
~ What do you think about the idea that struggles help people feel connected to others? Is connection easier or harder to achieve at upper economic levels than at lower?

4. For closure, ask for a summary of what has been discussed, or ask the group for insights, perspectives, or self-reflections prompted by the discussion.

FOCUS | The Future

Attitudes About Work

Background

This session provides group members with a chance to discuss the world of work, attitudes toward work, and the meaning of work. Even gifted teens who are quite engaged with planning for the future can benefit from discussion about employment—as an abstraction. The hope is that ultimately *all* group members will find a good fit and personal satisfaction in the workplace.

Objectives

- Gifted teens assess their attitudes about work.
- They look at what affects a person's attitude about work.
- They understand that there are many ways to view work.
- They consider that work, in itself, has personal value.

Suggestions

1. Ask the group to define *work*. Then ask these questions:

   ~ Does work have to involve pay? be outside of the home?

   ~ What is your view of work that people do in a home office, such as for home businesses? Are there differences between that work and work done in a place of business elsewhere?

   ~ Should a family or public attitude toward (or valuing of) household work (such as cooking, cleaning, buying groceries, washing clothes) be different from the attitude toward work done outside the home? What are you basing your opinion on?

   ~ Can money-earning work be enjoyable? Who do you know who obviously enjoys, and has fun doing, money-earning work?

   ~ Can household chores be enjoyable? If so, who do you know who enjoys them?

   ~ How important is work to feeling satisfied about life?

   ~ How do the media portray work—positively, negatively, rewarding, important? What are some examples from television programs, movies, magazines, or newspapers?

   ~ What is your attitude about the work that volunteers do in providing services to others? Do you see that as work? (You might mention that the United States has a somewhat unique and long tradition of volunteerism, which many community institutions depend on.)

~ Do you think it is work if someone pursues a personal interest or project and invests many, many hours in it, with no thought of pay? If so, can you think of an example?

~ Have you known anyone who worked a rather grim "day job," but devoted leisure time to acting, singing, a band, art, or some other satisfying expression of talents and interests? If so, how would you describe his or her personality and attitudes about work and life?

~ Have you known anyone who did difficult, heavy labor for many, many years and never seemed negative about it? If so, what kind of work was it? How do you explain this person's attitude?

2. Ask the group how they feel about work in general. Encourage them to elaborate, challenge, and be honest. After they have expressed views, ask the following:

~ How much do you think adults' feelings about work affect their families? their satisfaction with life in general?

~ Consider the idea of "attitude *habits*." In regard to work, can you think of examples of negative-attitude habits? positive-attitude habits?

~ How can people improve their attitudes about work? (Possibilities: Use positive self-talk; be rested, alert, and pleasant; enjoy the social aspect of work.)

~ What can work do for a person? (Possibilities: Provide wages, occupy time, provide social contact, contribute to society, give one a sense of pride for doing something well.) (Mention that some retirees have difficulty adjusting to not working.)

~ It has been said that teens and young adults today (especially the upwardly mobile) have a sense of entitlement—to special treatment by employers, to leisure, to material amenities, and to not having to exert themselves. What do you think about that perception of your generation?

3. Hand out "The World of Work" (page 247) and ask the group to complete the list of significant adults (anyone who is influential in their lives) and identify the workplace, position, and attitude toward work of each. Use the questionnaire as a springboard for discussion and also ask these questions:

~ How much will work be a part of your adult life?

~ What might you not enjoy about your career?

~ What do you expect to enjoy about your career?

~ Do you expect to work more than eight hours a day outside of the home? What kinds of careers probably require longer days? shorter days?

~ How do you think you might help yourself to have satisfaction in your future work?

4. For closure, ask one or a few to summarize what has been discussed. To help them formulate a comment, ask them if the discussion caused them to think about work in a new way. Dispose of the sheets or add them to the group folders.

The World of Work

Name: _____

Significant Adult	Workplace and Position	Attitude Toward Work
1. mother		
2. father		
3. a grandmother		
4. a grandfather		
5. an aunt		
6. an uncle		
7. a neighbor		
8. an older sibling		
9. another relative		

Have most of the people in your life been positive or negative about their work? _____

_____

Have most of them found satisfaction in their work? _____

_____

For those who have felt good about their work, what do you think helped them feel satisfied?

_____

_____

For those who haven't felt good about their work, what do you think contributed to their

dissatisfaction? _____

_____

The Future

Future Lifestyle and Gender Expectations

Background

Many gifted early teens think seriously, anxiously, and often about the future. In contrast, some do *not* focus much on their future, appropriately enjoying the last stages of the transition from childhood into adolescence and living comfortably in the present moment. Some gifted teens may similarly be either preoccupied with the future or oblivious to it. If the latter, this session may be useful for helping them consider adult life realistically at their stage of development, especially as related to gender roles, career, and family. Carefully choose suggestions and activity-sheet items according to your group's needs.

Objectives

- Gifted teens anticipate possible gender roles in their future.
- They consider how gender expectations affect career and family responsibilities.
- They imagine the future realistically in terms of lifestyle.
- They imagine being single as an adult.

Suggestions

1. Have students fill out "Images of the Future" (page 251). (If time is limited, and if you want the focus to be only on gender expectations, move immediately to #2.) Ask the girls, and then the boys, what is expected of women at home, at work, and socially as adults, and what is expected of men at home, at work, and socially as adults.

2. Ask for thoughts about the following. Whether achievers or underachievers, and regardless of socioeconomic status, gifted teens should have opinions here.

   ~ the intelligence of women
   ~ the intelligence of men
   ~ women earning money in a career
   ~ men earning money in a career
   ~ women in leadership/executive positions
   ~ men in leadership/executive positions
   ~ working mothers
   ~ working fathers
   ~ women in business suits

~ men in business suits
~ mothers staying at home with children
~ fathers staying at home with children
~ how girls and women talk and communicate
~ how boys and men talk and communicate
~ female moods
~ male moods
~ women who are single at forty
~ men who are single at forty
~ women in business, medicine, law, engineering, construction
~ men in nursing, teaching, childcare, fashion, secretarial positions

3. Direct their attention to the future.

~ What kind of life will you lead?
~ How traditional will you be as a man or woman? What do you think *traditional* will mean when you are an adult?
~ How likely will you marry or have a serious relationship in early adulthood? later?
~ How likely are you to have children? If likely, when? If likely, will you stop or slow down your career when children are born or ask for maternity/paternity leave if it is available? How long would you like to be home with the children?
~ What kinds of outside interests will you have as an adult?
~ What will you do to relax?
~ How similar will your skills and interests be to your same-gender parent's?
~ How much will you share household duties (cooking, laundry, cleaning, grocery buying, paying bills, yard work, mechanical fixing) with your partner or spouse?
~ How likely will you be to relax at home instead of going out when there is free time?
~ How fit will you be?
~ How dependent do you think you will you be on your spouse or partner and others for intellectual stimulation and emotional support?
~ What career(s) are you seriously considering?
~ How much education will be required for the career(s) you are considering?
~ If in a partnership or marriage, how able will you be to pursue further education when you want to pursue it?
~ What effect will your gender have on beginning or advancing in your career?
~ How able will you be to have the career you aspire to?

Many of the above questions warrant extended attention. You might ask the girls in the group how they feel about the aspirations and expectations of the male group members. Do they seem realistic, idealistic, naive? Ask the boys the same questions about the girls.

4. Move to a discussion of being single—whether from never marrying, divorcing, or losing a spouse or partner to death. Invite the group to consider what it means to be single at ages thirty, forty, fifty, and sixty. Encourage realistic thinking about

self-sufficiency. If divorce trends continue, half of marriages will not last. Ask the following:

~ What kind of lifestyle would you have as a single person who never married?
~ What kind of lifestyle would you have as a divorced person? (with young children?)
~ What kind of lifestyle would you have as a widowed person? (with young children?)
~ What kind of income would you have in each case above? (Be armed with statistics.)
~ How easy or difficult is it for you to imagine being single as an adult?
~ On a scale of 1 to 10, with 10 being highest, to what extent do you plan *not* to be single as an adult?

5. Invite the group to brainstorm some of the problems faced by dual-career couples. Mention the following if they are not mentioned during the brainstorming:

job transfers	jobs in different cities
child-rearing	dividing home responsibilities
conflicting work schedules	mutual exhaustion
little time together	different income levels

Then ask questions like the following. You might mention the importance of dual-career couples cooperating, supporting, and accommodating each other.

~ How would you deal with your spouse's job transfer, if it meant you had to leave a good job?
~ If you had children, what would be your role in child-rearing? your partner's role?
~ When your schedules conflicted, whose schedule would be most important?
~ If both of you worked outside of the home, what percentage of the housework would you likely do? How would you determine an appropriate level?

6. Invite the group to project into the future by asking the following:

~ What do you think men's and women's roles will be when you are an adult—at home, in the workplace, in the community, and in state and national leadership?
~ How do you see the roles of men and women changing in your lifetime?
~ How similar or different will your roles and attitudes be to those of your same-gender parent?

7. For closure, ask the group how they feel when they think about future gender roles. Excited? discouraged? apprehensive? eager? sad? anxious? scared? satisfied? Dispose of the sheets or file them.

Images of the Future

Name: _____

1. What are some of your mental images of yourself as an adult? How do you picture yourself?

   _____

   _____

2. What kind of work do you see yourself doing? _____

   _____

3. Where do you imagine yourself living? _____

   _____

4. If your parents or guardians have told you how they imagine you in the future, how old were you when they began to do that? _____

   _____

5. What did teachers suggest to you early in school about your future?

   _____

   _____

6. What have teachers and counselors suggested recently about your future?

   _____

   _____

7. What have you been hearing lately from your family about their expectations of you?

   _____

   _____

8. Who else in your life is giving you ideas for your future (for example, boyfriend, girlfriend, other peers, religious/spiritual leader, a boss at work)? _____
   What are they saying? _____

   _____

9. Have adults in your life been supportive of you as they talk about your future? _____

   _____

10. Are your wishes and dreams for yourself generally the same as the wishes and dreams others have for you? _____

    _____

11. What level of education will you need to pursue your goals? _____

    _____

FOCUS | The Future

Choosing a Career

Many gifted teens have a dilemma of too many choices—being able to do several things well, having many interests, and having the motivation necessary to succeed in any of the areas. This may be true even for the gifted underachiever who has many talents but little motivation, or who is "paralyzed" by multipotentiality.

In addition, these gifted adolescents are often burdened by others' expectations. They hear a lot about their potential. They receive advice about careers, and the advice is often conflicting. Should they consider engineering, just because they are good in math and science? Should they avoid the arts or humanities, even though their passion lies in those areas, because significant adults warn that they won't make a lot of money? Should they put job security first? How do they choose which interest to take seriously? Can they combine interests? Could one become a satisfying avocation? Gifted teens may foreclose early on a career, either because of the dreams of adults in their lives or because they find uncertainty hard to tolerate.

No one can predict exactly what the economy will be like, or what new job opportunities there will be, when today's youth are ready to enter careers. However, each person will likely make more than one career change during a lifetime, and there will be careers and specialties that don't currently exist. They can probably take some risks. Regardless, aspects other than ability should be considered, such as personality, personal needs, dreams, and even values. Sorting through these can be helpful. (Refer to "A Question of Values" on pages 82–83, and "Family Values," on page 229, to be reminded of personal values that may be pertinent to career decisions.)

Important

An option is to arrange for three to four adults from the community to visit the group and, as a panel, discuss finding satisfying careers. Try to find middle-aged people of both genders who have made thoughtful and successful career *changes* in order to address the issue of "fit"—and also to represent the reality that one does not have to find a perfect fit immediately or at all (often a concern of perfectionistic gifted students). If your group includes individuals at risk for poor outcomes, such as high-ability underachievers, locate speakers who once were "square pegs in round holes" or who had difficult home situations but who became successful as adults. Consider the needs and interests of your group, and invite panelists who represent various careers. Group members with little direction can benefit from hearing how a language major became a labor union leader, or how a chemistry major became director of hazardous waste transportation, or how someone with good mechanical sense ended up monitoring an oil pipeline. People do not necessarily know, when young, what they will find satisfying in the future and even what is available in their area of interest. For further ideas for this option, see suggestion #3.

Objectives

- Gifted teens sort out personality, needs, dreams, and interests and consider their importance for satisfaction in a career.
- They learn that there is no perfect career choice; several possibilities are worth considering.
- They consider that education and adulthood might include changes in direction.

Suggestions

1. Hand out "Career Needs" (pages 256–257) and ask the group to complete the questionnaire. Afterward, have them share their responses. (A show of hands might suffice for #5 and #6, or simply have them read their choices.) Ask who found that their responses for #5 and #6 matched careers listed in #1.

2. Explore group members' attitudes about needing to find a career direction before high school graduation. Ask the following questions:

   ~ How important is it to know what you want to do as a career before graduating?
   ~ At what age do you think most people figure out what they want to do for a career?
   ~ What advice have your parents and teachers given you about finding a career?
   ~ How much are you worrying about finding a career for yourself?
   ~ How might you respond to parents' college and career expectations that conflict with yours?
   ~ Do you think people who have many talents and abilities have more difficulty than others with finding direction in life? Explain your thinking.
   ~ Some experts believe gifted individuals experience loss and grief when they have to select one of many career options. What do you think about that idea?

   Encourage the group to relax about needing to find *the* direction right now. Even in college they can usually delay choosing a major for a year or more and can even change majors later. Encourage them to keep their options open and to expect to consider new possibilities during college. Professors, courses, and friends may give them new career ideas. Although late changes usually necessitate going extra semesters, the prospect of several decades in unsatisfying work probably justifies the investment. Remind them that it is not abnormal to change careers or directions within a career—even going back to school late in life. Therefore, it is good to develop a broad knowledge base, rather than narrow skills. Reading, writing, and thinking ability will continue to be key factors in career success and adaptability. Both gifted achievers and underachievers can benefit from this emphasis on broad-based education. Perfectionistic underachievers, stymied by anxiety or multipotentiality, might benefit from knowing that later changes are possible.

All careers have positive and negative aspects, but someone does not have to be in an unsatisfying career groove for forty or fifty years.

3. If you have invited a community panel (see "Important" below), have the group interview them, asking these or other career-development questions:

   ~ How did you get to the career you have today? Was it a straight path?
   ~ Which positions have been a good match for you, and which have not?
   ~ What risks did you face in making career changes?
   ~ What advice would you give to teens about career decisions?
   ~ What educational or life experiences were valuable for finding your career direction?
   ~ Who influenced you regarding career choices along the way?
   ~ What is most important to you now—income, social status, or work satisfaction?
   ~ Have your careers allowed adequate time for family and a life outside of your career?
   ~ What do you like best about your career? least?

4. To introduce a new dimension, ask what the group thinks is more important to find first—a satisfactory career or a satisfactory relationship? Why?

   Suggest that finding a satisfying career may be a higher priority, given the impact of job dissatisfaction on relationships. This may not be a popular thought. However, a relationship might come through the career, since work environments usually include people with similar interests. Satisfaction in the workplace is probably important to general happiness since it provides a sense of control. Making good academic choices, even during the early teen years, improves chances of having options and career satisfaction later. Making poor choices for social reasons might close doors.

5. Organize a brief career-shadowing experience as a group—a one-day (or half-day) experience, with each member focusing on one career, deciding on a community location for the experience, and researching the career. (See the following "Important" for guidance.) Gifted teens often do not know about career *contexts*. Many for whom engineering is being recommended might have no sense of what engineering looks like in the workplace, for example.

Important	For individual career-shadowing, it is best to have an adult make the call, in order to assure the professional that the experience will be relatively brief, that it will be prepared for, that only one teen will be observing, and that the teen will be learning about a typical half or full day at work, including, perhaps, the sore feet, the fifty phone calls, the research, the long hours, the interruptions, and the stress—in other words, beyond television portrayals. (Limited shadowing is usually best, since longer experiences can quickly use up willing professionals. One full day can be quite informative, especially in terms of seeing context. For various kinds of engineering, field trips for groups of gifted students work well, with a spokesperson in each context explaining activities and environment.) The person being shadowed

need not put on a show. Explain that the teen would like to do a fifteen-minute interview sometime during the half or full day about career preparation, path, and satisfaction. Young gifted teens are usually sufficiently serious about career exploration to invest. However, professionals might communicate more comfortably about career-related personal concerns to an older teen. Remember that a busy professional's day might be constrained by having someone "at the elbow" and that a service is being done. Emphasize to those who will participate that they be on time, dress appropriately, be attentive, and thank their mentor. It is also important that both you and the group member send a written thank-you after the experience.

6. For closure, have group members create a one-line bit of career advice for themselves. Remind them that it is wise to keep their options open, gain broad-based education and experience, pay attention to personality and needs, and be alert to pertinent career information, including on the Internet. Dispose of the sheets or add them to the folders—or encourage members to take these questionnaires home with them, for future reference or to share with parents/guardians.

Career Needs

Name: _____

1. List any and all career possibilities that you have considered in the past year:

   _____

   _____

2. How might your mother (or other significant woman in your life) imagine you in ten or

   fifteen years? _____

   _____

3. How might your father (or other significant man in your life) imagine you in ten or fifteen

   years? _____

   _____

4. Who (of anyone in your life) expects the most of you? _____

   _____

5. Personality and preferences: Check any of the following that describe you accurately:

   _____ like to be around people   _____ like to deal with scientific ideas

   _____ like to deal with writing   _____ like to perform in front of people

   _____ like to work with my hands   _____ like to deal with "fine print," details

   _____ like to help people   _____ like to teach others new things

   _____ like to research, find out things _____ like to sell things or ideas

   _____ like to deal with data, numbers   _____ like to figure out how things work

   _____ like to work outdoors, not indoors _____ like to meet new people

   _____ like to put things in order   _____ like to "get my hands dirty"

   _____ like to deal with machines   _____ like to make beautiful things

   _____ like creative activities   _____ like rules and regulations

   _____ like to construct, build things   _____ like to feel a sense of contributing
                                                  to the world

6. Personal needs: Circle those that will probably be important to you in a career:

   independence, making my own decisions

   to finish, not to have many unfinished projects

   order

   (continued)

Career Needs (continued)

a sense of play

achievement, rewards

being the center of attention

travel

contact with people

being in charge

helping/guiding others

to be done every day when leaving work

predictability; knowing what to expect

belonging to a group

guidance from others

advancement; going up the career ladder

flexible schedule

maternity/paternity leave

a quiet, calm environment

variety every day

adequate time to be a parent

living close to my extended family (such as parents, siblings, grandparents)

deadlines

adventure and excitement

an urban setting

a rural setting

teamwork; working in a group

solitude

many things happening at once

7. How firm is your career direction right now?

FOCUS The Future

Asking "Dumb" Questions About College

Background

This session can help to prepare students for the inevitable adjustments of college, if indeed they pursue higher education. It can also help to relieve current anxiety. Many gifted students do not know much about college. Perhaps they have no college-educated family members to learn from, or they assume that college is not financially an option. Others are from highly educated families, but they're still poorly informed about college. Regardless of background, many gifted teens do not ask questions about university life because they don't want to appear stupid. They may wonder even about basic terminology:

major	orientation	fraternity, sorority
minor	work-study	financial aid
credit hour	five-year program	colleges, departments, programs
advisor	liberal arts	presidents, deans, directors
scholarship	counseling center	

core course (or whatever is required by an institution or major)
quiet residence halls (or whatever term is applied to housing for serious students)

They wonder about other things as well:

~ where students study
~ how roommates are selected
~ where medical help is available
~ if a student can change majors
~ how accessible professors are
~ where students can get academic help
~ how students find their way around
~ what constitutes success in college
~ what the level of competition is
~ what adjustment problems are typical
~ public and private college differences
~ differences between large and small colleges/universities
~ differences between big-city and small-town colleges/universities
~ what a community college is
~ college teaching, testing, and studying styles

~ important courses as preparation for college

~ whether career direction is necessary before college

~ what an honors college is

Gifted students who believe they do not have enough money for higher education should be encouraged to apply for scholarships and other types of financial aid—and to check out a variety of institutions. Many colleges and universities are concerned about maintaining enrollment levels, and some readily develop good financial packages for those with ability. Today, too, a great number of young adults delay college or spread it out over several years so that they can work and attend classes.

For students whose parents' dream includes a prestigious institution, there might be more interest in the process of getting into college than in preparing for the social and emotional dimensions of college life, the latter often the key to first-year success. Sometimes even students with high intellectual ability, adequate finances, and good records are not successful during that time.

I recommend inviting a panel of four to six varied college students to be interviewed by you and your group—from large and small colleges and from a variety of socioeconomic, family, and high-school-success situations. You might also include someone attending a community college. This session should be scheduled for a time when concerns about college, high school course selection, or college applications are being expressed, although even young gifted teens may benefit from this experience. Just prior to the Thanksgiving holiday break is an ideal time for seniors who are working on applications. In addition, first-year college students will probably arrive home for break before middle schools and high schools dismiss. Sometime before the session, ask your group to write down questions they have about college, anonymously—about schedules, residence halls, orientation, courses, academic terminology, private versus public institutions, costs, financial aid, etc. Collect the questions and have them ready for the panel. This session can be particularly informative for nonmainstream students with high ability, regardless of whether they have been identified for a program or missed. If your group is part of a gifted education program, this session might be opened up to others for the sake of information and inspiration.

If you choose not to invite a panel of college students, you might address these concerns yourself. Find out, first, what the group knows about various aspects of college, and then fill in the gaps.

Objectives

• Gifted teens learn college terminology.

• They learn about college life and some of the challenges first-year students face.

• They learn that financial aid helps to make college possible for many.

Suggestions

1. If you have a panel, interview the college students, using the questions your group prepared earlier, some of the ideas mentioned in the background information, and new questions from your group. You might also pursue some of these directions:

- ~ experiences with homesickness, illness, loneliness, finding friends
- ~ food, weight gain, illness, fatigue, sleeping in noisy residence halls or apartments
- ~ adjustments to fewer and new kinds of tests, less teacher feedback, heavy reading assignments, mid-term pressures, a new level of competition, extent of preparation needed for exams, rapid pace of courses, note-taking
- ~ adjustment to roommates (especially if no experience sharing a room at home)
- ~ social life, comfort level, relaxing, finding people to eat with, alcohol/drug use
- ~ size of institution (as related to initial loss of identity), finding friends, access to professors, getting academic help, distance between classes
- ~ self-discipline and adjustments to less or more structure in life
- ~ time management: balancing jobs, social life, studying
- ~ money: how much is enough, budgeting, book costs (and how to find cheaper books)
- ~ personal adjustments to other cultures and lifestyles
- ~ taking advantage of speakers, programs, campus events, campus groups
- ~ which high school courses gave good preparation
- ~ grading
- ~ financial-aid processes
- ~ deciding on a major
- ~ "fit" of institution
- ~ personal growth and maturity (when and in what ways)
- ~ personal changes, in order to adjust
- ~ colleges visited, applied to, and how they made a choice (if they had one)

2. For closure, ask the group what was most helpful about this session. What feelings do they have when they think of college?

FOCUS | The Future

Anticipating Change

Background

People respond to change uniquely. Some people embrace it eagerly and even seek it out. When life becomes static, they feel they are in a rut and may make dramatic changes. Others resist change or strenuously avoid it. They like life to be predictable and familiar. Most people fall somewhere along the continuum between these extremes. This session provides an opportunity to examine attitudes about change—beyond the focus of the "Loss and Transition" session.

Objectives

- Gifted teens evaluate their ability to embrace change by looking at past changes.
- They think about significant changes that might occur in the next few years.

Suggestions

1. Introduce the discussion by referring to the ideas in the background information. Go around the group and invite members to finish this statement: "When there is a major change in my life, I usually react by _____." Then ask these two questions:

   ~ On a scale of 1 to 10, with 10 being "high anxiety," how would you assess your feelings about big changes?
   ~ On a scale of 1 to 10, with 10 being "very," how confident are you at the outset of a change that everything will eventually work out?

2. Ask the group to give examples of change in their lives. (If they have difficulty, steer them toward major life adjustments related to illness or accident, births, deaths, divorce, remarriage of a parent, moving, starting middle and high school, friendships. If these were discussed thoroughly in the "Loss and Transition" session, remind the group of them.) Ask these questions:

   ~ How did you respond to the change?
   ~ (If they've adjusted) When did you know you had coped well with the change?
   ~ What had you done to help the process?
   ~ (If they dealt well with change) What strategies do you use for coping with change?
   ~ Who are your role models for adjusting to change? How do these people adjust?

3. If you think your group would enjoy it and gain from it, ask those who have trouble adjusting to change to give a detailed "recipe" for how to have *difficulty* with changes. That request may sound bizarre, but it gives those group members an opportunity to speak as if they have control over their responses to change. Allow them to create their own examples; illustrate with one or more of the following *only if necessary*:

   ~ Be angry. Find someone to blame for the change.
   ~ Resist the change with all of your energy.
   ~ Become depressed.
   ~ Do something to show how bad the change is—sulk, run away, make others miserable.
   ~ Believe wholeheartedly that you will never adjust to the change.
   ~ Believe that nothing good will come of the change.
   ~ Lie awake at night and think of ways to change things back to how they were.
   ~ Get physically ill.
   ~ Change your personality so that no one will see how you used to be.

4. Encourage the group to anticipate changes in the future:

   ~ What major changes do you anticipate for yourself in the next year? two years? five years?
   ~ When you leave home for college, or after college (perhaps if attending college locally), or for another reason, how do you predict that you will handle that?
   ~ What kinds of changes do you think you will have the most trouble adjusting to?
   ~ What can you do for yourself during the time of change?
   ~ What can you rely on if there is a major, surprising change? (Possibilities: Your experience in life; your ability to adjust; knowing you have survived other changes.)

5. For closure, ask someone to summarize the discussion or give a one-sentence suggestion for how to change successfully, based on the discussion. What feelings did group members have during the discussion?

FOCUS | The Future

When and If I'm a Parent

Background

Both high- and low-achieving gifted teens may chafe, silently or otherwise, under the constraints of parents/guardians, eager for independence. Yet most are likely to remain financially and otherwise dependent beyond the high school years. During this sometimes stressful period, it is the parents' job to provide appropriate support and guidance. These are important responsibilities. Sometimes parents don't adjust their parenting to accommodate their teen's increasing maturity and competence, and indeed some parents fall short in other ways as well. However, even when parents perform their tasks wisely, there is potential for conflict.

This session gives gifted teens a chance to talk about parent-teen issues. Even if some believe they will never be parents, they can still be involved in the discussion. What do group members hope they will do—or never do—as parents?

If there are group members who already are parents, their opinions can be especially valuable in the discussion, which can be helpful to them as well. They are undoubtedly already aware of some of the challenges of parenting.

Objectives

- Gifted teens look to the future while assessing how they have been parented.
- They think about their personalities, beliefs, and values as they imagine themselves as parents.

Suggestions

1. Begin by having the group define *parenting*. Then proceed with broad questions:

   ~ What is the "job," or responsibility, of a parent?
   ~ When does parenting begin? When does it end?
   ~ What are some challenges of parenting? What is difficult?
   ~ What is important in parenting very young children?
   ~ What are some typical conflicts between parents and teens?
   ~ What conflicts are probably related to figuring out how to be separate from, yet connected to, parents? (Possibilities: Conflicts about privacy, curfews, clothes, friends, choices, direction, activities, behaviors, achievement, appearance.)
   ~ What makes parenting a teen particularly challenging? (Possibility: A sense of having less and less control as the teen moves into the peer culture and a separate identity.)

~ What kinds of fears and anxieties do parents probably have about their children?

~ How much independence is appropriate for a teenager?

~ What are the challenges of stepparenting? foster parenting? grandparents parenting?

~ What might be some challenges for parents when two families blend?

~ What is the most important positive quality in a parent? (Many possible answers.)

2. Encourage the group to look realistically into the future by asking this question: "What will you be like as an adult? Give three to five adjectives that you think might fit you someday." (If the group has difficulty here, suggest some of the following.)

restless	suffering	hard working
settled	tolerant	workaholic
moving often	critical	career focused
content	stable	balance of work and play
tense	unstable	spending as much time as possible
serene	wise	with your children
calm	impulsive	spending little time with your children
energetic	consistent	having no children
patient	inconsistent	involved in many conflicts with others
impatient	lazy	

3. Continue the discussion by asking the following:

~ What have you learned from your parent(s) about parenting?

~ How will you want to be like your parent(s) in parenting style?

~ How will you want to be different from your parent(s) in parenting style?

~ In your opinion, when is a good time for a couple to begin having children?

Mention that parenting behaviors, especially when under stress, often reflect how someone was parented. Parents are models, and, even if teens are convinced that they will never behave like their parents, they may indeed behave like them when under stress. Assure the group that they can change those behaviors through insight and effort. They have choices. If they understand themselves and stay poised even in difficult circumstances, they are more likely to choose wisely. Even learning to listen and respond in a discussion group can help in future parenting. Many communities offer parenting workshops to help parents become more effective.

4. For closure, ask the group what they are thinking or feeling. Tell them that they do not have to be perfect parents—just caring and responsible—if they choose to be parents.

FOCUS Final Session

FOCUS Final Session

Ending

Background

This book is designed to give facilitators the freedom to choose session topics from various sections of this book, according to the needs and interests of their groups, according to the length of a session series, and with no particular sequence. However, regardless of topics discussed and their sequence, it is important to conclude a series carefully, since group members may have sadness, anxiety, or other feelings about endings in general—or about ending the group experience in particular. Refer to the guidelines in "Endings" in the introduction (pages 19–20) as you prepare for the final meeting.

Be aware that as groups prepare to disband, especially at the end of a school year or summer experience, members may bring up serious matters for the first time. Some may have waited a long time to feel safe enough to do that. Others may still not feel comfortable enough to mention something in the group, but will arrange to speak with you individually. If something serious is mentioned in the group, use appropriate listening and responding skills (see pages 13–14), reflect what you hear, validate their experiences and concerns, and remind the group of the importance of confidentiality and trust. They have been trusted with information. Be ready to make a referral, if appropriate.

Objectives

- Gifted teens feel a sense of closure to their discussion experience.
- They interact positively.

Suggestions

1. Hand out "Ending" (page 268) and ask the group to write brief, genuine responses. (You might want to restructure the sheet, including only some of the items, depending on the composition of your group.)

   Invite the group to share their responses. If a particular item generates discussion, pursue it, although keep in mind that all members should have a chance to share their responses.

2. Instead of using the activity sheet, encourage members to share orally what they have gained through the group experience. Or use the first several minutes for them to summarize their experience in writing. Such feedback is valuable for a

leader, and writing gives members a chance to express private thoughts. Encourage them to identify themselves by name on the sheet, if they wish, as this is personal communication to you as facilitator. Assure them that their remarks will be kept confidential.

If it might be helpful for building support for discussion groups in your residential school, summer institute, or school district, invite group members to add a sentence for administrators or brochures (to be kept anonymous), about the value of the experience.

3. Encourage comments about ending the experience. This is perhaps the most important suggestion in this session, since endings are difficult for many people. Talking about feelings at this point is an important part of the group process. Ask these questions:

   ~ How does it feel to know that this is our final meeting?
   ~ Are endings usually easy or difficult for you? Can you recall an example or two?
   ~ How have you managed to cope with endings in the past?

4. As an alternative to #2, have group members fill out "Group Evaluation" (page 269). Emphasize that their opinions will let you know what has been valuable to them and how to improve the group sessions. Perhaps they can give you ideas that you can use when asking administrators for support of groups in the future. Point out that they should not sign this form; it is meant to be anonymous. If there are time constraints, limit the sheet to just Part 1.

5. For closure, tell the group you are glad they committed themselves to the discussion group, took it seriously, became a group, or whatever else is appropriate. Thank them for their special contributions. Wish them well.

Use your judgment about collecting and disposing of the "Ending" handouts. Group members might like to keep them as souvenirs and to look back at them sometime in the future.

Ending

Name: _____

1. As this group ends, I find myself thinking that _____
   _____

2. Based on this group, common concerns for gifted teens are _____
   _____

3. Concerns in this group that are probably common for other teens are _____
   _____

4. Discussing "growing up" with other gifted teens was _____

5. As I leave this group, I feel good about _____

6. I regret that I didn't _____

7. Someone in the group I'm glad I know better now is _____

8. An important discussion topic for me was _____

9. Something important that I learned in the group was _____
   _____

10. A memorable experience in the group was _____
    _____

11. Because of the group, I am now more aware of _____
    _____

12. I discovered that I _____

13. I learned that others _____

14. I was surprised that _____

15. I learned to appreciate _____
    _____

16. During this whole year, I've probably changed most in _____
    _____

17. I'm glad I was part of this group because _____

Group Evaluation

How was this experience for you? Your responses will help your leader plan for future groups.

PART 1
Circle the number that best describes how you would rate each of the following.

5 = excellent   4 = good   3 = average   2 = fair   1 = poor

5 4 3 2 1   My experiences in the group.

5 4 3 2 1   The leader's ability to guide the group.

5 4 3 2 1   The leader's warmth and concern.

5 4 3 2 1   The leader's respect for every member of the group.

5 4 3 2 1   The value of the group for me personally.

5 4 3 2 1   The emotional safety we had for sharing feelings.

5 4 3 2 1   The comfort and safety I felt personally.

5 4 3 2 1   The respect and appreciation I felt for the other members of my group.

5 4 3 2 1   Other members' respect for me.

PART 2 For each of these statements, circle your response and give a reason.

1. If I had it to do over, I (would, wouldn't) participate in this group because

_____

_____

2. I (would, wouldn't) like to participate in another discussion group because

_____

_____

3. In general, I (do, don't) think discussion groups are helpful because

_____

_____

PART 3

What was it like to be in a group? _____

_____

_____

Recommended Resources

Helplines

Boys Town National Hotline
800-448-3000
A 24-hour crisis line where teens can talk with professional counselors about any issue, including depression, suicide, and identity struggles.

LGBT National Youth Talkline
A confidential helpline for LGBT teens open Monday through Friday from 1 p.m. to 9 p.m. and Saturday from 9 a.m. to 2 p.m. (Pacific Time). They also offer an email peer counseling service: help@GLBThotline.org.

National Association of Anorexia Nervosa and Associated Disorders
630-577-1330
A helpline for anyone struggling with an eating disorder. Open for calls Monday through Friday from 9 a.m. to 5 p.m. (CST).

National Center for Victims of Crime Connect Directory
The NCVC's helpline is no longer available, but they do provide information for victim service providers throughout the country: www.victimconnect.org.

National Child Abuse Hotline
800-4-A-CHILD (800-422-4453)
A hotline for anyone suspecting that a child is being abused.

National Dating Abuse Helpline
866-331-9474
A 24-hour hotline that provides support, assistance, counseling, and other services for teens with relationship concerns. Text, email, and chat services available as well: www.loveisrespect.org.

National Suicide Prevention Lifeline
800-273-TALK (800-273-8255)
This is a confidential source of help 24 hours a day.

Substance Abuse and Mental Health Services Administration National Helpline
800-662-HELP (800-662-4357)
Offers confidential help related to substance abuse and addiction.

Abuse, Assault, and Harassment

Child Welfare Information Gateway
Children's Bureau/ACYF
330 C Street SW
Washington, DC 20201
800-394-3366
www.childwelfare.gov
Sponsored by the U.S. Department of Public Health, this organization promotes the safety and well-being of children and families. The Web site provides extensive information about abuse through its electronic publications, online databases, and links to outside sources.

Rape, Abuse & Incest National Network (RAINN)
1220 L Street NW, Suite 505
Washington, DC 20005
800-656-HOPE (800-656-4673)
www.rainn.org
The largest anti-sexual-assault organization in the country, RAINN provides extensive information about sexual abuse to the public. In addition, the organization sponsors a national hotline that connects callers to rape and abuse crisis centers in their area.

For Teens

TeensHealth
www.teenshealth.org
This Web site addresses many of the questions teens have about their mental and physical health. Includes information for teens about rape, bullying, abuse, and where to go for help.

In Love and In Danger: A Teen's Guide to Breaking Free of Abusive Relationships by Barrie Levy (Seattle: Seal Press, 1997). Describes the experiences of teens in violent or abusive dating relationships and offers advice on how to create relationships that are violence-free.

When Something Feels Wrong: A Survival Guide About Abuse for Young People by Deanna S. Pledge (Minneapolis: Free Spirit Publishing, 2003). Support and healing for teens who have experienced physical, sexual, and emotional abuse. Checklists, journaling exercises, and encouragement help the healing process.

Alcohol and Drug Abuse

Al-Anon/Alateen
1600 Corporate Landing Parkway
Virginia Beach, VA 23454
1-888-4AL-ANON (1-888-425-2666)
www.al-anon.alateen.org
The mission of Al-Anon is to help families and friends of alcoholics recover from the effects of living with a substance abuser. Alateen, sponsored by Al-Anon, is a recovery program specifically for young people.

Club Drugs
www.drugabuse.gov/drugs-abuse/club-drugs
An informative Web resource about the series of drugs prevalent in the young-adult party scene.

National Institute on Drug Abuse (NIDA)
6001 Executive Boulevard, Room 5213 MSC 9561
Bethesda, MD 20892
301-443-1124
www.drugabuse.gov
NIDA supports 85 percent of the world's research on drug abuse and addiction. The Web site contains a wealth of information in the form of articles, statistics, and research for parents, teachers, teens, and kids. Includes curriculum guides, education materials, and classroom tools for educators.

For Teens

NIDA for Teens
www.teens.drugabuse.gov
Created by the National Institute on Drug Abuse, this Web site contains facts, stories, and activities about the science of drug abuse. Includes a lengthy "Ask Dr. NIDA" section that addresses a wide range of teen questions about drugs.

Anger Management

American Psychological Association: Anger
750 First Street NE
Washington, DC 20002
800-374-2721
www.apa.org
A part of the APA Web site, this section defines anger, offers anger management strategies, and gives advice about when specialized help is needed.

Healthy Anger: How to Help Children and Teens Manage Their Anger by Bernard Golden (New York: Oxford University Press, 2003). This book helps adults identify the causes of child and teen anger and offers practical strategies that adults can use to help their teens with anger management.

For Teens

TeensHealth: How Can I Deal with My Anger?
www.teenshealth.org
A part of the TeensHealth Web site, this section on anger provides numerous anger management tips for teens and advice about when to seek more help.

Mad: How to Deal with Your Anger and Get Respect by James J. Crist, Ph.D. (Minneapolis: Free Spirit Publishing, 2008). This supportive book contains practical tools and strategies to help teens control their anger and avoid poor decisions and actions. Insights from real teens let them know they're not alone.

Bullying

Odd Girl Out: The Hidden Culture of Aggression in Girls by Rachel Simmons (Orlando: Harcourt, 2002). With data from 300 girls in thirty schools, this book debunks the stereotype that girls are the kinder gender. It closely examines acts of aggression and cruelty among girls and covers the topics of gossiping, ganging up, note-passing, the silent treatment, and more.

No Room for Bullies: From the Classroom to Cyberspace edited by Jose Bolton, Sr., Ph.D., L.P.C., and Stan Graeve, M.A. (Boys Town, NE: Boys Town Press, 2005). Stop abuse, reward kindness, and teach respect with help from experts from Girls and Boys Town. Practical and comprehensive, this book goes beyond defining the problem to providing solutions.

Careers

Best Jobs for the 21st Century by Michael Farr and Laurence Shatkin (Indianapolis: JIST Works, 2006). Contains over 500 job titles and descriptions. Includes numerous "best job" lists based on age, salary requirements, level of education, personality type, and more.

For Teens

Careers for Geniuses & Other Gifted Types, 2nd Ed. by Jan Goldberg (New York: McGraw Hill, 2007). Lets career explorers look at the job market through the unique lens of their own interests. Reveals dozens of ways to pursue a passion and make a living—including many little-known but delightful careers that will surprise readers.

Mapping Your Future
mappingyourfuture.org
A public service project of the financial aid industry, this Web site gives information to students and parents about college, careers, and financial planning.

Counseling Services

American Counseling Association (ACA)
6101 Stevenson Avenue, Suite 600
Alexandria, VA 22304
800-347-6647
www.counseling.org
The ACA is a not-for-profit professional and educational organization dedicated to the growth and enhancement of the counseling profession.

National Board for Certified Counselors (NBCC)
www.nbcc.org
This part of NBCC's Web site can be accessed to find counseling resources in your area.

Creativity/Fun

The Grey Labyrinth
www.greylabyrinth.com
This Web site challenges its visitors to solve some of the most difficult puzzles around and prides itself on having at least one unsolved puzzle posted at all times.

WebMuseum, Paris
www.ibiblio.org/wm
A place for teens and adults to learn about and view famous art before they explore art venues in their areas.

Hiking and Backpacking: A Trailside Guide by Karen Berger (New York: W.W. Norton & Company, 2003). This handy book is loaded with tips, photos, tutorials, and equipment guides for use on the hiking trail.

For Teens

Teen Knitting Club: Chill Out and Knit Some Cool Stuff by Jennifer Wenger, Carol Abrams, and Maureen Lasher (New York: Artisan, 2004). This book, highlighting an increasingly trendy hobby for teens, provides all of the information they need to start their own knitting club. Includes knitting basics for beginners.

Wise Highs: How to Thrill, Chill, and Get Away from It All Without Alcohol or Other Drugs by Alex J. Packer (Minneapolis: Free Spirit Publishing, 2006). Over 150 ways to achieve creative, safe, playful, legal highs without alcohol or drugs.

Depression and Suicide

National Institute of Mental Health (NIMH)
6001 Executive Boulevard, Room 6200 MSC 9663
Bethesda, MD 20892
866-615-6464
www.nimh.nih.gov
NIMH is the leading federal agency for the research of mental and behavioral disorders. The Web site contains a wealth of information on mental health topics, including depression, and provides a substantive collection of articles, resources, and research.

SAVE—Suicide Awareness Voices of Education
8120 Penn Avenue S., Suite 470
Bloomington, MN 55431
952-946-7998
www.save.org
An organization dedicated to educating the public about suicide prevention and depression.

Overcoming Teen Depression: A Guide for Parents by Miriam Kaufman (Buffalo, NY: Firefly Books, 2001). This book discusses the warning signs and treatment methods for depression in teens. It contains case studies and a thorough analysis of current research. Though written to parents, it offers good background information for a group facilitator to use prior to group discussion.

For Teens

Everything You Need to Know About Depression by Eleanor H. Ayer (New York: Rosen Publishing, 2001). Written for teens, this book explains the science of depression, the causes of depression, and the pros and cons of various treatment methods.

The Power to Prevent Suicide: A Guide for Teens Helping Teens by Richard E. Nelson and Judith C. Galas (Minneapolis: Free Spirit Publishing, 2006). With updated facts, statistics, and resources, this book gives teens the information they need to recognize the warning signs of suicide in peers. Includes advice on how to reach out and when and where to go for help.

When Nothing Matters Anymore: A Survival Guide for Depressed Teens (Revised & Updated Edition) by Bev Cobain, R.N.,C. (Minneapolis: Free Spirit Publishing, 2007). A classic book teens turn to, and teachers and counselors trust. It defines depression, described the symptoms, and explains that depression is treatable. Personal stories from teens speak directly to readers' feelings, concerns, and experiences.

Divorce/Family Change

DivorceNet
www.divorcenet.com
Provides extensive information about the legal aspects of divorce. Includes a resource page for every U.S. state.

For Teens

Families Change: A Teen Guide to Parental Separation and Divorce
www.familieschange.ca.gov
Developed by the British Columbia Ministry of the Attorney General, this Web site is a guide for any teen facing parental separation and divorce. Discusses family change, emotions, and legal issues and provides a list of resources and frequently asked questions.

Eating Disorders

Academy for Eating Disorders (AED)
11130 Sunrise Valley Drive, Suite 350
Reston, VA 20191
703-234-4079
www.aedweb.org
A professional organization that promotes excellence in the research, treatment, and prevention of eating disorders. The Web site contains facts, articles, resources, and links for professionals and the general public.

National Eating Disorders Association (NEDA)
200 West 41st Street, Suite 1203
New York, NY 10036
800-931-2237
www.nationaleatingdisorders.org
This organization provides information on various eating disorders and treatment options and offers referrals to doctors, counselors, and clinics. Helpline available 9:00 a.m. to 5:00 p.m. EST.

For Teens

Over It: A Teen's Guide to Getting Beyond Obsession with Food and Weight by Carol Emery Normandi and Laurelee Roark (Novato, CA: New World Library, 2001). Examines the social and cultural factors that foster weight obsession in girls and lists the kinds of behaviors that lead to eating disorders. Contains activities and quotations from teens.

Wasted: A Memoir of Anorexia and Bulimia by Marya Hornbacher (New York: Harper Perennial, 2006). Hornbacher talks about possible causes for her eating disorders and describes feeling isolated, being in complete denial, and not wanting to change or fearing change, until she nearly died. Young people will connect with this compelling and authentic story.

Giftedness

Center for Talent Development (CTD)
Northwestern University
617 Dartmouth Place
Evanston, IL 60208
847-491-3782
www.ctd.northwestern.edu
The mission of CTD is to identify and develop students with exceptional ability in academic areas. The Web site contains information about the Midwest Academic Talent Search, talent development programs, research, and advocacy.

Center for Talented Youth (CTY)
Johns Hopkins University
McAuley Hall
5801 Smith Avenue #400
Baltimore, MD 21209
410-735-6277
cty.jhu.edu
To find educational programs and learning opportunities for gifted students, contact the CTY. The Web site contains information about talent testing, summer programs, family programs, distance education, and more.

Hoagies' Gifted Education Page
www.hoagiesgifted.org
The Hoagies' Web site contains a great mix of informational resources about giftedness and links to fun Web sites chosen with the gifted audience in mind. A great resource for gifted kids and teens, their parents, and educators.

National Association for Gifted Children (NAGC)
1331 H Street NW, Suite 1001
Washington, DC 20005
202-785-4268
www.nagc.org
NAGC is an organization that unites parents, educators, community leaders, and professionals to address the needs of gifted children. The Web site offers a host of resources for anyone interested in the latest news and research on giftedness and provides links to the gifted organizations in each state.

Supporting Emotional Needs of the Gifted (SENG)
P.O. Box 1184
Schenectady, NY 12301
844-488-7364
www.sengifted.org
SENG is dedicated to addressing the emotional needs and emotional health of gifted children and adults. Check out their Web site for resources, guidance, and information and for a way to connect with a community concerned about the emotional needs of the gifted.

When Gifted Kids Don't Have All the Answers: How to Meet Their Social and Emotional Needs by Judy Galbraith, M.A., and Jim Delisle, Ph.D. (Minneapolis: Free Spirit Publishing, 2015). Takes a close-up look at gifted kids and topics such as identification, super-sensitivity, perfectionism, and underachievement. Includes first-person stories, easy-to-use strategies, survey results, activities, and reproducibles.

For Teens

More Than a Test Score: Teens Talk About Being Gifted, Talented, or Otherwise Extra-Ordinary by Robert A. Schultz, Ph.D., and James R. Delisle, Ph.D. (Minneapolis: Free Spirit Publishing, 2006). Drawing on the voices of thousands of gifted teenagers, this book is a real-life look at what being gifted means to teens today.

Giftedness in Diverse Populations

Special Populations in Gifted Education: Working with Diverse Gifted Learners by Jamie A. Castellano (Boston, MA: Pearson Education, 2003). Recognizing that gifted students come from all backgrounds, this book helps educators identify and nurture giftedness in students of various cultural, linguistic, and socioeconomic backgrounds. Includes examinations of giftedness in girls, GLBT students, and students with disabilities.

Teaching Culturally Diverse Gifted Students by Donna Y. Ford (Waco, TX: Prufrock Press, 2005). Helpful tips for educators on how to create a gifted program that serves children from all cultural backgrounds.

Gifted Underachievers and Twice-Exceptionality

Association for the Education of Gifted Underachieving Students (AEGUS)
6 Wildwood Street
Burlington, MA 01803
www.aegus1.org
A forum for information about the needs of under-achieving gifted students. The Web site includes helpful links and a list of suggested reading on the topic.

Council for Exceptional Children
2900 Crystal Drive, Suite 1000
Arlington, VA 22202
888-232-7733
www.cec.sped.org
The CEC is the largest professional organization dedicating to improving the education of students with special needs, including students with exceptionalities and disabilities and students identified as gifted. The Web site includes numerous articles and resources on twice-exceptionality.

Uniquely Gifted: Identifying and Meeting the Needs of Twice-Exceptional Students by Kiesa Kay (Gilsum, NH: Avocus Publishing, 2000). Chapters by forty-three authors discuss types of situations in which gifted students also have significant learning difficulties. Review the information online at www.uniquelygifted.org.

Grief/Loss

Centering Corporation
7230 Maple Street
Omaha, NE 68134
866-218-0101
www.centering.org
A nonprofit organization that provides guidance, education, and resources for the bereaved.

On Death and Dying by Elisabeth Kübler-Ross (New York: Scribner Classics, 1997). The classic, quintessential text on dying, death, and grief, this book gives insight into how imminent death affects patients and the family, friends, and professionals who care for them.

For Teens

Healing Your Grieving Heart for Teens by Alan D. Wolfelt (Fort Collins, CO: Companion Press, 2001). Offers 100 suggestions for dealing with grief.

When a Friend Dies: A Book for Teens About Grieving and Healing by Marilyn E. Gootman (Minneapolis: Free Spirit Publishing, 2005). With compassion and sensitivity, this book answers the tough questions teens have about grieving the loss of a loved one.

Identity

In the Mix
23 Stephenson Terrace
Briarcliff, NY 10510
212-288-2150
www.pbs.org/inthemix
A weekly PBS series that discusses relevant teen issues, including labeling, stereotyping, and cliques. Educators may purchase episodes online or by phone.

For Teens

The Courage to Be Yourself: True Stories by Teens About Cliques, Conflicts, and Overcoming Peer Pressure edited by Al Desetta (Minneapolis: Free Spirit Publishing, 2005). True stories from real teens about breaking stereotypes, standing up for themselves, and learning who they really are.

Internet Safety

Federal Bureau of Investigation: Cyber Investigations
FBI Headquarters
935 Pennsylvania Avenue NW
Washington, DC 20535
202-324-3000
www.fbi.gov
The FBI is actively investigating cyber crime in the United States. The cyber-investigation section of their Web site contains facts, resources, and news articles about online crime, as well as advice about Internet safety.

For Teens

SafeTeens.com
www.safeteens.com
This Web site contains information for teens about Internet safety. Covers blogging, emailing, chat rooms, bullying, instant messaging, privacy, and more.

Mentors/Role Models

Institute for Educational Advancement: EXPLORE Program
569 South Marengo Avenue
Pasadena, CA 91101
www.educationaladvancement.org
The summer apprenticeship programs offered by the IEA give gifted high school students the opportunity to work in leading universities, corporations, and research facilities and to learn from professionals in their fields of interest.

Who Mentored You?
Harvard Mentoring Project
Center for Health Communication
Harvard School of Public Health
677 Huntington Avenue
Boston, MA 02115
617-495-1000
sites.sph.harvard.edu/wmy
A collection of personal stories and insights by prominent public figures about the importance of their mentors.

For Teens

My Hero: Extraordinary People on the Heroes Who Inspire Them edited by the My Hero Project (New York: Free Press, 2005). A collection of first-hand essays by well-known public figures about the people who influenced their lives for the better.

Perfectionism

Being Perfect by Anna Quindlen (New York: Random House, 2005). In this short book, novelist Anna Quindlen describes how perfectionism affected her life as a young person and how she was able to overcome its debilitating effects.

Moving Past Perfect by Thomas S. Greenspon, Ph.D. (Minneapolis: Free Spirit Publishing, 2012). In this book for parents, a psychologist and therapist describes a healing process for transforming perfectionism into healthy living practices and self-acceptance.

For Teens

Perfectionism: What's Bad About Being Too Good? by Miriam Adderholdt and Jan Goldberg (Minneapolis: Free Spirit Publishing, 1999). Explains the differences between healthy ambition and unhealthy perfectionism and gives teens strategies for getting out of the perfectionist trap. Contains a quiz that can be used as a discussion prompt.

Relationships

Lifestories. A board game that encourages people to share stories about themselves to build interpersonal competence. Available through the Talicor Company at www.talicor.com or 800-433-4263.

How to Talk with Teens About Love, Relationships, & S-E-X: A Guide for Parents by Amy G. Miron and Charles D. Miron (Minneapolis: Free Spirit Publishing, 2002). Helpful tips and practical strategies for adults on how to talk to young people about love, relationships, and sex.

For Teens

Boy v. Girl? How Gender Shapes Who We Are, What We Want, and How We Get Along by George Abrahams, Ph.D., and Sheila Ahlbrand (Minneapolis: Free Spirit Publishing, 2002). This book invites teens to examine gender roles and stereotypes, overcome gender barriers, and be themselves.

Cool Communication: From Conflict to Cooperation for Parents and Kids by Andrea Frank Henkart and Journey Henkart (New York: Perigee Books, 2002). Advice for adults and young people on how to bridge the parent-teen communication gap.

The Teen Survival Guide to Dating & Relating: Real-World Advice on Guys, Girls, Growing Up, and Getting Along by Annie Fox (Minneapolis: Free Spirit Publishing, 2005). Designed to help teens build healthier relationships with everyone in their lives, this book gives thoughtful, frank advice on feelings, boyfriends, girlfriends, sex, parents, and more.

Self-Image

Media Education Foundation
60 Masonic Street, Suite A
Northampton, MA 01060
800-897-0089
www.mediaed.org
The nation's leading producer of educational videos that encourage young people to critically analyze the messages and images presented by the media.

Uniquely Me! The Girl Scout/Dove Self-Esteem Program
www.girlscouts.org
A program developed by the Girl Scouts of America and Dove to promote positive self-esteem in adolescent girls between the ages of 8 and 17.

For Teens

Focus on Body Image: How You Feel About How You Look by Maurene J. Hinds (Berkeley Heights, NJ: Enslow, 2002). Contains personal stories from girls and guys about their experiences related to body image.

Self-Mutilation

"**Adolescents Who Self-Injure: Implications and Strategies for School Counselors**" by Victoria E. White Kress, Donna M. Gibson, and Cynthia A. Reynolds (*Professional School Counseling*, February 2004, Vol 7: 195–201). Strategies for school counselors on how to manage students who self-injure. Covers intervention, education, advocacy, and prevention.

A Bright Red Scream: Self-Mutilation and the Language of Pain by Marilee Strong (New York: Viking, 1998). Rejecting the classic psychiatric wisdom that views self-mutilation as a species of suicidal behavior, Strong links the phenomenon instead to the will to live—often in the face of overwhelming childhood abuse. Contains interviews with more than 50 self-injurers.

Secret Scars: Uncovering and Understanding the Addiction of Self-Injury by V.J. Turner (Center City, MN: Hazelden, 2002). This groundbreaking book demystifies self-injury by explaining it as a treatable addictive disorder. An important resource for parents, educators, and mental health professionals.

For Teens

Teenbreaks.com
www.teenbreaks.com
This Web site for teen real-life issues addresses the truths about cutting, includes stories from teens who cut, and advises cutters on how to stop when they're ready and willing.

Sex and Sexuality

American Association of Sexuality Educators, Counselors, and Therapists
1444 I Street NW, Suite 700
Washington, DC 20005
202-449-1099
www.aasect.org
A nonprofit organization devoted to promoting healthy sexual behavior and an understanding of human sexuality. The Web site contains articles, links, and referrals to professionals all over the country.

Parents, Families and Friends of Lesbians and Gays (PFLAG)
1828 L Street NW, Suite 660
Washington, DC 20036
202-467-8180
www.pflag.org
A national nonprofit organization for parents, families, and friends of lesbian, gay, bisexual, and transgender individuals. PFLAG's mission is to promote the health and well-being of GLBT persons through support, education, and advocacy.

Planned Parenthood Federation of America
123 William Street, 10th Floor
New York, NY 10038
800-230-PLAN (800-230-7526)
www.plannedparenthood.org
Planned Parenthood is the world's oldest family planning organization and is dedicated to promoting sexual health and sexual education. The Web site contains extensive resources and fact sheets, as well as a section for teens.

The Sex Lives of Teenagers: Revealing the Secret World of Adolescent Boys and Girls by Lynn Ponton (New York: Dalton, 2000). This book explores the topic of sex from the teen perspective with a goal of helping adults and teens better communicate about dating and sexuality.

For Teens

Info for Teens
www.plannedparenthood.org
An award-winning sexual-health Web site for teens created by Planned Parenthood. Contains answers to frequently asked questions, advice, and an "ask the experts" section. The site is available in English and Spanish.

GLBTQ: The Survival Guide for Gay, Lesbian, Bisexual, Transgender, and Questioning Teens (revised and updated 2nd edition) by Kelly Huegel (Minneapolis: Free Spirit Publishing, 2011). This frank, sensitive book is for any queer or questioning teen—and any straight friend or caring adult who wants to understand. Topics include coming out, getting support, staying safe, making healthy choices, and accepting oneself.

Stress
· · · · · · ·

American Psychological Association
750 First Street NE
Washington, DC 20002
800-374-2721
www.apa.org
A scientific and professional organization that represents psychology in the United States. The Web site contains the latest information and research on various topics in psychology including stress.

For Teens

Mind Your Mind
www.mindyourmind.ca
Created for teens and by teens, this Web site provides information and resources to help young people manage their stress. Contains real stress stories, tools for handling pressure, and tips for healthy stress relief.

Too Stressed to Think? A Teen Guide to Staying Sane When Life Makes You Crazy by Annie Fox and Ruth Kirschner (Minneapolis: Free Spirit Publishing, 2005). In teen-friendly language, this book examines the effects of stress on the mind and body and discusses how stress interferes with decision-making. Includes activities, resources, real-life stories, and stress-busting tools.

Index

•••

Page numbers in **bold** indicate reproducible activity sheets.

About the Author

Jean Sunde Peterson, Ph.D., was a classroom teacher for many years, was involved concurrently in teacher training, was named State Teacher of the Year, and developed summer foreign language day camps for children prior to graduate work in counseling and development at the University of Iowa. Now a professor in the Department of Educational Studies at Purdue University, she has directed school counselor preparation and focused most of her research on counseling concerns related to the social and emotional development of high-ability children. Her national and international workshops, conference keynotes, and presentations address those areas, as well as academic underachievement, bullying, negative life events, development-oriented group work with children and adolescents, and listening/responding skills for teachers and parents. A licensed mental health counselor, she continues to be involved in clinical work with gifted children and adolescents and their families. She has authored over 100 books, invited chapters, and journal articles; has received seven national awards for scholarship; and has received numerous awards at Purdue related to teaching, research, or service.

More Great Products from Free Spirit!

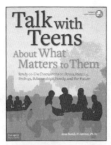
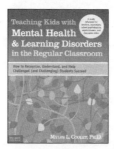